Studies in Islamic History

No. 17

A BAGHDAD CHRONICLE

[*Photo: Hasso Bros. Baghdad*

RUINED MINARET, SÚQ AL-GHAZL, BAGHDAD

A BAGHDAD CHRONICLE

BY

REUBEN LEVY, M.A.
Lecturer in Persian
in the University of Cambridge

PORCUPINE PRESS
Philadelphia

First edition 1929
(Cambridge: At the University Press, 1929)

Reprinted 1977 by
PORCUPINE PRESS, INC.
Philadelphia, Pennsylvania 19107
By arrangement with Cambridge University Press

Library of Congress Cataloging in Publication Data

Levy, Reuben.
A Baghdad chronicle.

(Studies in Islamic history ; no. 17)
Reprint of the 1929 ed. published at the University Press, Cambridge.
Bibliography: p.
Includes index.
1. Baghdad--History. I. Title. II. Series: Studies in Islamic history (Philadelphia) ; no. 17.
DS79.9.B25L48 1977 956.7'4 77-10580
ISBN 0-87991-466-1

Manufactured in the United States of America

CONTENTS

Preface . . . . *page* xi

Introductory 1

CHAPTER I

The Building of the City 11

CHAPTER II

The Expansion of the City 26

CHAPTER III

"In the Golden Prime of Good Haroun Al-raschid" 42

CHAPTER IV

City Life under Hárún 59

CHAPTER V

The First Siege of Baghdad 70

CHAPTER VI

The Reign of Ma'mún 86

CHAPTER VII

Baghdad without a Caliph 98

CHAPTER VIII

Baghdad Restored 119

CONTENTS

CHAPTER IX

Baghdad under Persian Masters . . *page* 154

CHAPTER X

The Greater Seljúqs and Baghdad . . . 184

CHAPTER XI

The Seljúq Decline 205

CHAPTER XII

Two Sieges 219

CHAPTER XIII

An Indian Summer 228

CHAPTER XIV

City Ideals and Accomplishments . . . 244

CHAPTER XV

The Downfall of the City 252

Notes 261

Bibliographical List of Authorities . . . 271

Index 275

ILLUSTRATIONS

Ruined minaret, Súq al-Ghazl . *Frontispiece*

View from minaret, Súq al-Ghazl. Shorja Bazaar running across . *to face page* 33

The Upper Bridge, Baghdad, looking east . 161

Kaẓimain Mosque 248

The accent (′) over a vowel denotes that it is long.

To

M. H.

WHO
ENCOURAGED
ALWAYS

PREFACE

If one were to judge from the standard histories—both Oriental and European—of the Abbasid Caliphate, of which Baghdad was the capital, the only sounds that ever issued from the "City of Peace" were those of strife and battle. The attention of the political historians seems to have been captured almost exclusively by the records of conflict, which are indeed very difficult to disregard. Yet fighting can only have been an occasional accompaniment to the daily life of the mass of the citizens, and there seemed to be room for some record of what may be called the social history of Baghdad under the Abbasid Caliphs. But the political side, which gave rise to most of the fighting, could not be left out of account, and if it takes what may appear to be a disproportionate amount of space in the present work, it is not only because the sources demanded it but also because strife left obvious marks on the daily life of the city. Yet one may hope that the effect of the present work is not altogether that of a drum and trumpet history, and that the sketches of Baghdad's manners and customs and the descriptions of typical citizens are not obscured by the martial record.

As will perhaps be seen from the notes—which have been relegated to the end of the book in order not to interrupt the current of the narrative—it is not so much the political annalists as the biographers who have provided the materials most in accord with the scheme of the work. Even they are stereotyped in their methods, so that, to believe them, every man they described was a paragon of all the virtues rather than an ordinary mortal. There had to be careful search for the "touches of nature" which made characters recognizable, and all whose business it is to deal with Arabic and Persian authors will appreciate the relief which greeted any mention of a weakness normal to human beings. It may be not without significance that the most convincing biographies are the work of Yáqút, who was of Greek origin.

For the preparation of the MS. of this volume for press—perhaps her least contribution to the work—I am indebted to my wife. To my friend and colleague, Professor R. A. Nicholson, my thanks are due for help on numerous difficult points and for useful criticisms, and to the Master of Christ's College (Mr N. McLean) I owe my gratitude for the material way in which he lightened my task. The problem of illustrations for the work was solved for me by my friend Dr R. Campbell Thompson, whose company once made two Mesopotamian summers tolerable.

Finally I should like to express to the readers of the Cambridge University Press my appreciation of a remarkable vigilance and of a great helpfulness in suggestion.

R. L.

CAMBRIDGE

INTRODUCTORY

There are few cities, even in the storied East, that hold the imagination like Baghdad. As becomes the background of the *Arabian Nights* and the scene of Hárún al-Rashíd's nocturnal adventures it has a special character combining with its mundane reality a mystery and fancifulness that put it outside the sober records of history and make it a capital whose annals should be sought not in the humdrum narratives of the scribe but in the unfettered imagery of poet or painter.

Events have made reality more prominent than the romance, and tourists have brought reports eloquent of disillusionment. They went perhaps to behold marble palaces and "shrines of fretted gold" and found a town of mud-brick houses and monotonous palms. Soldiers returned associating the place with prostrating heat and devastating sickness. Yet even with actual contact it is not impossible to recapture the feelings engendered by the tales of the *Thousand and One Nights*. Approach the city neither by the railway from Basra, nor by motor from Beirut—the one lands you in a crude railway station far from the town, amid a clamorous mob of ragamuffin porters, and the other leaves in one the desire for a bath, to the exclusion of all else—but by river, either by *kellek* (the raft made of inflated sheep skins) from Mosul or by steamer from Basra. The time to reach the town is in the spring, in early morning before most of the citizens are awake; and the place for the anchor to drop is between the two bridges. The traveller's mind will have been attuned to the spectacle he beholds either by sight of the mighty ruins of Persian Ctesiphon or by the gilt domes of the mosque and shrine at Kazimain. The growing light, like a seal upon soft wax, impresses upon the dusky surface of the world the outlines of flattened domes and tall minarets, of waving palms and level-roofed houses, with mystery lying in the sombre recesses between. Round coracles, black and very solid, appear on the surface of the river. The pattern of them dates from most ancient Babylon, and the solitary fisherman who occupies each vessel quavers a tune probably as antique as he draws net or paddles his rudderless craft forward by spiral turns alternately to right and left. The river itself will be flowing strong and yellow, washing high up the retaining walls of the houses that rise straight out of the water, for there are no docks or quays.

As it grows lighter, the points where the city lanes come down to the river edge will be marked by little crowds, mostly of women, crouching down to wash clothes or to fill jars with water, and always on their guard to draw veil against too close scrutiny. There will be men too, either boatmen to ferry the early trader across the river, or water carriers shovelling the muddy liquid into the sheep skins in which it is transported. Around the newly arrived paddle steamer black-headed gulls will be wheeling and whistling, dropping with a swoop to the water after any likely morsel.

With the traveller's landing, romance may recede for a time before the babel that greets the process everywhere from Calais eastwards. By the time he is on his way to his quarters the city will be awake and he will find motor cars in plenty, mainly of American manufacture, roaring along the only two streets that are wide enough for carriages. Yet they will be sharing the roadway with donkeys, horses, mules, camels or ancient four-wheeled '*arabánas* drawn by two horses. All will be laden; the camels, mules and pack horses with boxes and bales of merchandise from most of the countries of the world; the donkeys with glistening black water skins of the *saqqá*, though these may be replaced by a grave and reverend senior seated far back on the animal's rump, his legs, bare from the knee, swinging out wide and at each beat landing heavily on the poor creature's ribs. Sometimes a string of mules will be carrying the huge fishes caught in the Diyala river and locally known as *biz*, a name which seems to imply a species of tunny. They are caught with drag nets, and each fish makes a mule-load. Occasionally there will be a couple of pack animals in the charge of a Persian muleteer; to be recognized as such from his loose baggy trousers unrestrained at the bottom, and from his hat, a high cone of felt, truncated and inverted. Swinging on either side of each animal will be a long, tapering case covered with rough canvas. These will contain the remains of pious relatives, anxious for their bones to rest in the proximity of the saints, and they will have been brought, it may be, from the furthest limits of Persia for burial in the sacred places of Kerbela and Nejef.

In the '*arabána* a couple of female figures may be

seated, shrouded in black from head to foot if they are Moslem ladies, for in Baghdad they have not yet by any means found "emancipation", and it is reported that there was much ado when even King Faisul's own consort appeared unveiled at a public reception. But the occupants of the carriage may be Jewish or Christian girls cloaked in '*abás* of a cheerful blue, pink or yellow, or perhaps of black silk embroidered in gold thread, and interest in a stranger will not be entirely concealed even by a veil or horsehair vizor.

On the pavements will be the crowd going to its business in the bazaars, either of selling or buying. The *effendís* in European suit and fez; the less up-to-date citizens—the bearded bourgeois—in tailor-made coat and skirt under an '*abá*; sayyids, whose green turbans proclaim them descendants of the Prophet, '*ulamá*, mullahs and shaikhs—clerics all—in white or blue turbans of all sizes; in between, an occasional negro—probably not long emancipated from slavery—or a fellaḥ with his bare legs showing through the piece of rough sacking that, with a long white shirt, forms his wardrobe. Here and there an Arab girl will be carrying a copper water-jar on her head. In her nose is a ring and on her forehead a greenish blue amulet, while the lift of her arm raises the hem of her '*abá*, disclosing a row of little blue crosses tattooed round each bare ankle.

Except in detail the spectacle cannot have altered much for a thousand years or more. The conquering Arab is no longer distinct from the descendant of ancient Babylonians and Assyrians; Mongol types are rare except in visitors, and for the time being there are individuals from the West with an influence disproportionate to their numbers here.

For full appreciation of the picture it is necessary to go back in time and examine some of the component details. The native annalists begin the story of the city with its foundation by Manṣúr the Abbasid as the capital of the Caliphate. Its origin however goes back much further. How long there has been a human settlement on the site is a matter of dispute. Lying at a point where the Tigris and Euphrates approach one another to a distance of less than thirty-five miles and within the area bounded by the Persian plateau on the east and the Syrian desert on the west, the place is well suited for the location of the country's chief city. On or near it the alluvial plains of the Two Rivers have for thousands of years had their seat of government. In historical times at any rate there have been Akkad, the capital of the great Assyrian King Sargon; ancient Babylon the Mighty; Seleucia, from which the successors of Alexander the Great ruled Babylonia; Ctesiphon of the Sassanians; and now Baghdad, which has lasted longer than any of them. The proximity of the Two Rivers and the consequent fertility of the district encouraged trading caravans from all directions to include it in their itinerary, and Baghdad's importance as a trade centre was the result.

Long before Baghdad was the capital of Iraq, however, there were human habitations on the spot. A boundary stone of the reign of Merodach-Baladan I (1201–1189 B.C.) has been found inscribed with cuneiform characters that most scholars read *Bag-da-du*. In 1848,

Sir Henry Rawlinson in the course of some excavation on the west bank of the Tigris near the mosque of Khidhr Ilyás which lies opposite the Citadel of Baghdad, found part of a quay wall built of Babylonian bricks. They were inscribed with the name of Nebuchadnezzar II (604–561 B.C.) and were cemented together with bitumen in the Babylonian fashion. The wall is still visible, but that must perhaps be discounted as evidence for the reason that Baghdad's builders were in the habit of utilizing the ancient materials which they found close at hand.

There is no definite proof that a settled community inhabited the site until after the Christian era, but the Babylonian Talmud, which was completed by the end of the fifth century, mentions Baghdad as the birthplace of a certain Rabbi Hóná and also speaks of a Baghdadí mathematician and astronomer. According to the historian Ya'qúbí[1] a village called Baghdad existed in Sassanian times in the district of Bádúrayá. Later on, when the capital was built, the village formed the quarter of Abú 'l-'Abbás al-Fadhl[2]. On the whole, tradition goes to show that the majority of the inhabitants were Christian. Al-Karkh, which is now the official name of that portion of the city lying on the west bank, is derived from the Aramaic *Kàrká* ("The City"); and the fact implies fairly definitely that the village which originally bore the name and occupied that site was either Christian or Jewish, and so existed before Moslem times. It is said to have been founded by the Sassanian king Shapur II, "The Broad-Shouldered" (A.D. 309–379)—thus the Persian geographer Ḥamdulláh Mustawfí in his *Nuzhatu al-Qulúb* or *Delight of Hearts*. But, as might be expected, Persian tradition claims that the city of Baghdad is of Persian origin and that it, as well as the city of Babylon, "was built by the kings of Persia of the first dynasty...and that Zuhak, who is the Nimrod of the Jews, was its first founder; that Afrasiab, king of Turkistan and conqueror of Persia, enlarged it and called it Baghdad, which is to say, Garden of Dad, from the name of the idol which he worshipped".[1]

A piece of evidence that comes from rather nearer home is a road chart compiled by the geographer Ptolemy, who lived in Egypt in the second century. The chart shows a village called *Thelde* on the location that was later covered by Baghdad, and it is likely that this was the Ptolemaic version of *Súqu al-Thaláthá*, "the Tuesday Market", the Arabic name of a village that was afterwards incorporated in the Abbasid capital.

Nearly all the Moslem geographers and historians who deal with the foundation of the city speak of a village or settlement on the site of Baghdad before the coming of Mohammed. For example the Persian historian Ṭabarí, writing between A.D. 875 and 915, says that under the Sassanian rulers of Persia, who reigned from A.D. 226 until the time when the Moslem invaders subjugated the country, Baghdad was a village on the right bank of the Tigris. It was occupied chiefly by Nestorian Christians, amongst whom were a good number of monks, and it had a flourishing market.

The name "Baghdad" is itself of pre-Islamic origin, but what it means and how it came to be applied to the city are questions that have never been determined. The Babylonian *Bag-da-du* is of uncertain meaning. The derivation of the name given by D'Herbelot comes from Ḥamdulláh Mustawfí who says: "On the east bank of the Tigris (opposite Karkh) was a village known as Sabat, one of the dependencies of Nahrawán. Khusraw Núshírwán made a garden, *bágh*, in the open spaces surrounding the village and called it 'Bágh Dád', i.e. the 'garden of Dád'". But there is no known person or god of that name and he would seem to be a myth specially invented to explain it. If the name Baghdad is Persian, as some Moslem writers have asserted, it might mean "Given by God". Yet this also is doubtful because there is the further complication that the name is sometimes written *Baghdáḍh* or *Maghdád*.[1] Whatever its origin, the Caliph Manṣúr decided to have none of it when he built his city, and he thought to remove the ill omen of a pagan nomenclature by calling his capital *Madínat al-Salám*, "The City of Peace". It was this title that the Greeks adopted when they called the city "Eirenopolis"—thus Gibbon. It is said that the new name was taken from that of the Tigris, which was locally known as the "River (or Valley) of Peace". The name Baghdad however has survived, though other titles were applied to various parts of the city; such as *Madínat Manṣúr*, "the City of Manṣúr", to the portion actually constructed by that Caliph, and *al-Zawrá*, "the Crooked", to the eastern half of the town lying on the left bank.

When it is considered how famous the name of Baghdad now is and how widespread its repute during the days of the Caliphate, it is an amazing fact that for centuries during the middle ages the name was lost in Europe or mangled or else confused with Babylon. The rabbis of the Geonic period often speak of Baghdad as "Babel", but they seemed to do so of set purpose, well knowing the difference; and the European rabbi Benjamin of Tudela identified the site of the more ancient city when he visited it in 1173. But during the centuries after the city fell to the Mongols the error is due to pure confusion. Thus Sir Thomas Roe, who was the British ambassador at Constantinople from 1621 to 1628, in his despatches reports the sieges which the Persians in his day were laying against "Babilon", by which of course he meant Baghdad and not the ancient capital, that had long been in ruins. Even later, the courageous French traveller Tavernier in describing his journey down the Tigris in 1651 tells us that he arrived at "Baghdad, qu'on appelle d'ordinaire Babylone". And twelve years after that, the encyclopaedic geography book of Jean Blaeu—published in Amsterdam in 1663—calls the capital of "Chaldaea and Babylonia" the city of "Baghdad, which is also called Baldach and Baudras by some". From the former of these two variants came the name of the brocade known as baldachin which used to be made in the city. By the splendid adventurer Marco Polo Baghdad was called "Baudas" and he describes the city though he probably did not visit it; while Longfellow's Spanish Jew speaks of "Baldacca's" Kalif. It was the Roman traveller Pietro Della Valle who first made it clear that Baghdad and Babylon were not identical. He visited

Mesopotamia in 1616 and his researches on the spot led him to reaffirm what had so strangely been forgotten. Not however until 1704 did the western world begin to take any real interest in the city of Baghdad. In that year the French orientalist Antoine Galland translated the *Arabian Nights* into French, so for the first time making the stories available for general consumption in a European language. Their popularity was immediate and the city of Hárún al-Rashíd sprang into fame; and though it may be that the *Thousand and One Nights* were—as one critic had it—Persian tales told after the manner of Buddha by Queen Esther to Hárún al-Rashíd in Cairo during the fourteenth century of the Christian era, yet the ordinary reader will ever associate them with Baghdad.

CHAPTER I

The Building of the City

It was no accident that led to the foundation of Baghdad as the capital of the Caliphate. Religious and dynastic struggles were inevitable when the vast Mohammedan empire became too unwieldy for one man to govern, and the centre of government had changed more than once in the century after Mohammed. In the early days of the empire the power had lain, naturally enough, with the Arabs, whose soldierly qualities and religious enthusiasm together had succeeded in spreading the faith of Mohammed over a far larger field than he himself could ever have imagined to be possible. When, after an unpromising beginning at Mecca, the Prophet in 622 took refuge from his enemies at Medina, it was from this city that operations were directed and it remained the capital of the growing domain of Islam for about forty years. The first great wave of conquest received its impetus from this small town in western Arabia. The Caliph Omar had his residence here when, in 637, Iraq, the province which contained Ctesiphon, the capital of the Persian empire, was subdued by Khálid ibn Walíd, "The Sword of Allah". Almost as soon as he arrived at the Euphrates after some hard fighting on the way, he was told that it would be worth his while to turn his attention to the rich village of Súq Baghdád, or "Baghdad Market" on the Tigris. Accordingly a raiding party was despatched under his lieutenant Muthanná. The historian Ṭabarí describes the raid as follows:

> There said a man of Ḥíra to Muthanná, "We will guide you to a village to which there come the merchants of the cities of Khosroes (i.e. the twin capital Seleucia-Ctesiphon), and in which they assemble with their goods once a year, making it as rich as a treasure house. Their market is being held during these very days, and if you can fall upon them while they suspect nothing you will light upon wealth that will be rich booty to the Moslems". He asked: "How far is it from that place to the cities of the Khosroes?" and he was told that it was part of a day or perhaps a whole day.

Having obtained guides and put out advance guards to arrest anyone who might give news of them, the company set out upon their march and

> they came upon the village in the early morning, at a time when the markets were at the height of their activity. And they slew the merchants and seized everything they desired. But Muthanná said to his men: "Take nothing but gold and silver, and let no man of you take any merchandise except what he can carry upon his own charger". The people who belonged to the markets fled and the Moslems filled their hands with the yellow (gold) and the white (silver) and the best of everything. Then they departed at full speed until they reached the canal of Saylaḥín at Anbár.[1]

Medina remained the capital while the four so-called "orthodox" Caliphs ruled. The last of them was the Prophet's son-in-law 'Alí, who was murdered by a fanatic in A.D. 661 and was succeeded by Mu'áwiya, the Arab military governor of Syria. He had long been awaiting his opportunity, and in spite of considerable opposition he seized the Caliphate. The force which had enabled him to realize his ambition came from his own

Arab troops on whom the continuance of his power depended. At Damascus, from which he ruled Syria, he could be sure of their loyalty and at the same time be at a safe distance from his enemies in Arabia. Damascus moreover would provide him with a better capital than Medina for his growing empire, and the transference was accordingly made.

The Ummayad dynasty which Mu'áwiya founded lasted for a century, but long before the end of that period the Arabs of Arabia were seeking a return of power to themselves, while the Persians and other non-Arab Moslems too were beginning to assert themselves out of dissatisfaction with the conditions of inferiority under which they remained members of the Caliphate. The Persians in particular, with a traditional faith in the hereditary principle, had an immense loyalty for 'Alí, Mohammed's son-in-law and cousin, whom they regarded as the one rightful heir to the Caliphate. They looked upon the Ummayads, who had succeeded to office only by election, as usurpers, and sought some other object for their religious and political affections. In the family of the Prophet's uncle 'Abbás they found what they wanted. These Abbasids were as eager for power as any other oriental princes, and when, in A.D. 747, during the reign of the weakling Caliph Merwán II, a certain Abú Muslim, who was a loyal slave of theirs, raised the black standard of his master's house in revolt in the Persian province of Khurásán, the Persians flocked to it in thousands. Three years later, the last of the Ummayads was defeated in battle. He was caught and slain after many of his followers had been butchered, and Abú 'l-'Abbás, "The Blood-pourer", reigned as first Caliph of the Abbasid line.

If the Umayyads derived their power from the Arabs of Syria, the Abbasids, as we have seen, owed theirs no less to the loyalty of their Persian supporters. The first Caliph of the new line recognized the fact, and determined to move the seat of authority from Damascus to a point nearer Persia. His first step was to settle in the town of Anbár near Kufa and on the Euphrates. There he built an imposing palace which he called the Háshimíya after his ancestor Háshim, and thence he directed the bloodthirsty operations which earned him his sinister title of "The Shedder of Blood". He seems not to have succeeded altogether in his purpose of shaking off his enemies, for Kufa was overrun by the 'Alids and by supporters of the house of 'Alí, who were rival claimants with himself for the Caliphate. He died in A.D. 754 before he had time to carry out his purpose, and his brother and successor Manṣúr (Abú Ja'far) made up his mind to escape from the neighbourhood of Kufa, whose inhabitants he mistrusted, and to move nearer still to Persia.

The historian Ṭabarí relates that Manṣúr had no intention of leaving the choice of a locality for his new city to chance. He set out himself one morning with a few followers to find a site that would be suitable not only for his own palace but for a large camp, in which he hoped to garrison his army. The first locality which attracted his attention was the village of Jarjarayya on the Tigris, fourteen leagues below the ancient twin capital of Seleucia-Ctesiphon. From there he ascended the river by the west bank, to the village of Baghdad, situated at a point near where the old Sarát canal joined the Tigris. His first view of the place did not attract him and he continued his search along the river as far north as Mosul, but without finding anything more to his liking. Accordingly he returned to Baghdad, which on consideration seemed to him the safest place for his camp.

Legend relates that when report of the Caliph's intention to build a city near the site of their monastery came to the ears of the Christian monks who lived there, one of them approached a member of the imperial retinue and questioned him on the project. He asked first who it was that had undertaken to build the city and was told in reply that it was: "The Commander of the Faithful, the Caliph of Mankind". "Has he any other name?" asked the monk. The courtier knew of none except the Caliph's patronymic "Abú Ja'far" and his title of "al-Manṣúr" ("the Victorious"). "Then", said the monk, "go to him and tell him not to weary himself with the building of this city, for we find it written in our books that one named 'Miqlás' is to build a city here, and it will be one of the most resplendent in the world. No one but he has the power to build here." The courtier thereupon returned to the camp, and, approaching Manṣúr, who happened to be on horseback, related to him what had occurred. The Commander of the Faithful at once dismounted and remained for long prostrated in prayer. Then he rose and said: "By Allah, I used to be called Miqlás. When I was a boy there was a famous robber called Miqlás who was notorious for his thieving prowess. Now we had an old woman who brought me up, and it chanced that one day the boys from school came to our house and insisted that it was my turn to play the host. I had nothing to spend on their entertainment; but the old woman had some spun thread and I took this and sold it so that I could provide hospitality for them. When she discovered I had stolen her thread, she called me 'Miqlás'. I had forgotten this, but now I am assured that it is I who am to build this city".[1]

Another equally legendary argument that led Manṣúr to decide on the site is put into the mouth of a Christian philosopher who met him on his first coming to the place. The holy man expatiated on its excellences.

"You will be on the Sarát canal", said he, "between the Tigris and the Euphrates. If anyone should attack you, the two rivers will be moats to your city. Moreover, stores can reach you by the Tigris from Diyár Bekr, or from across the sea, from India and China, or from Baṣra; and, by the Euphrates, from Raqqa and Syria. By the river Tamarra [the modern Diyala] also, supplies can come to you from Khurásán and the provinces of Persia. You will be in the centre of the country, between Baṣra, Kufa and Wásiṭ in the one direction and Mosul in the other; right in the midst of the alluvial lands of Iraq. You will therefore be near to open plain, sea, and mountain."

Ṭabarí[2] tells still another story in connection with Manṣúr's search for the place in which to put his capital. When he was in the neighbourhood of the future city, he summoned the heads of all the Christian villages and monasteries near by. He questioned each closely with a view to discovering how each was situated with regard to heat and cold, rain and mud, mosquitoes and venomous reptiles. Not content with that, he gave orders to the various members of his retinue that each was to go to a village, spend the night there and bring back a report on his experiences. When the reports had all been presented, Manṣúr, after due consideration, decided to erect his new city on the site of the village of Baghdad. It is not unlikely that one of the reasons which finally determined the Caliph's choice was Baghdad's comparative freedom from mosquitoes, which are a plague in the rest of Iraq.

It must be remembered that in Manṣúr's day the ancient system of canals, dating from far back in Babylonian history, was still, in part at any rate, in working order, and the desert which at the present time surrounds the city was then a patchwork of fertile fields. Ṭabarí tells us that the ground on which the foundations of the city were actually laid covered the arable lands of sixty villages, to which Manṣúr made suitable compensation. The fields themselves were divided by a network of canals, some of which were broad enough to carry the vessels that came up the two rivers. Also, as has been seen in the story of the early raid on Súq Baghdád, the trade of the district was already vigorous.

In devising the plan for the city the Caliph seems to have been inspired by his constant fear of assassination or of attack by his numerous enemies. His whole idea apparently was to build himself a fortress that should be as strong as he could make it, and with this object in view he laid out the city in a circle, after a plan which all the Moslem historians and geographers proclaim to be unique. His own house was to be in the centre and on all sides there was to be an open space which he could easily command with his bodyguard. Once he had chosen the site he began to work with a will. The village and surrounding country were made to swarm with workmen in readiness for the building. As a first step he levelled the whole area, then cut out the ground-plan of the city in the surface of the sand and filled in the excavated lines with ashes. The ashes in their turn were covered with bales of cotton soaked in naphtha. When all was ready the bales were set alight, so that the whole plan stood revealed in lines of fire.

The Caliph had been careful to take a horoscope in order to find a favourable time for the building, but he also attended to more practical matters. We are told by the eleventh-century biographer who is known as Al-Khaṭíb, "The Preacher", who was a native of Baghdad, that as soon as Manṣúr had worked out his plans

> he sent for engineers, architects, and men skilled in the knowledge of measurement, surveying, and apportionment. When they were assembled he described to them the plan which he had conceived and then brought from a distance artisans and craftsmen, carpenters, smiths and diggers. For all he provided daily rations. Further, he wrote to every town giving instructions that any inhabitant who knew aught of building was to be sent to him. And he began nothing of the work of construction until there were assembled before him many thousands of craftsmen and artificers.[1]

Ṭabarí says that places as far afield as Damascus, Mosul and Baṣra were laid under contribution.[2] Over the workmen officers were appointed, of whom one was the famous theologian Abú Ḥanífa, founder of the earliest of the schools of Sunní thought. Another account says that Manṣúr brought Abú Ḥanífa from Kufa, which was his home, and wished to appoint him cadi, but that the learned theologian refused the office. After the completion of the city, when Manṣúr had taken up his residence there, his son, the prince Mahdí, went to live outside the city walls and on the opposite, the east, bank of the river. He built a mosque there at Ruṣáfa and asked Abú Ḥanífa to act as cadi. But the shaikh again refused the honour and Mahdí descended to threats. "If you do not accept", said he, "I will have you flogged until you do consent." Abú Ḥanífa was thus forced to undertake the duties, but his unwilling and grudging performance of them landed him in prison, where he died in A.D. 767. "He was buried in the Khayzurán cemetery (on the east bank) and his tomb, which is a well-known monument, is much frequented by pious visitors."[1] The tomb of this saint—for as such he came to be regarded—still exists, about two miles north of Baghdad in the village of Mu'aẓẓam. It is one of the few remaining links with old Baghdad, and though its two gilded domes and its minarets are of comparatively recent construction, there is no reason to doubt that the saint lies buried under them.

But that is anticipating the completion of the city. There was, and is, no stone to be found nearer to Baghdad than the hills of the Jebel Hamrín, eighty miles away. Accordingly the next stage in the building operations was the making of bricks. They were of enormous size and weight, some being cubes that

2-2

weighed nearly 200 pounds apiece and measured a cubit (twenty inches) each way, while others were of about half that thickness. When the astrologers had pronounced that the stars were favourable to the enterprise, the actual work of building was begun. It is said that Manṣúr himself laid the first brick at the end of the year A.D. 762. The work took three years, but might have been completed earlier if the various rivals of the Abbasid house had allowed the work to proceed without interruption.

It is more than probable that in deciding on the architecture of the city the Caliph was inspired by the grandeur of the ruins at Babylon and Ctesiphon. In his day these must have retained enough of their old splendour to encourage him to rivalry with their builders. He was not above trying to demolish part of the palace of the Khosroes at Ctesiphon to obtain what he thought would be cheap materials for his own capital. Characteristically he first asked the advice of his vizier and counsellor Khálid ibn Barmak—first of the famous clan of the Barmecides that rose to power—and when he advised against it, Manṣúr taunted him with having retained a sympathy with things Persian which could only have come from his fire-worshipping Persian ancestors. But Khálid had a reply ready, and said that to leave such a noble monument standing would enhance the glory of Islam by proving that people with a great past had become subject to it. When, after demolishing about a third of the great palace, the Caliph found that it was cheaper to make bricks at Baghdad than to transport the materials from Ctesiphon across country, he ceased operations, again contrary to the advice of his minister, who said that to desist now was an admission of his defeat by the handiwork of a non-Moslem people.[1]

The main wall of the city was made tremendously strong and thick, and though the top measured less than a third of the width of the base, it carried a roadway twenty-five cubits (about forty-two feet) wide, to which there was approach by inclined pathways permitting horsemen to ride up. From the base to the tip of its pinnacles was a distance of sixty cubits. Four gateways pierced it: on the south-west the Kufa gate, on the north-west the Syria gate, on the north-east the Khurásán gate—leading to the huge Persian province of Khurásán—and on the south-west the Baṣra gate. Each was strongly defended against attack and was lofty enough to allow the passage of mounted men without any need to lower banners or spears. The iron gates with which the gateways were fitted were so heavy that a company of men was required to open or close them. Ṭabarí has a curious legend about them. He says:

At the time when Abú Ja'far (Manṣúr) came to need gates for his city a certain Abú 'Abd al-Raḥmán mentioned to him that Solomon son of David had once built a city in the neighbourhood of Wásiṭ. The *Shaytáns* (Demons) had built some magnificent gates of iron for him, the like of which no man could fashion to-day. They remained in the position in which he had placed them till Ḥajjáj [the conqueror of Iraq], coming to build Wásiṭ, destroyed the old town and took possession of the gates. Manṣúr took them for his own town, using four of them for the inner gateways and the fifth for the outer gate of his own castle.[2]

Surrounding the main rampart, and at a distance of about fifty yards from it, Manṣúr put another wall, not quite so thick, but protected by a moat. The gateways of the new wall were topped by strongly defenced structures which housed troops, and they corresponded in position to those in the main wall. The distance between gateways is given as 5000 cubits and the circumference of the outer wall may be taken therefore to be rather more than six miles.

Between each gateway in the inner wall and the one opposite to it in the outer wall, Manṣúr laid paved roads beginning and ending in square open spaces in front of the gateways. At first these roads were regarded as paths leading to the Caliph's domain, which was the whole space inside the main wall, and no one but the Caliph himself was allowed to ride on them. But arcades came to be built on each side of them, and when the city's population began to flow in, the arcades were found to be convenient depositories for the display of merchandise, and before long were converted into regular bazaars. Even in the early days of the city the traders in the various classes of goods separated themselves into groups, so that all the slave dealers, for example, were to be found occupying a place in the arcades apart from that of the leather sellers; the silk merchants were separated from the silversmiths, and so forth. As a consequence, it must then, as now, have been difficult to buy a completed garment in the bazaar, for the cloth had to be bought in one place, trimmings in another, needles and thread in another, and the whole had to be transported to the tailors to be made up.

In the rest of the space between the two walls the artisans of the city—the craftsmen, tradesmen, scribes and mullahs—the beggars and all the various kinds of minor officials that go to make up the "masses" in an Eastern town, began to find a lodging and to build their homes. The arcades and the strong walls of the city divided the multitude of dwellings into four districts, each rigorously shut off from the other except for gateways, which were strongly guarded and could be closed to prevent any concerted action in case of a rising. Moreover, in accordance with the Caliph's plan of safeguarding himself, there was no free access to the central portion of the city, so that he could live in complete privacy if he so desired. Each quarter was put under the authority of a special official or elder, whose business it was to maintain order in his section. Of planning within the various quarters we hear nothing. Presumably the houses were huddled together and built wherever their owners fancied, and lack of space, together with the necessities of the climate and absence of good building materials, made for narrow streets and blank mud walls.

The main streets were fifty cubits in width and the smaller ones sixteen cubits, but these were the streets actually laid out in connection with the walls and gates. In among the private houses, public buildings such as mosques and baths began to be erected to fulfil the needs of the inhabitants, and a sufficient water supply was provided by means of canals taking off, for the most part, not from the Tigris but from the Euphrates, for ease in engineering. These canals were also used for the supply of water to numerous gardens outside the walls or laid out within the courtyards of many of the richer houses.

Inside the main wall the chief building was of course the Caliph's palace, which, from its gilded entrance way, came to be known as the Golden Gate. To contain all the separate apartments required by his many wives and slave girls and the numerous households of his children, it had to be a large building, and in fact it covered an area of over one-eighth of a square mile. Amongst its public rooms were two main audience chambers. In one or other of these the Caliph sat to receive in state the numerous people who had a claim on his attention; visiting ambassadors, erring governors of provinces, wandering dervishes in search of alms, or poets, philosophers, historians and other men of letters in search of a patron.

Each of the chambers had a dome, one rising behind the other. The taller one was 130 feet high, and its green outlines could be seen from every part of the city, dominating all the minarets and pinnacles. Tradition in later times had it that the dome was topped by the figure of a mounted man holding a lance, and that in time of trouble the figure pointed in the direction from which danger to the capital might be expected. The historian al-Khaṭíb al-Baghdádí, when discussing the ultimate fate of the dome, says: "It has been related to me that the dome fell in the year A.H. 329 (=A.D. 941). On the night of its collapse the rain descended in torrents, and thunder and lightning filled men with awe. The dome was the crown of Baghdad, the standard of the realm and the most considerable monument of the Abbasid sovereignty".[1] Some pious Moslems disliked the legend of the figure on the dome and strenuously denied the truth of it, and the setting up of an image was certainly against the Koranic law. The geographer Yáqút, who was a converted Greek, said that the story was "a lie, an extravagant invention. Such things are told only of the Egyptian magicians...Moslems are too serious minded for such fables....The figure had of necessity to be turned in one direction, and, if the legend is true, enemies would be constantly crowding in from that direction. But Allah knows best".[2]

The palace did not occupy the whole of the interior circle, although no other building but the royal mosque intruded on the open space provided by the Caliph for his greater security. But within the wall there were erected the palaces of the Caliph's children and the various government buildings. One of the earliest of these was the mint, and the British Museum possesses coins minted in A.D. 763, just one year after the city's foundations were laid. Other such buildings were the treasury, the armoury, the secretariate, and even a public bakery. A third wall separated these public buildings from the extensive quarters of the royal princes and their servants.

CHAPTER II

The Expansion of the City

There seems to have been no difficulty in providing the new capital with inhabitants. People flocked to it from all parts of the Moslem empire, attracted not so much by the reports of the beauty of its architecture or the healthiness of its situation—about which the common folk probably cared very little—but by the prospect of gain, and the fact that the city meant something new in Islam. The original Mohammedans had been Arabs, men of the desert or inhabitants of small villages or of military camps. Here was a city which was not a fortified dépôt for troops and which as yet had no traditions and few vested family interests, so that for a time it was without any internal conflict of policies. The consequence was the growth of a new citizen class, which created a fresh standard and ideal of life not only for the Arab but for the Moslem world generally.

Although Moslem Arabs and Persians formed the bulk of the immigrants, men of other faiths came too. Amongst the newcomers to the city was the Patriarch of the Nestorian community. In Persian times he had lived at Ctesiphon, but when that royal city was destroyed he moved to Baghdad and erected the patriarchal headquarters on the west side of the river where the church of St Mary was also founded. A Christian community built itself up round the church, later to be transferred to the east side, where it still exists, probably in the very spot where it was originally established.[1] At the same time Jewish traders and others, descendants of the Jews exiled by Nebuchadnezzar from Palestine and long domiciled near the Euphrates, began to make their homes in the city.

Together with the traders, craftsmen, teachers and beggars, came those new citizens who earned a livelihood by amusing the rest of the population in their leisure hours. Amongst the entertainers were the singers and musicians who are to be regarded as the artists of the new community. Some had already made a name for themselves in Mecca or Medina, where their art flourished, but they came to the capital in search of new conquests and increased wealth. They had no difficulty in finding patrons amongst the nobles and chief officers of Manṣúr's court: the Caliph himself however had little use for them, for in addition to being miserly he was entirely insensible to the charms of music. One of the best of the musicians was a certain Ḥákim al-Wádí, who had begun his career as a barber, but afterwards found he possessed a good voice and put himself under a skilled singer for training. In Baghdad he discovered the merits of the *hazaj* rhythm, a quick and lively measure, well adapted to songs of frivolous *galanterie* of a kind that appealed to the crowd. His success was immediate. Manṣúr used to hear of the enormous sums paid to the singer and was astonished at the prodigality of his patrons, several of them members of the royal family. "What is Ḥákim?" he would ask. "Only a man who recites pleasantly. That is all. How can he be worth such presents?" One evening while Manṣúr was taking the air on a balcony he saw opposite his palace, issuing from a house that was occupied by one of his generals, a personage clad in a superb robe, seated on a fine mule and preceded by a slave carrying a lighted torch. "That mule", said the Caliph to the courtiers standing round him, "is the general's. But who is it riding the mule?" He was told that it was the singer Ḥákim. "Oh yes!" said the Caliph, wagging his head, "now I see that he deserves the gifts that he receives." "How does the Commander of the Faithful see that?" one of the courtiers inquired. "I know the general," said Manṣúr, "he is a thrifty person and gives money only for good value."[1]

Towards the end of Manṣúr's reign the political importance of Persia began to have its effect on the life and fashions of the capital. The Caliph himself was the model upon whom the populace fixed its eyes, and by natural inclination and for political reasons he was greatly influenced by Iran. His chief minister was Khálid the Barmecide, a man of Zoroastrian origin, and similarly in every one of the great households Persian scholars were to be found teaching their own literature, history, astronomy and medicine. Persian theologians were in especial demand, for the conversion of large numbers of Zoroastrians to Islam helped the spread of Iranian culture in the new capital, to which Persians streamed as soon as they realized that they were regarded with favour there. Indeed they held so great a place in the Caliph's esteem that we hear of an Arab of some standing waiting in vain for admission at the door of Manṣúr's palace, whereas men of the province of

Khurásán went freely in and out and jeered at the old man who stood watching them.[1] With the Persian doctors came pilgrims and merchants who settled in the old village of Karkh outside the city walls, and made it an abiding outpost of the land of their origin.

The constant influx of new inhabitants in time caused the question of supplies to become a serious one. Long before the end of Manṣúr's reign the bazaar arcades had proved too small for the needs of the city. The abundant wares of the merchants overflowed into bazaars outside the city to the south, where they became the chief market of the Middle East. It attracted such great numbers of foreign traders from all parts of the Moslem empire and outside it that at last the situation began to give Manṣúr cause for uneasiness. He saw in these foreigners a possible menace to his city, and asked advice on the point from a Greek ambassador, who told him that by admitting anybody and everybody into the city he must, at some time or other, be letting a possible enemy enter within his gates. At the ambassador's suggestion he ordered the bazaars to be entirely removed and placed outside to the south, in the suburb of Karkh. Here the market could expand as much as was necessary, and in fact it grew rapidly, more bazaars and houses being erected round it until it formed an integral part of Baghdad; and its importance finally was such that it gave its name to the whole of that part of the city which lies on the right bank—a name which is still retained. Here, even at the present day, are to be found the *alwás*, or grain warehouses, and the chief markets for the fresh fruits, dates and vegetables that form the main food of the Moslem inhabitants.

The palace of the Golden Gate, like the original bazaar, soon outgrew its purpose. The Caliph's harem and retinue, which had never been small, increased steadily, while in addition the numerous members of his family who were growing up began to have households of their own. A certain amount of unrest amongst his troops, due to the stinginess for which he was notorious, led Manṣúr to transfer a section of them to the left bank. There he put them under the command of his son Mahdí, who was to succeed him on the throne and for whom he built a house on the site known as *Ruṣáfa*, "The Causeway", that was later to grow into the most important section of the city.

Of Manṣúr's parsimony, already mentioned, many stories are told which incidentally depict the life of the city. Ṭabarí, for example, tells how the prince Mahdí once rewarded a sycophantic poet with the sum of 20,000 dirhems—over 400 pounds—for some flattering verses. Manṣúr summoned the panegyrist and made him read his composition. When the poet had done he was gruffly told that he had been paid five times too much for his work, and he was made to disgorge four-fifths of his honorarium on the spot. Yet we are told by the same historian that in spite of Manṣúr's meanness he spent on his city not less than 4,800,000 dirhems, which would be roughly equivalent to a quarter of a million pounds sterling at a direct calculation of exchange, though it would probably be worth ten times that amount in actual value.

On his own residences alone the Caliph must have expended huge sums. When the middle of the Round City began to be crowded he looked about for a site for a new palace. He chose one outside the walls, on the river bank near the Khurásán gate, on a spot that had once been occupied by a Christian monastery. The beauty of the place and the freshness of the air which he found there after the stuffy atmosphere of the crowded town delighted him and all who visited it. Manṣúr himself expressed his approval by calling his new palace *Qaṣr al-Khuld* or "Paradise Castle", though the magnificence of the architecture and the gorgeousness of the decoration no doubt had something to do with the name. Inevitably the castle became the nucleus of a city quarter, for the houses of servants and courtiers had to be built near it, and a bazaar, mosques and public buildings came into being with the increase of population.

Naturally enough, Baghdad occupied an important place in the mind of its founder, and indeed he gave it his last thought on his death-bed. While on a pilgrimage to Mecca he fell sick, and had his son Mahdí summoned. To him he gave much good counsel on various matters and then came to the subject of Baghdad.

> "Behold this city", said he. "Beware of exchanging it for another, for it is your home and your strength. In it I have gathered for you treasures so abundant that even if the land revenues were cut off for the space of fifteen years, you would still have sufficient for the supply of your army and for expenditure of all kinds.... And beware of building up the eastern part of the city, for you will never complete it."

So far as the capital of the empire was concerned, the new Caliph did not pay much attention to his father's dying wishes. The palace on the left bank which had primarily been intended for a secluded pleasure-resort —at a safe distance from the disapproving glances of the rigid citizens of Baghdad—was turned into the headquarters of a large body of troops. A high and massive wall was built round the camp and an independent water supply was provided by a channel specially dug from a branch of the famous Nahrawán canal, an ancient waterway that itself took off from the Tigris about a hundred miles upstream from Baghdad and watered an immense tract of territory lying between the river and the Persian mountains.

Soon there began to cluster round the "Camp of Mahdí", as it came to be called, the superfluous population of the older part of the city, which, even though capable of containing great masses of inhabitants, was yet unable to house all that were attracted to it. Ruṣáfa, which was the other name of Mahdí's camp, soon expanded into three flourishing suburbs, and the city's prosperity was now well on the way to being established. An indication of Baghdad's wealth is given by the fact that already one whole bazaar was devoted exclusively to the sale of Chinese silks.

"We know", says an authority, "that hither came all the products of the world in constant stream. Spices of all kinds, aloes and sandal-wood for fumigation, teak for ship-building, ebony for artistic work, jewels, metals, dyes and minerals of all kinds from India and the Malay archipelago; porcelains and—what is indispensable to the oriental—musk from China; pearls and

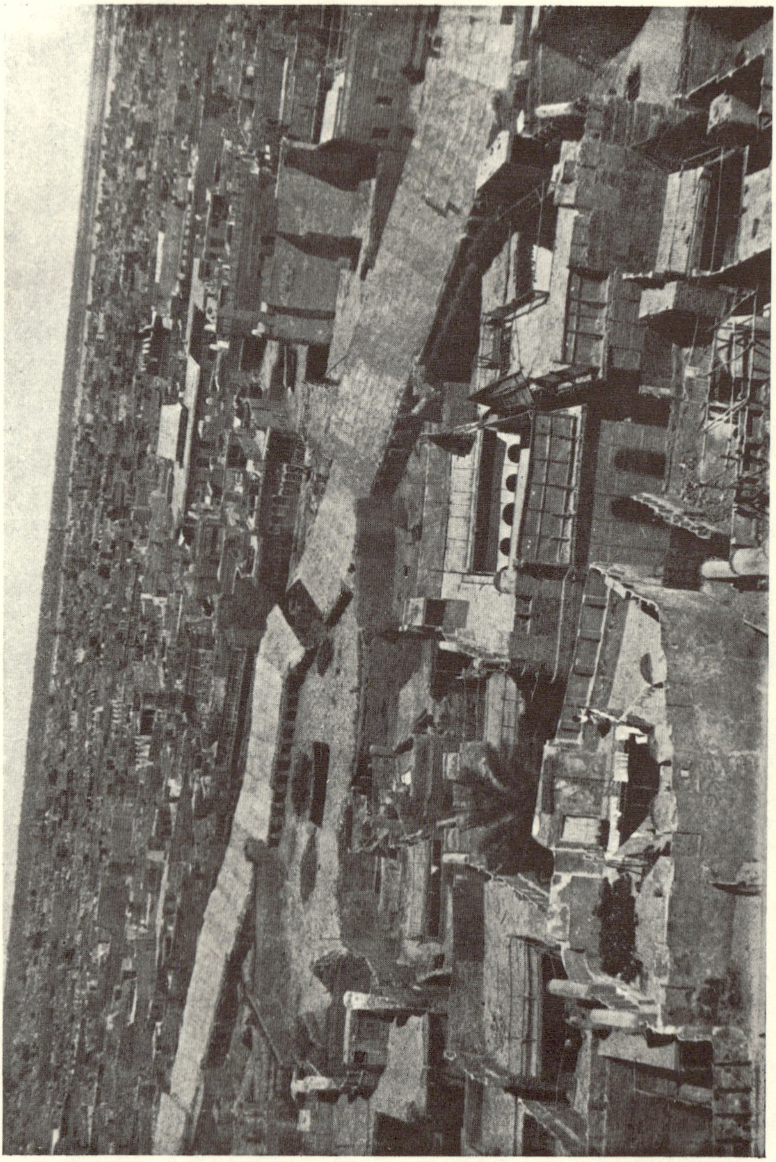

white-skinned slaves from the lands of the Turk and the Russian; ivory and negro slaves from East Africa;—all were brought here by traders and navigators after long and arduous journeys by land and sea. At the same time the city merchants carried on a profitable trade with China in the products of the Caliphate; dates, sugar, glassware, cotton and iron. Even more brisk was the internal trade between the various provinces of the empire, all of which trade flowed through Baghdad. Egypt's rice, grain, linen and paper; Syria's glass and metal ware, Arabia's spices, pearls and weapons; Persia's silks, perfumes and garden produce, all found their way here."[1]

Mahdí was not slow to take advantage of the wealth that came pouring in. First of all the Caliphs to do so, upsetting all precedent, he levied a tax on the bazaars. Medina and Damascus, the former capitals of the Caliphate, though they did not equal Baghdad, were yet flourishing centres of trade, and the native historians remark on the fact that until Mahdí no one had thought of making them productive of revenue. It scarcely needs saying that his successors did not surrender this profitable source of income. It was a sane and justifiable step, and Mahdí followed it by giving the inhabitants of his city a freedom rarely to be found either in the East or West until quite modern times. It was such that merchants who had come for purposes of business remained to become citizens, and so further enhanced the prosperity of the city. And it was not merely the utilitarian arts that the Caliph encouraged. Poetry and music, for which his father had had little use, began to be heard in his palaces and in those of his nobles. Also, since he set the fashion, the art of good living began to flourish in the city; but there the Caliph may have had an ulterior motive—one that would not have been beneath the traditions of his family—for he is said to have collected a certain amount of revenue from taxes on taverns, even though Islam forbade the drinking of wine or other intoxicating liquors.

Of the artists who enlivened the capital in Mahdí's time was the singer Siyáṭ, who came from Mecca and became popular in Baghdad. His accompanists were two of his friends, "one of whom played the flute and followed his singing, and the other played the lute and marked the rhythm of his airs". The names of these three artists formed a strange group. Siyáṭ means "whips" in Arabic; the flute player was called Ḥibál, i.e. "ropes", and the name of the player on the lute was 'Iqáb, i.e. "torture". They were names that lent themselves to jests, and the story is told that one night, before their fame had spread, Mahdí, while at drink with some of his friends, called Salám al-Abrash, his chief eunuch, and gave him an order in low tones. All that the company could hear was, "Go and bring... whips...ropes...torture". Knowing something of their sovereign's character, they had some excuse for feeling with considerable uneasiness that he was going to exact vengeance from one of them for some offence. After a painful quarter of an hour's wait they saw Siyáṭ and his two assistants armed with their musical instruments. Only then were they reassured, while the Caliph laughed loudly at the fright he had given them.[1]

But though Mahdí liked music for himself he refused to allow either of his sons, Músá al-Hádí or Hárún, to be seduced by it, and gave express orders that no musicians were to be permitted to enter into their presence. He discovered one day that two of Siyáṭ's pupils, Ibrahím al-Mauṣilí and Ibn Jámi', had visited the young princes. He promptly had the artists brought before him. Ibrahím received 360 lashes, and Ibn Jámi', though successful in entreating the Caliph to forgo the corporal punishment, was banished from the city in disgrace.

Inseparably connected with the freedom of life in the capital was the safety of the roads throughout the empire. This security not only encouraged trade but induced an ever-increasing number of pious Moslems to undertake the pilgrimage to Mecca, a sacred expedition required to be made by every true believer at least once in his lifetime. At that time, as at the present day, the pilgrim trains from the north and east generally passed through Baghdad. Those that started from the capital itself were supplied with an amazing number of luxuries, and it is said that when the Caliph Mahdí set out to make the journey in the late summer of A.D. 776, he provided ice for nearly one-half of the very large company that travelled with him.

Another side of the picture is given in that charming book on the history of the Caliphs and their viziers that goes under the name of *al-Fakhrí*. According to this authority, Mahdí for some years left the management of his affairs to a certain vizier called Ya'qúb ibn Dá'úd, who seems to have pleased the Caliph very well until there occurred an incident which gave Ya'qúb's numerous rivals cause for rejoicing. Mahdí one day summoned the vizier and had him ushered into a delightful garden where the audience was to take place. The trees were in full bloom, the blossoms were of many colours, and the part of the garden where the Caliph sat was covered with a rose-coloured carpet on which a beautiful slave girl stood before him. As the vizier entered, the Caliph asked him what he thought of the *al fresco* sitting-room. He pronounced it pleasant in the extreme and prayed Allah to grant his sovereign full enjoyment of it. "It is all yours", said Mahdí, "together with a hundred thousand dirhems; and, to complete your happiness I add the slave girl." Ya'qúb cried out in his amazement, but the Caliph silenced him, and said: "There is something I need from you in return. I require your assurance that you will give it". The vizier replied: "Commander of the Faithful, I am your slave, obedient to all that you command". The sovereign then mentioned a particular individual, a descendant of the Caliph 'Alí, and said he would be glad to see the man put out of the way because he showed symptoms of being a possible traitor. Mahdí forced the minister to swear an oath that he would do what was necessary, and gave orders that everything in the place of audience, including the slave girl, was to be transferred to the vizier's house.

The minister had the proposed victim brought before him and found him a man of the highest character and intelligence, who pleaded with him and warned him against shedding the innocent blood of a descendant of 'Alí, the Prophet's son-in-law, and of Fáṭima, the Prophet's daughter. Moved by pity, the vizier gave the man a sum of money and told him to escape to some place of safety. Unfortunately for Ya'qúb, the slave girl had been spying on him, and sent a secret messenger to the Caliph telling him of what had occurred. Mahdí at once covered the roads with his agents and had the refugee stopped and brought back. He put him into a room near the audience chamber and sent for his vizier. "Ya'qúb," said he to the unsuspecting minister, "what did you do with the 'Alid?" "God has given the Commander of the Faithful relief from him", was the reply. "Is he dead?" then asked Mahdí. "Yes", said Ya'qúb. Turning to his servants the Caliph ordered them to bring before him a man whom they would find in the next room. As soon as the 'Alid appeared Ya'qúb knew that his own career was over, and remained silent. He was sent to the dungeons, where he was let down by a rope into a deep pit into which no light penetrated. There he was left, just enough food being given him from day to day to keep him alive. When someone remembered him in the reign of Hárún al-Rashíd, many years afterwards, his sight had failed, and he was brought up out of his pit only to die.[1]

Like all the members of his line, Mahdí seldom bestowed his favours for very long in the same quarter. He once punished the court poet, Abú 'l-'Atáhiya, for the crime of forsaking his art in favour of the less dangerous occupation of selling water jars, which had been his business before he took to writing panegyrics. Yet while he was at court he was enough of a favourite with Mahdí to venture a request for a certain slave girl known as 'Utba, who was in the royal harem. He had been much smitten with her charms and wrote most of his amatory verse to celebrate them. His method of making his request was characteristic of the time. One New Year's Day he obtained permission to give his royal patron a present and brought a specimen of his wares in the shape of a large porcelain vase. This contained a perfumed robe, round the hem of which were embroidered some verses hinting at his desire for the girl. Mahdí seemed pleased at the device and was for giving the girl to Abú 'l-'Atáhiya, when she cried out: "O Commander of the Faithful, treat me as a woman and a member of your household! Would you give me up to a nasty man who sells pots and gains a living by his verses?"[1] The appeal was successful and the poet transferred his affections elsewhere.

About the life of the ordinary citizen of the day not a great deal is to be gathered. The great contrasts of wealth and poverty which were to appear later had not yet made their presence felt. The Caliph set all the fashions, which those in the vicinity of the court followed. But the lesser people lived their own lives, probably very little different from those of their pre-Islamic ancestors, except that they had changed the object of their worship and substituted Mohammedan teachers and holy men for the priests of Zoroastrianism or other religions. The merchants very early formed an important part of the community and the professions of ecclesiastical law and medicine were well established in Mahdí's reign, though it cannot be said that there was a high standard of professional morality. A well-known story in illustration is told in connection with a negro called Abú Duláma, who had a reputation as a wag in Mahdí's time:

He once called in a physician to attend to his son who had fallen ill, and agreed to pay a certain sum in the event of the patient's recovery. When his son was restored to health, Abú Duláma said to the physician: "I call heaven to witness that we have nothing in the world to pay you with. However, cite the rich Jew so-and-so before the judge, and I and my son will go before him and swear that the Jew owes you money". The physician immediately brought the Jew before the *cadi* of Kufa, one Ibn Abí Laylá, claiming a certain sum of money. The Jew naturally denied the debt, and the claimant, saying he had witnesses to prove it, went out to bring Abú Duláma and his son. The elder of these two scoundrels had anticipated that the judge would make some inquiry about the character of the witnesses, and in the ante-chamber he recited in a loud voice for the *cadi* and all to hear:

"Such men as screen me find in me a screen;
But if men pay I run their sins to ground.
Wouldst cleanse my well, thine own though far from clean?
Then all shall know what filth in thine I've found".

He then entered the court and gave his evidence. The *cadi* listened carefully, and having apparently given it due consideration, he said: "I have accepted your declaration and admit your evidence". Being convinced however that they were false witnesses, he himself paid the sum in question out of his own pocket and dismissed the Jew out of fear for Abú Duláma's tongue.[1]

Mahdí's building policy in the new part of the city led, as has been seen, to the establishment of three flourishing suburbs. Of these Ruṣáfa lay in the angle made by a bend in the river, between it and the desert on the east was the suburb of Shammásiya, while along the river bank to the south-west and facing the Round City on the opposite side, lay the Mukharrim quarter. Between the two latter suburbs the boundary was marked by the great Khurásán highway, an ancient trade route that carried most of the merchandise that came from Persia and China.

Protecting the new suburbs on the land side, a wall was built, but enough room was left for expansion. It was here that the Barmecides or Barmakites, who were to become famous in Baghdad's history, came to build their homes, which rivalled the Caliph's palaces in magnificence. Here also the Caliphs themselves later built their chief residences. Between East and West Baghdad communication was assured by three bridges built on boats or pontoons, much as the Baghdad bridges are to-day. It is probable that the lack of a permanent bridge over the Tigris is due to the fact that the cost would be prohibitive, for the reason that there is no stone nearer than the Jebel Hamrín hills, over eighty miles away. Then, as now, the absence of a permanent structure was felt as more than an inconvenience, since in times of high flood the pontoon bridges were liable to be swept away, often with loss of life.

The main bridge in Mahdí's day formed a continuation to the Khurásán highway which led through the great bazaar in East Baghdad. On the west bank the "Paradise" palace faced the bridge-head and was separated from it by a wide open space. Lower down the river, but within the grounds of the palace, the western end of another bridge was moored, while the northern parts of the city were served by still a third bridge about a mile north of the main one. Somewhere near the site of the upper bridge the Turks in fairly recent times had a bridge joining the modern suburbs of Muʿaẓẓam and Kadhimain, but that is no longer in existence.

CHAPTER III

"*In the Golden Prime of Good Haroun Al-raschid*"

Towards the end of Mahdí's life the matter of the succession began to be prominent and there arose the usual intrigues that such a situation breeds in the East, with the consequent hurt to the peace and quiet of the capital. Mahdí's favourite slave girl, Khayzurán, had borne him two sons, Músá al-Hádí ("Moses the Guide") and Hárún al-Rashíd ("Aaron the Upright")—the prince of the *Thousand and One Nights*. Músá, as the elder of the two, was entitled to the throne, but in the year 772 the younger prince greatly distinguished himself during a struggle with the Byzantine empire. On an expedition in Asia Minor, with Khálid the Barmecide as his counsellor, he had marched along the coast as far as the Bosphorus and compelled Irene, queen of Byzantium, to submit and pay him a large sum of money as a tribute. With this and a vast quantity of booty which his troops had acquired in enemy territory, the young warrior returned in triumph to the capital, where his delighted father bestowed on him the honorific title of "al-Rashíd", and determined that he, and not Músá, was to be the next occupant of the throne.

However, on the death of his father, Hárún loyally permitted his brother Músá to ascend the throne as Caliph. The troops in Baghdad disapproved and revolted in favour of Hárún, rioting in front of the house of the new Caliph's minister, and releasing the prisoners he had in confinement. Only by a promise that they would receive their pay, long deferred, were the mutineers persuaded to disperse. After his accession Músá was not restrained by any feelings of gratitude to his brother from trying to retain the succession in his own immediate family. As soon as he could do so he appointed his son Ja'far to be his heir, in the hope that Persian adherence to the hereditary principle would assist him in his scheme. As a further measure he summoned Yaḥyá the Barmecide, Hárún's secretary, and son of that Barmecide who had been Hárún's adviser at Byzantium, and tried by the offer of a bribe to win his support. Yaḥyá however had that sense of loyalty which made his family a power in the land and which all the Abbasid monarchs lacked. He refused Músá's approaches, and the Caliph, in a fierce rage, threw him into prison and would have had Hárún himself assassinated if that cautious prince had not anticipated trouble and fled the city. In a mad search for some victim to satisfy his wrath, the Caliph turned on his own mother, Khayzurán, whom he accused of favouring Hárún. The story goes that with a bloodthirstiness not unknown in his family, he plotted, though without success, to have her poisoned, and that she revenged herself by bribing some of his slave girls to smother him with pillows in his sleep. Whatever the truth of that may be, his reign was a short one and ended suddenly. In the year A.D. 786 Hárún al-Rashíd, at the age of twenty-two, became the next Caliph or "Successor" of the Prophet on earth.

Legend and history have combined to put the most brilliant period of Baghdad's career in the reign of Hárún whose attribute "The Upright" has already been explained. Critical examination does not always bear out the praises bestowed on that monarch by the professional panegyrists whom he gathered around him. Casual hints and odd stories incidental to the main course of the narratives told by the historians make it evident that he could be cruel, treacherous and mean. But there are good qualities that cannot be denied him. The success of his campaigns against Byzantium prove him to have been a good soldier, while a certain measure of administrative ability, of a kind rare in his day, brought security and wealth to the empire and its capital. It was then that Baghdad became in very special degree "a city of palaces and offices, hotels and pavilions, mosques and colleges, kiosks and squares, bazaars and markets, pleasure grounds and orchards, adorned with all the graceful charms which Saracenic architecture had borrowed from the Byzantines".[1] By that time also, with the increase of population and trade, the city had become a very important shipping centre. Along its miles of wharves lay vessels of every description and tonnage, from Chinese junks that had been towed with great labour up the Tigris from Baṣra to native *kelleks*—primitive rafts, built up on inflated sheep skins—of the kind that could not be propelled against the current, but had been floated down from Mosul. In addition there were ships of war, bitumen-covered *quffas* or coracles, and gaily coloured pleasure craft.[2] Trade poured into the city from the various provinces of the empire and the bazaars were more crowded than ever with merchandise from the four quarters of the world, so that to men living in the leaner days that came afterwards Hárún's reign was looked back upon as the Golden Age. Even then it cannot have been anything of a paradise for the poor man. The rich and powerful followed the example set by the Caliph, and extravagant luxury and display with immense expenditure on amusement were the fashion amongst those who had relationship with the court. It was an amazing establishment that Hárún maintained in his palace and its numerous annexes, which occupied altogether about one-third of the Round City. His wives and *odalisks* each had to be provided with separate quarters, and his taste for singing-girls necessitated huge harems, generally ruled over by an old slave woman. The Caliph's satellites were constantly on the watch for new talent to please him, and the "trade" was so large that one of Hárún's favourites, Ibrahím al-Mauṣilí, himself a singer, generally had a stock of eighty girls in training at a time.

There were others also who flocked round him in the hope of reward. Panegyrists, wits, physicians, gardeners, trainers of fighting-cocks and dogs, in fact all who could flatter, amuse or interest him were certain of his favour and of largess. But his singers gave him most pleasure. Of these, three, already mentioned, in particular competed for his recognition, Siyáṭ, Ibrahím al-Mauṣilí and Ibn Jámi', of whom the two latter had been Siyáṭ's pupils. Ibrahím was a Persian by birth and seems to have been intended originally for the profession of cadi. At the age of twenty-three, however, he fled from the seminary in which he was pursuing his studies and went to Mauṣil (Mosul), from which place he received his name of Mauṣilí. There, for lack of better employment, or perhaps to indulge a natural propensity, he became a highwayman, and, during his wanderings with various gangs, learned the songs of his comrades. In course of time he had surpassed all his acquaintances in the number and variety of the tunes at his command, and finally, hearing of the demand for singers at Baghdad, he had made his way there and succeeded in attracting the attention of Hárún's father, Mahdí, who was then Caliph.

Ibrahím's great rival, Ibn Jámi', was an Arab by origin and a member of the aristocratic tribe of the Quraysh, to which Mohammed himself had belonged. Like Ibrahím, he had first come to the capital in the reign of the Caliph al-Mahdí, who, as has been noted, banished him from the city for disobeying the command that no singers were to be allowed in the company of the young princes Hárún and Músá. After his banishment he returned to his home in Arabia, and at the time when Hárún came to the throne he was living at Mecca in great poverty, having squandered all his money on dogs and gambling. Soon afterwards he left Mecca for Medina in order to try and restore his fortunes. In the famous collection known as the *Kitáb al-Aghání* or *Book of Songs*, which contains much valuable biographical material about early Arab singers and poets, he tells the story of his subsequent adventures. In abbreviated form it runs:

I arrived at Medina with only four dirhems in my pocket. On my way to the house of an acquaintance of mine, I overtook a negress walking about two paces in front of me and singing a plaintive ditty. The tune was delightful and very original. I marvelled at it, but as I had not been able to catch it, I begged the negress to repeat it, which she did. But it again escaped me. "Once more", I begged. "Oh", said she, "that is enough. I must go and do my work." I offered her the four dirhems which was my entire possession, and she accepted them, though not without hesitation. She stopped, put down her pitcher on the ground, and sang the tune once more. This time I caught the air, having applied all my wits. "It has cost you four dirhems," said she, "but I predict it will bring you four thousand pieces of gold." With these words she picked up her pitcher and went on. I continued my way, humming the tune until I had fixed it in my memory.

One of the friends whom I visited assured me that the Caliph was well disposed towards me and advised me to go to Baghdad. When, at the end of a long journey, I arrived, the caravan set me down in a suburb of the capital. The day declined and I knew not where to go. I was following some people who were walking across the bridge, when I found myself in one of the main streets. There I saw a mosque, and entered. After the sunset prayer I remained in my place for about an hour without stirring. I was starving of hunger and utterly weary. The mosque gradually emptied until there remained only one person, well dressed, behind whom were several slaves and eunuchs. He prayed for a little while longer and then turned towards the door. As he passed he looked at me, and said: "You are doubtless a stranger?" "Yes," I replied, "I arrived in Baghdad this evening and I have no lodging." "Your profession?" "A singer." "I will make myself responsible for you", he said, and entrusting me to one of his men he left the mosque.

My guide led me to a great building, which he told me was the part of the imperial palace inhabited by his master Salám al-Abrash, chief of the eunuchs. We traversed various rooms and at last found ourselves in a long corridor at the end of which we reached a small room. There I was given a meal which I sorely needed. As I was nearing the end of my repast I heard hurried footsteps and a voice that said: "Is he in here?" "Yes", replied another voice. "Then", said the first, "let him be suitably clad and perfumed and let him be brought in." These orders were immediately executed. I was mounted on a mule of which a eunuch took the bridle. We passed through several courts, under lofty vaults, and finally reached a last court more spacious than all the rest. By the lamps which shone everywhere, and by the guards that were stationed near the doors and sent back and forth to each other the cry *Alláhu Akbar*, I knew that we were near the dwelling of the Caliph, and I dismounted. I was introduced into a vast and splendid hall, at the back of which hung a curtain of silk. Seats arranged in rows in front of the curtain occupied the middle of the chamber. Upon four of them were seated four persons, namely three women and a man. The women began to play and the man to sing. They were indifferent artists. When my turn arrived I begged the person nearest me to be my accompanist, and asked her to tune her instrument to a higher pitch. "Now", said a page to me, and I sang an air of my own composition. Five or six pages came running out from behind the curtain and asked me: "Whose composition is that?" "My own", I replied. Promptly they departed as quickly as they had come. Then Salám al-Abrash himself, coming down from behind the curtain, approached me and said: "You lie. That composition is Ibn Jámi''s". I remained silent and the chief of the eunuchs withdrew.

Soon the singing began again, in the same order, and my turn arrived, after I had been given wine. This time I sang another of my tunes and with more spirit than the first time. The hall resounded with the strong echoes of my voice. As soon as I had finished, the same pages leapt from behind the curtain and hurried towards me, crying out: "Whose composition is that?" "Mine!" I said. And they departed at the run. The chief page again came from behind the curtain, and said: "You lie. That tune is the composition of Ibn Jámi'". "Yes," said I, "I am Ibn Jámi'." Hardly had I spoken these words when the curtains parted and the great chamberlain Fadhl ibn Rabí' appeared, and announced: "The Commander of the Faithful", and Hárún al-Rashíd came forward leaning on the arm of Ja'far the Barmecide. The Caliph asked me: "Are you Ibn Jámi'?" "Yes, Commander of the Faithful." "How long have you been in Baghdad?" "A few hours." "It gives me pleasure to see you. Count on my generosity to fulfil any desire you may have." "May Allah, who is almighty", I replied, "overwhelm the Commander of the Faithful with prosperity and may he make the glory of his reign eternal."

Then Hárún sat with Ja'far upon a couch and asked me to sing some new air. The song of the negress came to my mind, and when I had sung it Hárún turned to Ja'far, and said: "Have you ever heard anything so original?"...I then told him the story of the song, and what the negress had said about the four thousand pieces of gold.

The singer's tale then goes on to say how the Caliph, in delight, three separate times gave him a bag containing a thousand gold pieces, and finally made the sum four thousand gold pieces, in order that the negress might not lie. He continues:

The night was far advanced when Hárún rose and went to his own apartments in the interior of the palace. I too got ready to go, heavily embarrassed with my four thousand pieces of gold. An officer of the palace bade me follow him and led me to a house richly furnished, fitted indeed with everything that could be useful or pleasurable. I found there also several male servants and two beautiful slave girls. "Everything here belongs to you," said the officer to me, "it is a gift from the Commander of the Faithful." Thereupon he left me, and I gave thanks to Heaven for having made me pass at a bound from poverty to wealth.[1]

Ibn Jámi' and Ibrahím al-Mauṣilí appear to have been generous rivals. Ibrahím one morning went to visit Ja'far the Barmecide, with whom he was very well acquainted, and asked him what he had done the night before. "I spent the whole day with friends," replied Ja'far, "amusing ourselves, drinking and listening to Ibn Jámi'." "We noticed", he added with meaning, "that he did not always keep the rhythm." "You think to please me by saying that," remarked Ibrahím, "but you do nothing of the kind. Ibn Jámi' not keep the rhythm! Impossible! For thirty years he has not walked, spoken or coughed except in rhythm. How could he leave out the rhythm in singing?"[2]

It was on occasions of ceremony that the wealth and magnificence of the court found their fullest display. Hárún's own audience chamber seems at all times to have been adorned with the richest fabrics of the East, but when he was receiving the representatives of foreign potentates, the Caliph surpassed himself, so that the historians vie with each other in their descriptions of the brilliant scenes. Among the envoys thus received legend puts an ambassador from Charlemagne and another from the king of China. According to the chronicler Eginhard, the envoys of the great king of the West returned home with rich presents that included a number of elephants and also a cunningly contrived water clock of bronze that marked the time by means of numerous little knightly figures which opened and closed various little doors. Another occasion for display was at the Persian New Year festival of Nawrúz, when the Caliph ceremonially received all his high officers of state at a banquet that lasted six days. Hárún was seconded in his love of parade by his chief and favourite wife, Zubaida, who would have at her table no vessels that were not made of precious metals and who set the fashion of ornamenting her shoes with jewels.

Not far behind their royal master in their riches and luxury came the Barmecide family. From amongst the legends that have gathered about them it may be gathered that they were of Persian origin and that they probably derived their name from the Iranian title "Barmak", which was bestowed on the head of the Buddhist monastery of Naw Bahár in Bactria. Later Persian tradition, by the same process of apologetics which made Alexander the Great the son of a Persian mother, came to regard this temple as belonging to the Zoroastrian cult and claimed that the "Barmaks" were descended from the viziers of the Sassanian kings. It may well be that they held some kind of official position which facilitated their acquaintanceship with the Abbasid family. There is no record of the beginning of this acquaintanceship nor of the date of the Barmecides' conversion to Islam. Khálid the Barmecide, who was adviser to al-Saffáḥ, first of the Abbasid dynasty, bore an Arabic and hence a Moslem name, and the probability is that the family were early converts. Khálid continued in the office of chief minister to Manṣúr, the founder of Baghdad, and Khálid's son Yaḥyá became the adviser of Manṣúr's son Mahdí, and also, as we have seen, of Hárún al-Rashíd, when, as a youth, he made an expedition to Asia Minor.

The long connection between the royal family and that of its now princely counsellors led to such close intimacy that Yaḥyá's son Fadhl, who was born within a week of Hárún, was said to have been nursed by the queen Khayzurán, while Hárún often fed at the breast of Fadhl's mother. Ja'far, another son of Yaḥyá, became the Caliph's brother-in-law—a relationship that was ultimately to have disastrous consequences for the vizier's family. Further, the Barmecide houses occupied one side of the *maydán*, the great parade ground fronting the Abbasids' palace of Khuld. The family also had large estates near the Shammásiya quarter on the east bank, near the palace of Ruṣáfa, and some time during the early part of Hárún's reign Yaḥyá built himself a mansion there, which however, from its name *Qaṣr al-Ṭín*, "Clay Castle", would seem to have been only a temporary structure.

There is little need to dilate on the wealth and influence of the family and, though it is certain that the Caliph's subjects had extortionate sums wrung out of them to provide the Barmecides with their riches, they seem to have used what they acquired in a more generous and often more public-spirited manner than the Caliphs themselves. Thus, on the death of the Caliph Mahdí, when the troops in the city mutinied for payment of the arrears of their hire, Yaḥyá, who was vizier at the time, distributed two years' pay to each man and kept all quiet while he sent off his son Fadhl to hasten the arrival of the new Caliph, Músá al-Hádí.

Like his royal masters, Yaḥyá had a passion for building. A famous house of his stood on the east bank directly across the river from the Khuld palace. According to the historian Mas'údí, Yaḥyá built it for his son Ja'far, of whose convivial habits he did not approve, and whom he therefore advised to have a house on the east bank as he could not restrain his frivolous conduct. There he could entertain his licentious friends to his heart's content out of sight of people in the capital, who disliked their irreligious ways. This house was so magnificent on its completion that prudent friends told Ja'far he would be wise to forestall the too-ready jealousy of the Caliph by telling him that it was ultimately intended for Ma'mún, the young heir to the throne. The stratagem succeeded, and Ja'far was able to enjoy the luxuries of his new home at the expense of occasional visits from the stripling prince.

Of the kind of life led in the house we gain an idea from *al-Fakhrí*, the entertaining history of the Caliphate which has already been quoted. For example:

Ja'far, son of Yaḥyá the Barmecide, was one day seated at wine with a group of boon companions, whose company he wished to enjoy undisturbed. The assembled guests were all clad in garments of bright hues, for it was their custom when they sat at wine to don festive robes of red or yellow or green. Meantime Ja'far had warned his head chamberlain to admit no single mortal except one friend who was still to come, and whose name was 'Abd al-Malik ibn Ṣáliḥ. And the company sat down to their feasting and the cups passed round while the lutes made merry music. Now there was a relative of the Caliph's known as 'Abd al-Malik ibn Ṣáliḥ ibn 'Alí, a person very grave in manner, exceedingly religious and of the highest dignity. Hárún al-Rashíd had often invited him to feast with him, but he had always refused, even though the Caliph had offered him considerable gifts in order to persuade him to be his drinking companion. It chanced that this 'Abd al-Malik ibn Ṣáliḥ presented himself at Ja'far ibn Yaḥyá's gate to consult with him on a matter in which he needed his assistance. The chamberlain, thinking that this was the friend whom Ja'far had bidden him admit, allowed him to enter, and he came towards Ja'far, who on seeing him was almost distracted with confusion and understood at once that the porter had been confused by the similarity of the names. 'Abd al-Malik also saw from the shamed look on Ja'far's face what had occurred, and cried out merrily: "Good fortune to you. Let me also have one of those coloured cloaks". A brilliant-hued robe was brought to him, and he donned it and sat down chatting and jesting gaily with Ja'far. He then asked for wine, and a goblet being filled for him he was invited to remain as one of the company. He sat in merry conversation till he saw that Ja'far's restraint and confusion were entirely dissipated. Indeed his host's pleasure at his coming was now unbounded, and he asked his guest what need had brought him. "Heaven prosper you," was his reply, "I have come on three matters in which I desire you to approach the Caliph on my behalf. The first of these is that I am in debt to the tune of a million dirhems, which I am being compelled to pay; the second is that I desire for my son a province which will be suited to his station; the third that I desire you to arrange for the marriage of my son with the Caliph's daughter." To this Ja'far replied: "Allah has already satisfied these three needs of yours. The money will this very hour be taken to your house; for the province, I have appointed your son to Egypt, and as for his marriage, I have already betrothed him to so-and-so, the daughter of our master, the Commander of the Faithful, and have allotted for him out of the royal revenues the sum of such-and-such. Go therefore now, with Allah's protection".

The story continues that when Ja'far presented himself before the Caliph next day and informed him of what he had done, Hárún seems to have expressed astonishment, but agreed both to the marriage and the appointment.

It was not in the nature of things that so treacherous and suspicious a monarch as Hárún would permit the power of the Barmecides to grow into what might become a danger to his own prestige. In fact he had, soon after his succession, begun to be jealous of the authority wielded by his minister Yaḥyá, even though he had delegated it himself. The time came when Hárún was only waiting an excuse to be rid of the family that had helped his line to greatness. *Al-Fakhrí* graphically describes the monarch's change of attitude in the course of the account of the Barmecide fall. The narrative reads:

Bukht Yishú', the [Christian] physician, relates that he was one day in attendance upon al-Rashíd, who was then residing at his palace of Khuld in the City of Peace [Baghdad]. The Barmecides were at the time living exactly opposite him on the other side of the river, with only the width of the river between the two palaces. It chanced that al-Rashíd on that occasion glanced across the river and beheld the press of horses and the crowd of men at Yaḥyá's gates, and he said: "May Heaven requite Yaḥyá with good. He has undertaken with courage all the business of the state and has freed me from exertion so that I am able to devote liberal time to my own pleasures". Upon a later occasion when the physician was again in attendance on Hárún, he again chanced to see the crowd of horses and men, but this time he burst out angrily: "Yaḥyá transacts all the business of state in entire independence and without consulting me. In reality the Caliphate is his; it is mine only in name".

The numerous rivals and enemies of the Barmecides were not slow to notice the Caliph's changing attitude, and accusations of Barmecide high-handedness and independence of action began to pour in to him. The occasion for which he was looking came at last. The story is told with considerable embroidery by various historians, but it is given in its simplest form by Ṭabarí. He tells us that the relationship between Hárún and the Barmecides had been so close that the Caliph had given his favourite sister 'Abbása in marriage to Ja'far, son of Yaḥyá. The primary object of the marriage had been to enable Hárún to have the pleasure of the company of both his sister and of Ja'far at one and the same time. He was passionately fond of both of them, but unless the two were connected by marriage, the harem system made it impossible for Ja'far to enter the women's quarters. The marriage, however, was to be one in name alone, and Hárún made it very clear that he did not wish them ever to meet except in his company. But he could not prevent 'Abbása from falling in love with her husband, whom, in spite of the Caliph's commands, she contrived to meet, and to whom she bore a son. The child was sent away to Mecca in charge of a trusty servant, and for a time all appeared to be going well. Some months after the birth of the child however, 'Abbása, during a squabble in the harem, gave a beating to one of her slave girls. This girl knew of the birth of the child and in revenge for her beating told the story to Hárún's favourite wife Zubaida. She had always been jealous of the influence borne by Ja'far over her husband, to whom she promptly went with the tale. He soon afterwards set out for Mecca, ostensibly on a pilgrimage, but in reality to have proof of what had been told him. The production of the child satisfied him that he had been betrayed and he determined on vengeance. He delayed action until he and his pilgrim train had reached Anbár on the Euphrates, and there he sent his black eunuch Masrúr, who was his executioner and his constant companion, to Ja'far's tent, with orders to cut off his head. The unfortunate man's pleadings were in vain; even if Masrúr had been inclined to be merciful, his master was inexorable. Ja'far's body was divided into three parts and, with the head, these were gibbeted on the middle bridge connecting east and west Baghdad, for the city to see that the Barmecide power was fallen.

The narrative may be continued from Ibn Khallikán, who reports the story of what happened immediately afterwards from the lips of one of Hárún's officers, al-Sindí ibn Shakík:

"I was one night sleeping", says the officer, "in the upper room of the guard-house which is on the west side of Baghdad, and I saw in a dream Ja'far, who stood before me in a robe dyed with saffron and inscribed with verses. [Here a number of verses of doleful import are quoted.] I awoke in terror and related my vision to one of my friends, who answered: 'Not all that a man sees in sleep will bear interpretation'. I then returned to my couch but had scarcely closed my eyes when I heard the challenge of the sentries, the ringing of the bridles of post horses and a loud knocking at the door of my chamber. I ordered it to be opened and the eunuch Salám al-Abrash (whom Hárún never sent out except on important business) came upstairs. I shuddered at his sight and my joints trembled, for I imagined he had some orders for me....The eunuch handed me a letter telling me to seize and imprison Yaḥyá and all his relatives."[1]

The prisoners were sent to Raqqa on the Euphrates where they were kept in an appalling state of misery until their deaths. The absence of the guiding hand of the family of wise counsellors was to have bitter consequences for the capital of the empire, which was thrown into a turmoil after Hárún's death over the matter of the succession.

CHAPTER IV

City Life under Hárún

The stories of luxurious living and of dissipation in the reign of Hárún derive generally from the pages of the court historiographers. Yet life in the city was by no means confined to the court, though the enormous mass of the population found few to chronicle their doings except incidentally. It would appear that such persons as came into contact with the court—even the lesser fry, the singers and hangers-on of all kinds—tried to imitate what the great were doing. The rest lived, according to their means, by the rules laid down in the Koran and the traditions of the Prophet as interpreted by the learned jurists, for there were no priests. The large majority must have been people of restricted means, and for them life was as uncomfortable as in any other great city where extremes of wealth and poverty exist together. We have the lament of more than one poet that while wealth was a key that opened all doors in Baghdad, poverty admitted man to little but discomfort or distress, and the cadi 'Abd al-Wahháb likens a poor man wandering in the streets of the rich city to a Koran lost in the house of an atheist.[1] Those of the population who were not beggars were people of simple and industrious habits—though beggars undoubtedly swarmed in a city whose inhabitants were good Moslems that numbered the giving of alms among the four cardinal virtues.

If Abú Nuwás, the libertine poet who was the companion of Hárún al-Rashíd on his nocturnal rambles, showed in his work the contemptuous attitude of the court towards Islam and the morals which it inculcated, there was another poet, Abú 'l-'Atáhiya, who expressed the feelings of the humbler citizens of Baghdad. Abú Nuwás could say with impunity that the mosque was "Satan's rat-trap".[1] Abú 'l-'Atáhiya, on the other hand, filled his poems with praises of Allah, with thoughts on contentment and self-denial, and with bitter words on earthly vanities. These sentiments must be taken to be characteristic of many of his fellow-citizens even though he himself cannot be called a pattern Moslem. It is true that he practised asceticism, which he praises in his odes—a friend once found him dressed in two baskets—but he counterbalanced it with outrageous meanness.

Abú 'l-'Atáhiya had a neighbour who used to gather date-stones, a sickly man in poor circumstances who was nevertheless a man clad in the garments of piety. He used to pass Abú 'l-'Atáhiya twice every day and the poet each time would pray: "O God, free him from the need that is in his path; for he is a weak and poor old man, and clad in the garments of piety. O God, aid him, benefit him and bless him". He continued this practice until the old man died after about twenty years, without Abú 'l-'Atáhiya's ever having bestowed on him a dirhem or even a dániq; nor did he ever add to his prayer. I said to him one day: "O Abú Isḥáq [another name of the poet], I see you multiplying prayers over this old man, saying that he is poor and needy and yet you never bestow any alms upon him". He replied: "I fear his becoming accustomed to alms, which are the last resort of a slave. In prayer however there is great good".[2]

It will have been seen from the preceding chapter that women played a large rôle in the household of Hárún; some as slave girls who could be bought, sold, or given away at his pleasure; others, his own kinsfolk, such as Zubaida who was his cousin and wife; and 'Abbása his half-sister. Family prestige gave to these two women, and probably to others like them in the households of the more important inhabitants in the city, a more or less independent status which was not held by the vast majority of the female population. Even the regular wives, whose children were freeborn and entitled to inherit from their father, were in complete subjection to the head of the household. The fair amount of freedom that women had in nomad days never had a chance to exist in Baghdad, though amongst the earlier inhabitants of the city the seclusion of women was not so rigid as it later became. Two causes led to the increase of restriction: firstly the change in marriage custom brought about by the introduction of Islam, whereby it was made lawful for wives to be chosen, or taken, from anywhere that was found possible, and not merely from amongst groups of tribes related by kinship; secondly the practice fostered by the polygamous habits of the Abbasid Caliphs of shutting off the women of the household under the charge of eunuchs. Incidentally the low opinion of women expressed by the Moslem doctors could not fail to have its effect at a time when religious authority counted for much. Very occasionally the biographers mention a talented woman, e.g. Shuhda, daughter of al-Ibárí, who acquired an extensive reputation for learning and wrote a beautiful hand,[1] but normally the education of women was almost unknown. Learning to read in order to know the Koran was in general encouraged, but for the most part women were concerned with household duties, particularly with the care of the comforts of the master of the house, and that even among the richer classes.

Amongst the poor monogamy was imposed by economic necessity, and since the wife shared with the husband the toil of earning a livelihood she was apt to be freer than her richer sisters and was apparently treated with greater consideration. Ibn Khallikán's Life of Ibrahím ibn Isḥáq al-Ḥarbí quotes a statement which he made that when his daughter was ill, his wife remained with her for a whole month, and during that time he denied himself to such an extent that his meals for the whole month cost no more than a dirhem and two dániqs and a half.

The training of boys was a little better than that of girls, though there was no system of general education, except for those who were to become *cadis* (ecclesiastical judges) or *imáms* (leaders of prayer in the mosque) or for such boys whose natural ability in letters showed itself clearly. These might secure the favour of a patron and acquire simultaneously a training and a rich competence. The elementary schools that were attached to some of the mosques did about as much in Hárún's day as similar institutions do now in Moslem countries. They taught the Koran by rote—without explanation or comment—and also the simple formulas of prayer. Outside the schools there were popular tales and legends that went the rounds in addition to those more picturesque narratives told in great detail by the *ráwís*, or professional storytellers. Poetry too was not unknown, and there were satirical rhymes on popular characters or events of the day.

On a lower level, the compositions and songs of the humbler citizens, the boatmen, water carriers, masons, and others at their work, went to enliven the scene, and there can have been no lack of spicy conversation. Often it had a political interest and was reported to the Caliph himself by courtiers, who sometimes seated themselves on the bridges for the purpose of overhearing what passers-by were saying. It may not always have been to provide the sovereign with amusement that led to this form of espionage. The government of the city lay ultimately with him, and information gathered at first hand must have been of considerable assistance in keeping a check on viziers and the minor officials who formed the executive.

For purposes of administration the city was divided into a number of separate quarters, in each of which was a head responsible for the maintenance of order. For the whole city there was a police force that was part of the system of espionage, and the function of the officers, who were known as *muḥtasibs*, was to see that the laws were obeyed and that the public were protected. The *muḥtasib* was allowed wide discretion in the performance of his duties. He could concern himself as much with seeing that a merchant had weights and measures of an agreed standard as that a legal adviser or a public speaker was properly equipped for his profession. Mawardí, the Arab authority on public law and administration, lays it down that if a professional man is notoriously incompetent, the *muhtasib* may expose him, and he may examine any man who is not known to him. He was empowered to make tardy debtors pay their debts, to see to it that beasts of burden were not overloaded, that widows did not remarry before the proper time and that public decency was observed. He had to stop the open selling of wine, to apprehend drunkards and prevent the playing of musical instruments except in certain specified localities. Also he could prevent and punish other illegal acts, such as usury, sales of forbidden commodities, extortion and so on. Moreover, he had to maintain the established laws of privacy and to see that no one overlooked his neighbour and spied upon his womenfolk, just as in Baghdad to-day the man who owns a house higher than that of his neighbour is required to surround his roof with some material—generally sheets of tin—that will prevent any overlooking. Mawardí also mentions among the duties of the *muḥtasib* the responsibility for punishing men who dyed their beards black for the sole purpose of making a better impression on the fair sex. Only the military *mujáhids*, or "fighters in a holy war", had that privilege, though others might stain their beards red with henna.

The *muḥtasib* differed in his powers from the cadi, who was a superior official of the law, principally in this respect, that he could try no cases in which the charge was disputed. Where witnesses had to be sworn, or where a complaint had to be investigated, the trial was before the cadi. The *muhtasib* could investigate on the spot any irregularity which he came upon in the course of his rounds and could deliver summary justice, though he could not cross the threshold of a private house to prosecute his investigations. The mysteries of the harem were secure even from him.[1]

Where the case was of political importance, it was investigated by the Caliph himself, very rarely with any regard for equity. Sometimes, and particularly in the days of later Caliphs who were incapable of transacting public business, the viziers sat to receive reports of criminal offences.

Where a charge was proven it may be presumed that justice was done, though sentences were harsh. In doubtful cases there seems to have been no thorough investigation or consideration. The case is reported from the reign of Muqtadir of a man who was brought before the vizier 'Alí ibn 'Ísá on the charge of claiming to be a prophet. On being questioned, the man said he was Aḥmad the prophet, and that he proved it by having the seal of prophecy on his back. This was found to be a small wound, and though the man was obviously a lunatic in the vizier's opinion, he committed him to prison. Neither here nor in other cases was the length of the sentence ever specified. Release came when a friend or a relative could find enough money to bribe an official to carry a petition on his behalf to the Caliph, though often enough a man was forgotten for years together.

An important duty of the *muḥtasib* was to enforce the wearing of a special distinguishing mark by Christians and Jews. Hárún is the first Caliph recorded as having instituted the discriminating ordinance. By his time the "protected" peoples had become so assimilated to their Moslem fellow-citizens, outwardly at any rate, that the mark was found to be necessary to identify them. Even more irksome in that city of luxury and display was the ordinance that the value and style of non-Moslem dress were to be restricted and that no Jewish or Christian house was to be higher than neighbouring Moslem houses.

Jews and Christians had for centuries been settled in the districts round Baghdad and moved into the capital when it was built. The number of synagogues and churches had been limited from the beginning, but in the year 807 Hárún decided in a fit of zeal that there should be none at all, and ordered every non-Moslem place of worship to be razed to the ground. His edict, however, did not long remain in force, for we know that under his successors "protected" Christians and Jews gained almost complete liberty for themselves and that even under Hárún himself the Jewish exilarch maintained some show of authority and had certain privileges. Moreover, if there was discrimination against non-Moslems on the social and religious side, they had great freedom on the other hand so far as trading and choice of professions was concerned. Indeed in matters financial, in medicine and the arts, they seem to have had the city to themselves. The principal traders in the bazaar were Christians or Jews, and so high was the reputation of "unbelievers" in the realm of medicine that Hárún had a Nestorian Christian as his personal physician. This was the famous Bukht Yishú', who had learnt his art at the great hospital of Gunday Shápúr in the Persian province of Khuzistan, and whose income, incidentally, was said to be not less than 280,000 dirhems, or about 10,000 pounds sterling per annum.

Another product of the school of Gunday Shápúr who came to practise at Baghdad was the Christian Masawaih Abú Yoḥanna. His early efforts at finding patients were not very successful, and at the advice of the bishop he rented an alcove in the *Dár al-Rúm* (the "Greek House,") which was a large caravanserai frequented by Christian merchants and near which the bishop himself had his house. Near by also was the palace of the vizier. Abú Yoḥanna set out his stock of medicaments in his alcove and waited for patients to arrive. For a period custom lagged, then he had the good fortune to be successful in the treatment of a slave belonging to the vizier's household. That brought him more patients, and at last he was introduced by Bukht Yishú' to Hárún himself whom he cured of some malady of the eyes, thereby establishing his own fortunes.[1]

It has already been seen that in the bazaars the members of each craft and trade had their shops together, distinct from those of other craftsmen and tradesmen. Quite early there is mention of tailors, shoemakers, tanners, butchers, dyers, glaziers—craftsmen whose tasks were once carried out by slaves—and others who were more usually to be found in a great city than in villages, for example, water-carriers, brokers, masons, carpenters, gilders, goldsmiths and others. These craftsmen formed themselves into guilds and there is mention even of a thieves' guild with properly accredited officers.[1]

In addition to the organized and more reputable professions we may be sure that nimble-fingered and glib-tongued fraternities were not absent and that the credulous and the simple were interested or amused at the expense of their purses. The *Fihrist* or *Index*—an encyclopaedic bibliography composed in A.D. 988 by Abú 'l-Faraj the bookseller of Baghdad—contains a catalogue of a bookseller's stock-in-trade, amongst the items of which are numerous works dealing with the arts of hypnotism, sword-swallowing, glass-chewing, and the like.[2]

Such minor diversions as were provided by the professors of these arts were needed in the life of the majority of people in the capital, where existence seems by modern standards to have been exceedingly dull and humdrum. There were, of course, celebrations such as weddings and circumcisions, carried out with feasting and joyous ululations; such occasions being doubtless frequent enough in a city of prolific population. There were also festive occasions of a public character when the inhabitants of the city forsook their houses in thousands to rejoice in the streets. These were the times when the Caliph returned in triumph from campaigns against infidel foes or rebellious governors. The monarch would ride through streets and bazaars gaily hung with carpets and festooned with coloured robes, and following him would come a procession of captives and a booty train, with the rebel chief or perhaps the enemy king seated backwards on a double-humped Bactrian camel or on an ass. To add to the pleasurable excitement there might be elephants in the procession and the festivities would be crowned with the torture and execution of the captives, whose bodies would remain gibbeted on the bridges for weeks or years, to remind the citizens of their holiday.

Towards the close of the reign of Hárún the huge empire of the Caliphate began to show signs of breaking up under its own mass, and risings in distant provinces disturbed the peace of the capital. In the early part of A.D. 809 the Caliph determined to go in person to Khurásán in order to quell a serious rebellion of religious sectaries that had broken out there. He left in charge of Baghdad his son Amín, whose mother Zubaida—Hárún's favourite wife—was a person of pronouncedly weak and pleasure-loving nature. Another son, Ma'mún, accompanied the Caliph to Khurásán, of which he was made governor. The campaign had not lasted many months when Hárún, falling sick, was compelled to surrender the command to his son, whom he sent forward with a large force while he himself took to his bed at Ṭús.

It soon became obvious to the physicians and to the Caliph himself that his condition was serious. He repeated an old wish—which had been embodied in a formal agreement at Mecca some years before (in A.D. 791)—that Ma'mún who was his favourite son, though the son of a Persian slave girl, should succeed Amín on the throne, and, having had a grave dug to his satisfaction and chosen his burial robes, he died before his son could be called back.

CHAPTER V

The First Siege of Baghdad

The new Caliph, Amín, was a man who cared for little beyond his own pleasures. His main object in life lay in bringing together and housing musicians, dancers, mountebanks, male and female, and others who could entertain him; and upon them he spent a colossal fortune. The poet Tha'álibí[1] gives the measure of Amín's extravagance when he says that this Caliph "squandered all the wealth that al-Saffáḥ, Manṣúr, Mahdí and Hárún had collected". Ṭabarí pictures him as "tall, bald at the temples and pale, with small eyes and a hooked nose. Also he was pleasant mannered, mighty of bone and broad shouldered".

Sometimes the citizens benefited by his extravagances, being allowed occasionally to visit the gardens of the Khuld palace, and they flocked to the spectacle which he provided for them on the Tigris in the shape of a fleet of five boats built in the grotesque shapes of a lion, an elephant, an eagle, a horse and a serpent. A wild celebration in one of the gardens is reported by Ṭabarí in the words of a court poet called Mukháriq who says:

> One night as I was sitting at home, a messenger came and fetched me at a run from the house to the palace. When I was admitted I saw that Ibrahím al-Mahdí (a half-brother of the Caliph, renowned as a singer) had also been brought, in the same way as myself. We walked towards one another and the guide led us to a gateway opening on to a large courtyard. The court-

yard was filled with lighted candles...and it was as though there were daylight in it; and there was the Caliph, mounted on a wooden horse. The house itself was filled with slave girls and servants, and while the revellers were playing there was the Caliph in the midst of them, prancing about on his hobby-horse. Unexpectedly a messenger came to us telling us to remain stationed at the gateway leading into the courtyard and to raise our voices in tune with the oboes, singing loudly or softly and following what they were playing. Suddenly the oboe players and the girls and the revellers with one accord shouted out following the music: "These gold coins will forget me, but I shall remember them" [which seems to have been the chorus of the popular song of the day]. And, by heaven, I and Ibrahím did not cease to stand there, bursting our throats over this until the dawn came. Meanwhile the Caliph rode on his hobby-horse, of which he never tired, till morning; sometimes he approached us and we could see him, at other times he was lost to view in the crowd of girls and servants.[1]

A taste for real wild animals as well as for toys is numbered amongst the extravagances of the Caliph and it formed an extra hazard in the lives of the unfortunate Baghdadís condemned to his service. Yet his hobby sometimes gave him an opportunity of showing that he was not entirely lacking in manly qualities. Mas'údí tells the story of a lion which the Caliph's bodyguard had brought one day and set down in a cage outside his door. When he appeared he at once ordered the attendants to open the cage and let the animal loose. It was a particularly savage beast, and the Caliph had been told so, but he persisted in his command and the servants fled in terror as soon as they had opened the cage door. Amín, however, sat quietly finishing the drink which he had in his hand, until he saw the beast ready to spring. He then seized a cushion which he held in front of him as a shield, and as the lion leapt on him he plunged his dagger into it and despatched it.

Amín was for a time allowed to indulge his fancies in peace. But the inevitable intrigues about the succession were soon afoot. Persuaded by his vizier Fadhl ibn Rabí', who had reason to hate Ma'mún, then acting as governor of Khurásán, the Caliph appointed his own son to the succession. Ma'mún's friends at court were not slow to carry him the news, and when Amín wrote asking him to cede part of Khurásán for the purpose of increasing the royal revenues, Ma'mún refused. As a further step, when hostilities became more open, he cut off all communication between Khurásán and Baghdad.

Towards the end of the year A.D. 810, Amín despatched an army of 40,000 against his brother in Khurásán. It was routed by a body of 4000 men under the redoubtable Ṭáhir "the Ambidextrous"—who was later to be the founder of an independent dynasty in Persia—and Ma'mún was saluted as Caliph by his troops.

The messenger who hastened to Baghdad to report the disaster found the Caliph on the Tigris bank, fishing. His comment was: "Ill luck to you! Leave me alone! Kauthar has caught two fishes and I have caught nothing yet".

A second army which Amín sent out suffered the same fate as the first, and Ṭáhir began to march on Baghdad. On reaching Hulwán, about a hundred miles to the north-east of the city, Ma'mún suddenly changed his plans and put his general, Harthama, in charge of the troops advancing on Baghdad, while Ṭáhir was ordered to occupy Ahwáz in south-west Persia. Meanwhile disputes had broken out in Baghdad between Amín and one of his generals over the question of supplies, throwing the city into a state of confusion that gravely weakened its defences. The advance was now being made from two directions, Harthama marching down from the Persian mountains on the north-west, while Ṭáhir—his objective gained at Ahwáz—was making his way northwards along the Tigris by way of Wásiṭ. Soon he had reached the part of Madá'in (the old Seleucid twin-capital) lying on the right bank opposite Ctesiphon, about eighteen miles downstream of Baghdad. Ma'mún had numerous friends in the city and sympathy grew with his success. The sacred cities of Mecca and Medina too declared in his favour and the governor of Yemen yielded the province to him. There was a slight check to his advance however when dissension broke out in Tahir's army and 5000 of his men deserted to the Caliph on the report, which Amín was secretly spreading, that large pay was being given to the Baghdad forces. In general the report was false, but for the new recruits that came to his army Amín brought out such remaining treasure as he had and gave each man an advance of pay. With incredible folly he allowed his own veterans at the same time to remain on the verge of starvation. This conduct aroused fierce resentment in the older troops and Ṭáhir was able to retaliate on the Caliph by bribing some of the troops in the city to revolt and to spread mutinous ideas amongst the rest.

His efforts succeeded so well that the city troops were divided into two camps, who differed fiercely in their loyalties, so that at times brother fought against brother and father against son.

Scanty supplies and unfair treatment were the ostensible reasons for the desertions from either side. In reality the causes of dissatisfaction lay very much deeper, for Amín, as an Arab, commanded the loyalty of his Arab troops while Ma'mún had a Persian mother and represented the Iranian ideal. From the foundation of the city the two nationalities had occupied different quarters and shown tacit hostility to one another. The Arabs, who had held the supremacy under the Umayyads resented being put into the second place by the Persians, for whom they had a wholesome contempt, while the Persians lorded it without regard to Arab feelings. Differences of nationality were further accentuated by differences in religious opinions, and the conflict now raging was an opportunity for which both sides were looking to put their strength to the test.

In August, A.D. 812, Ṭáhir, joined by Harthama and Zuhair, another general of Ma'mún, proceeded to lay siege to the city. It was a rich prize. On the right bank the old Round City of Manṣúr was intact with many wealthy houses in it; to the east of it, and nearer the river was the Khuld ("Paradise") Palace, and to the south lay various flourishing suburbs. On the opposite bank several rich city quarters surrounded the palace and mosque of Ruṣáfa, and downstream of them were the mansions and gardens that had not long before been the property of the Barmecides. In the plan of campaign undertaken by the besiegers Ṭáhir decided to dig trenches on the west bank outside of the Round City; Harthama sat down outside the Nahrawán gate on the east bank, while Zuhair set up his mangonels and other engines of war at Kalwádhí in the bend of the river to the south of the city. Here he was able to command the approaches to Ṭáhir's camp and prevent any advance upon it. He was further in a position where he could stop all merchandise that was passing into the city and take tithe of it before it went on, and he could also levy tolls on all ships that came upstream with supplies. Feeling for his fellow-Moslems in the besieged city and the probability that he had friends in it, prevented him from the logical step of cutting off supplies altogether. Even as it was, complaints of Zuhair's ruthless methods were carried to Ṭáhir, with the result that he stood at one period in danger of losing his command.

For a time life in the city continued in the old, haphazard and ill-regulated manner. Those who had the means used bribery to have their supplies brought through the enemy lines, while those who had to depend upon what they could buy in the city after a time began to feel the pinch of hunger. It did not require a very high degree of intelligence to discover that the possession of money meant being well fed in spite of the siege, and soon gangs of ruffians, many of whom had broken out of the prisons, were roaming the streets of the city in search of plunder. In that respect they were in competition with the troops of Amín, and they came into conflict not only with the soldiers but with the bodyguards that rich merchants hired for their own protection, with the result that the streets of the city became battlefields more bloody than those outside.

In spite of all his difficulties Amín was able for a period of several months to maintain supplies to his forces, but the time came when he had to melt down some of his vessels of gold and silver for the pay that would enable the men to buy food for themselves. Before taking that extreme step he had tried to exact levies from the more wealthy inhabitants, who in the course of the siege had gathered themselves together on the west bank for their common protection. They evaded his officers, however, by contriving at odd times to leave the city, it being possible for them to pass through the enemy lines if they gave the pretext that they were going on a pilgrimage to Mecca.

Meantime the besieging mangonels and other engines of war were destroying many of the city's fine buildings, and from the fact that the state archives were consumed by fire it may be inferred that the royal quarters did not escape undamaged. The troops who remained loyal to Amín were bearing hardships not only from enemy aggression but from lack of supplies, and were reduced to the last degree of destitution. Yet desperation made their resistance all the fiercer, as the siege continued, and their constant effective sorties forced Ṭáhir to dig deep trenches as additional protection for his troops. Mas'údí describes the strange "army" which was helping to defend Baghdad after the siege had lasted about a year. Few of the men had any sound garment to wear. They went into battle naked to the waist but wearing on their heads sham helmets of leaves and carrying shields of the same material covered with bitumen. In spite of their ragged equipment their organization was very carefully arranged. Ten men were commanded by an *'árif*, ten 'árifs by a *naqíb*, and ten naqíbs by an *amír*. Supernumerary troops were allotted to each officer for various duties, all strange; but strangest of all perhaps was that of having to act as "mounts" in place of the horses that had long disappeared from the besieged city. The "mounts" of the amírs had bits and bridles. They were provided with tails made out of brooms and fly whisks, and round their necks were hung strings of bells and ropes of red and yellow wool. In this travesty of equipment the troops went into battle against the well-provided cavalry of Ma'mún, with their coats of mail, good shields and lances and fine horses. The ragged battalions nevertheless fought bravely. Mas'údí, with what seems to be considerable exaggeration, says that in one battle a hundred thousand of them, armed only with sticks and similar weapons, issued from the city and did not retire until ten thousand of them had been slain and many thousands more had been driven into the Tigris to drown.

The siege had dragged on for almost two years when Amín finally decided that surrender was his only means of escaping with his life. He chose to negotiate with Harthama rather than with Ṭáhir, whom he hated, though his courtiers strenuously opposed his choice on the ground that Harthama, who had once been one of themselves, would treat them with the contempt of familiarity, while Ṭáhir would accord them the treatment fitting their rank. Amín finally compromised by agreeing to send the royal insignia to Ma'mún by the hand of Ṭáhir, though he continued in his determination to give himself up to no one but Harthama.

Ṭáhir, however, was cunning enough to know how to lay his plans when the city fell, and long before the end of the siege he had sent a message to Ma'mún for permission to kill Amín. He had received a favourable reply in the form of a shirt having no opening at the neck—implying that it was "suitable only for a headless man".[1] He was not disposed, when the time for surrender came, to be robbed of the culminating triumph of the siege, and decided on a stratagem. On the night set for the surrender, the date of which had been reported to him by his spies, he posted a body of troops in ambush to await Amín's exit from the city. Meantime Harthama, who was on the left bank, had sent a boat across the river at the appointed time to receive the Caliph. It returned immediately to report that Ṭáhir's troops were in the way and Harthama thereupon sent a messenger through to the Caliph deferring the surrender to the next night. Amín however had already let most of his troops go, and, in great fear of capture by Ṭáhir, insisted on having the original plan carried out. Harthama at once decided to go himself with one or two picked men and endeavour to rescue Amín from Ṭáhir's hands. But for the merest chance the enterprise would have succeeded. The party with the Caliph in it had penetrated Ṭáhir's lines and were in the boat well away from the bank, when some noise attracted the attention of the men in the ambuscade, who pursued and sank the boat by hurling large stones at it. Amín managed to swim to the bank, where he concealed himself in a house. But a search was set on foot, and the Caliph was soon discovered, betrayed by the odour of the musk with which he was in the habit of scenting hinself. A gang of Persians dragged him from his hidingplace, stabbed him to death and sent his severed head to Ṭáhir, who next morning took possession of Baghdad in the name of his master Ma'mún. The head of Amín remained exhibited in the public places of the city for several days and was then sent with the crown jewels to Khurásán.

Amín, it may be said incidentally, was one of the few Caliphs that died in Baghdad. According to al-Khaṭíb, he was killed in the street of the Anbár gate, and was the first Caliph since the foundation of the city to die in it.[1]

Though the capital had fallen, Ma'mún remained in Khurásán and appointed one of his favourites, Ḥasan ibn Sahl, to be viceroy of Arabia, Iraq and neighbouring provinces, instead of Ṭáhir, who had been in charge of Baghdad. There were people who considered that the Caliph had delegated too much authority to Ḥasan and risings broke out at Kufa and elsewhere. Baghdad however was too exhausted immediately after the siege to take any active part in the revolt, but in the next year the trouble came to a head when Ḥasan, who had taken up his residence at Madá'in (the ancient Seleucia) ordered the governor of Baghdad to delay payment of the troops, whose sympathies were against him. In reply, the troops mutinied, demanding the removal of Ḥasan from the capital. Not content with that, they themselves appointed Isḥáq, a grandson of the Caliph Mahdí, to be Ma'mún's representative in the city. The inhabitants on both sides of the river, forsaking their normal antagonism, were at one over this step and accepted the new viceroy. But they were reckoning without Ḥasan, who understood the nature of the people with whom he was dealing, and by intrigues and promises soon had the two sides at one another's throats again. Nevertheless, when his promises failed to materialize, and the troops continued to be without the pay that was due to them, the governor he had nominated was sent in full flight out of the city and Ḥasan himself was compelled to follow as far as Wásiṭ.

In the same year that the city fell (813), Ma'mún appointed 'Alí ibn Músá, of the line of the Prophet's son-in-law 'Alí—and hence a member of the heretical Shí'a—to be his heir to the sovereignty of the Moslem empire and to be Caliph after him. As the outward and visible token of the change of dynasty from the Abbasids to the 'Alids, he bade all who were under his authority, including the inhabitants of Baghdad, to discard the wearing of black, which was the Abbasid colour, and to wear green—the 'Alid colour—instead. To further his cause he offered the soldiers the payment of a month's supplies and gave the promise of a further ration at the next harvest. The members of the Abbasid clan in Baghdad, who were at the time a numerous body, met together in great indignation to discuss the situation and after some months' delay came to the decision that Ma'mún himself was no longer worthy of the Caliphate and should be deposed. In his stead they elected as

Caliph his father's half-brother Ibrahím, a son of Mahdí by a negro slave girl. Their action was assured of considerable support in Baghdad, for, though the name of 'Alí bore great weight in the rest of Iraq, the capital owed its origin to the Abbasids and the citizens themselves did not forget the fact. Yet there were many men of moderate opinion in the city who, though disliking the 'Alid intrigues, were not desirous to go to the length of deposing the legitimate Caliph Ma'mún. Ibrahím's proclamation as Caliph was to have taken place on Friday, July 17th, A.D. 817, in the great mosque of Baghdad, but before the announcer could utter the name of Ibrahím in displacement of Ma'mún, the opposition made itself felt, and in the subsequent disturbance in the mosque the *khuṭba* was omitted. This was an important point, for the *khuṭba*, being the prayer for the sovereign in which the acknowledged Prince of the Faithful is mentioned by name, indicates the legitimate sovereign; and the people, ceasing to be a congregation, individually uttered the prescribed prayers and departed to their homes without hearing the official prayer pronounced. On the following Friday, however, after a week's wrangling, the *khuṭba* was pronounced in the name of Ibrahím, whom Baghdad now acknowledged as the Caliph.

Before two months had passed, the new monarch, who was a trained professional singer knowing nothing of government or finance, was in serious monetary difficulties. His "army", a rabble of the lowest class of Beduins and villagers who had hoped for an easy livelihood in the service of this easygoing prince, began to clamour for their pay. He was able at first to satisfy them from his own resources by giving each man 200 dirhems, but as further instalments fell due and were not forthcoming, the "army" at last refused to believe Ibrahím's promises and forcibly demanded their pay. On one particular day when their demonstrations began to look serious, an officer of the palace came out and confessed that the treasury was empty. Promptly an impudent member of the crowd called out: "Then bring out our Caliph and let him sing to us; three songs for the men on this side of the city and three for those on the other side. We will take them instead of pay".[1]

It was a bad beginning to the reign and before long Ibrahím moved to Ctesiphon, leaving the management of the city to two governors, of whom one was to be in charge of each bank of the river.

The long siege and consequent disorder had left a large part of the city in ruins, while the relaxation of discipline after the death of Amín had permitted the formation of a powerful gang of ruffians, some of whom belonged to the old army, which had not yet been disbanded. Women and children were openly attacked in the streets; houses, bazaars and neighbouring villages were robbed and the plunder openly exposed for sale. The governor was powerless, and the peaceable citizens of every quarter suffered until they at last determined to take matters into their own hands. The lead was taken by a certain Khálid the Dervish, who lived on the Anbár road. Summoning his neighbours and others in the quarter who were of the same mind as himself, he called on them to appoint him "to command the right and forbid the wrong".[1] They agreed to this proposal and he proceeded to carry out his commission by attacking the culprits wherever he found them, beating some, imprisoning others and carrying still others of them before the governor; though that proceeding appears to have had little effect. He was superseded in the leadership of the party of law and order by one Sahl ibn Saláma, who was by origin a Persian from Khurásán. "He too called upon men to command the right, and forbid the wrong, to act according to the book of God and the practice of His Prophet, and round his neck he hung a copy of the Koran."[2] Having secured a considerable following from amongst the more respectable classes of the population, he went about Baghdad from bazaar to bazaar, from suburb to suburb and from road to road, putting an end to various wrongs. He singled out for special treatment a peculiar form of blackmail which consisted in a man's going to the owner of a garden and saying, "Your garden is under my protection. I will guard it from anyone who attempts any damage to it in return for so many dirhems a month". The owner, very unwillingly, would pay the money to avoid further trouble.[3]

The preaching of Sahl ibn Saláma continued under the governorship of Ibrahím. But his objurgations now went beyond the vulgar lawbreakers and were aimed at the city authorities themselves, who began to regard the enthusiasm which his words aroused with considerable misgiving. One of Ibrahím's generals, 'Ísá, was amongst those attacked. He had been defeated in an insurrection of ‘Alids at Wásiṭ, and returning to Baghdad in the middle of Sahl’s preaching campaign he cast about for a means of revenge. During a demonstration at which Sahl was haranguing a crowd outside a mosque, ‘Ísá contrived, by bribing some of the preacher’s confederates, to isolate him from his followers and attempted to cut off his escape by any of the numerous lanes that led to the mosque. By some means Sahl discovered he was in danger, and suspecting who his enemy was, he threw away the weapons he was carrying and by mixing with the crowd of onlookers he was able to escape unharmed to his own house. But a watch was kept on his movements and he was captured one night in one of the streets near his house. He was taken before the prince Isḥáq (son of the Caliph Músá al-Hádí), who had been appointed heir to the throne in succession to his uncle Ibrahím and who was then in the city. Isḥáq cross-examined the prisoner and accused him of finding fault with the Abbasid government and exciting the people against them. Sahl’s reply was that his only offence was to summon people to live according to the Koran and the tradition of the Prophet, and that he still did so. Isḥáq refused to accept the excuse. He ordered Sahl to be taken outside, with instructions that he was to tell the people that his preaching had been false. When Sahl however faced the crowd, he said: “I called upon you to live by the Book and the Tradition, and I do so again now”. The words had no sooner been spoken than the guards fell on him with blows and struck him in the face. He was taken in again before Isḥáq, bound in chains and sent to Ibrahím, who imprisoned him. In order to prevent any popular ebullition the rumour was spread abroad that he had been executed.[1] It was not until some years later that he was released, in the reign of Ma'mún.

While discord was thus raging in the capital, Ma'mún's ministers had kept him in Khurásán in ignorance that he had been deposed in favour of his uncle, Ibrahím, who was regarded as orthodox, while he himself with his Persian sympathies was looked upon as a heretic. Not until nearly five years had passed after Amín's death did news come to Ma'mún which made him realize what was happening. The lethargy which seems to have possessed him during most of that time fell away and he set out in haste for the capital. Meanwhile the enthusiasm for Ibrahím was expiring. He had brought little peace to the city, and the disturbances culminated in a rising which compelled him to flee from his house at night and to make his way in disguise through the tortuous streets to a hidingplace in the city where hc could be certain of security. It is an astonishing commentary on conditions of life in Baghdad that he was able to remain undiscovered and undenounced for six years after Ma'mún's entry into the capital.

CHAPTER VI

The Reign of Ma'mún

The capital on Ma'mún's arrival in A.D. 819 was in need of considerable restoration. Such portions of the city as were not too hopelessly damaged were put into repair, but there were parts so badly dilapidated as to be beyond further inhabitation. We hear little more of the Round City after this time, doubtless because its walls had been so battered that their original outline was now no longer recognizable, though a further reason may be that the Caliph now had his residence on the east bank. The Khuld Palace on the right bank had been given by the Caliph to his father-in-law Ḥasan ibn Sahl, after whom it came to be known as the "Ḥasaní" Palace. The house on the left bank in which Ma'mún himself lived, was the old Ja'farí Palace, originally built for the unfortunate Ja'far the Barmecide. In its gardens the new resident laid out a spacious *maydán*, or parade ground, where he could run horseraces and play polo away from the vulgar gaze. Near by he kept a menagerie of wild beasts for the delectation of himself and his friends, and for his greater freedom he had a private gateway built on the east side of the palace by which he could gain immediate access to the desert. His friends and courtiers were now attracted to the east side of the city so that another quarter, called after him the "Ma'múniya", came to swell the growing importance of the left bank.

With a certain degree of peace and the restoration in part of the old way of life, there began a period of literary brilliance for which the Caliph must be given much of the credit. "Of the Caliphs of the Abbasids", says the poet Tha'álibí, "the 'opener' was Manṣúr (who founded Baghdad), the 'middle' was Ma'mún, and the 'closer' was al-Mu'taḍid." It is sufficiently true that under Ma'mún the city was at one of the peaks of its prosperity and that after him there was a rapid decline. He gathered together at Baghdad the best known poets, scholars and historians of the day and sent men to the old Byzantine provinces in search of the works of the classical philosophers and physicians. Many had already been rendered into Syriac, from which tongue Ma'mún had them translated into Arabic, thus introducing to the scientific world the works of Hippocrates, Euclid and Galen that had been all but forgotten in Europe.

Ma'mún's efforts were seconded by private individuals in the city and there is special mention of three brothers, known as the Banú Músá, i.e. the Sons of Moses. Their father, who had been a friend of the Caliph in Khurásán, was a geometrician, but he was better known as a warrior and a brigand who would attend the early evening service in the mosque and then depart to hold up travellers on the roads.[1] His three sons

were extreme in their search for ancient sciences, expended fortunes on them and wearied themselves out for them. They sent to the land of Greece people who would procure scientific works for them and brought translators from various countries at great expense, and so brought to light the marvels of wisdom. The chief subjects with which they occupied themselves were geometry, mechanics, the movements of the heavenly bodies, music and astronomy, but these were the least of their activities.[1]

Men of every faith were numbered amongst Ma'mún's own favourites, and as a consequence savants like al-Kindí the Jewish astrologer and philosopher were assured of a large clientèle even amongst the Háshimites, members of the Prophet's own family.[2]

As a centre for his scholars the Caliph founded at Baghdad a magnificent institute equipped not only with a fine library but with an observatory that attracted the learned from all over the Moslem empire. Through their labours the Arabs were enabled to become the science teachers of Europe in the middle ages and to be in some measure the forerunners of the Renaissance. Amongst these savants, so long as they did not secede from Islam, complete liberty of thought and speech was allowed, Ma'mún's Persian antecedents being doubtless responsible for the encouragement he gave to doctrines and discussions that appeared heretical and abominable to all who followed Arab thought and tradition. In Khurásán he had been so tolerant of heterodox opinions that he had been given the title of *Amír al-Káfirín*, or "Commander of the Unbelievers", and though he promptly put the inventor of the title to death, it nevertheless clung to him. Through his influence it became fashionable to confess in public to mildly heretical opinions. Generally it was a pose, and the poet Ibn Munádhir satirizes his friend Ibn Ziyád as follows for indulging in the practice:

O Ibn Ziyád, Abú Ja'far,
You display a faith different from that which you have in your heart,
Outwardly in your speech you play the heretic,
Being inwardly a youth of Moslem piety.
No heretic you; all you desire is to be called a smart fellow.[1]

Amongst the scientists living in Baghdad during the period of Ma'mún was the Christian doctor Ḥunayn ibn Isḥáq. Ibn Khallikán's biography of him permits us a glance at the daily life of some of the learned fraternity of the day, and from the details given it may be gathered that scholarship and scientific skill had considerable market value at the time. We are shown Ḥunayn, after his ride every day, going to the baths. There he would lie at his ease while the attendants poured water over him. On emerging from the bath he put on a bedgown, drank a cup of wine, ate a biscuit and lay down to rest—sometimes falling asleep. The siesta over, he burned perfumes to fumigate his person and ordered his dinner. This generally consisted of a large fat fowl and a cake of bread. He would sup the gravy and eat up the fowl and the bread. Then he resumed his sleep and on awaking drank four pints of old wine to which he added Syrian apples or quinces, if he felt the desire for fresh fruits.[2]

A "character" of the reign was Di'bil ibn 'Alí. Though he was a good poet he had the reputation of being a scurrilous rogue, addicted to satire and ever ready to utter slander without sparing any person, even the Caliph.[3] One of his sayings shows him to be a worthy prototype of W. S. Gilbert's "Disagreeable

Man". "For fifty years past", he said, "I have gone about with my cross on my shoulder but have found no one to crucify me on it."

Music was amongst the arts encouraged by Ma'mún, and he used to spend two hours every day cleaning his teeth, while poetry was recited to him.[1] He kept on at his court in great honour some of the singers who had made their home there originally and maintained their families. Ibrahím al-Mauṣilí, for example, had a son Isḥáq, who was not only an excellent singer but an accomplished scholar with a good private library. Ma'mún thought so highly of him that he permitted him to appear at the royal receptions amongst the savants and not amongst the mere singers, who occupied a humbler position. This honour was not sufficient for Isḥáq and later on he asked permission, which was given him, to be introduced amongst the learned jurists; and the other musicians with amazement saw him walking alongside the noted judge Yaḥya ibn Aktam, and familiarly holding the hand of the great man, who was dressed in his costume of state which jurists wore[a]—a long black robe and a high black sugar-loaf hat of marten-skin. Not content even with that, Isḥáq some time afterwards asked that he too might be allowed to wear this costume on Fridays and take part in the prayers from the royal pulpit. Ma'mún smiled at this

[a] Incidentally it may be mentioned that during the Abbasid period the "Khaṭíb", or preacher, was always dressed in a long black robe; his head was covered with a black turban over which, during the address, he drew the tall conical cap. A sword was slung around his shoulders, and in the pulpit was erected the black standard, the emblem of the reigning dynasty (von Kremer, *Culturgeschichte des Orients*, II, 33).

bold request. "Stop there, Isḥáq," said he, "I will buy your abstinence from this request for 100,000 dirhems."[1]

If the composition known as the '*Iqd* of Ibn 'Abdi Rabbihi († A.D. 940) is to be believed, the nocturnal adventures of Hárún's day, of the kind made familiar by the *Arabian Nights*, were not unknown in Ma'mún's time. Isḥáq the singer tells the story of an adventure of the sort in which he was the hero. He had spent the whole of one day with Ma'mún drinking, playing and singing, and when night fell Ma'mún left him, promising to return in a short while. Isḥáq waited with growing impatience, and at last, when most of the night was gone, he realized that Ma'mún had forgotten about the appointment, and got up to leave for home. When he reached the door of the palace, the house-slaves and men of the watch came up to tell him that his slaves had left some little while before. They had come with a mount to take him home, but when they heard that he was spending the night in the palace they had gone home again. "No matter," said Isḥáq, "I shall walk home alone." "Let us bring you one of the mounts belonging to the guard", said they. "I have no need of that", he replied. "Then," said they, "we will go in front of you with a torch." "No," he replied, "I do not want it." He set out in the dark, and as he was going along a narrow street he caught sight of something hanging down from the wall of a house and descending almost to the level of the street. On approaching he found that the suspended object was a large basket with four handles, containing an embroidered robe and four silken cords. In his half-drunken state he stood and contemplated it for a short while, reflecting that it must have a reason and must mean something. At last he said to himself: "By Allah, I will venture and seat myself in it, whatever may happen".

Continuing his tale, he says:

I wrapped myself in my cloak and seated myself in the middle of the basket. When the people on the other side felt the weight in the basket they pulled until I reached the top. There stood four maidens who welcomed me politely and asked me to alight, saying: "Are you an acquaintance, or someone new?" I said I was someone new, and they called for a candle which one of them brought and, carrying it in a holder, she walked down in front of me into a cleanly chamber in which there was a beauty and grace that astonished me. She then led me to various sitting-rooms covered with rugs and having couches adorned with coverings of which I had not seen the like, even in the Caliph's palace. I seated myself upon the nearest of them. After that (for a time) I continued to hear shouts and mysterious noises coming from somewhere in the house; and then suddenly there appeared before me a number of maidservants, some carrying candles and others braziers in which aloe wood and ambergris was smoking. Amongst the slave girls was one who had the appearance of a statue cut in ivory and who carried herself in the midst of them like a full moon rising in full glory disdainfully above the branches. At seeing her I was deprived of power to move.

The maiden then approaches and welcomes him as an unaccustomed visitor and asks how he happened to be there, to which he replies explaining his presence as has been narrated, adding that the wine he had drunk had emboldened him to his action. She replied that no harm had been done and hoped he would have cause to be pleased with the outcome of his adventures. The narrative continues:

"What is your profession?" she asked.
"A draper", I replied.
"And where were you born?" she continued.
"In Baghdad", I replied.
"Then of what people are you?" she asked.
"Of respectable middle-class people", I replied.
"Do you recite poetry?" she then asked.
"A little", I replied.
"Then mention something of what you have learned", she said.

He replies that he is a little nervous about taking the first step and persuades her to begin, so that in the meantime he may recall something to recite. She declaims one poem after another, going from old poets to new and back again until he is amazed and does not know which to admire more, her accuracy, her beauty of diction or the fine quality of her learning. He himself then recites, putting forward all his powers to please. When he has finished, she says: "You have indeed not disappointed me. I did not suspect that amongst ordinary merchants and traders in the bazaar there was anyone with your talents. How did you acquire your knowledge of the traditions and the 'Days' [famous battles] of the [Arab] people?" He returns a vague reply, and then she orders a table with food and wine to be brought in.

Over the food and drink they converse and she again calls out in wonder that a mere merchant should know so much of romance and life at kingly courts. They keep up their conversation and their competition in capping each other's feats of memory until the dawn, when an old woman appears and hints it is time for him to depart. The next day the Caliph apologizes for his neglect of the poet, who replies, after various complimentary phrases: "I had bought a slave girl in the bazaar and my heart was set upon taking my pleasure with her, and when I saw that the Commander of the Faithful was occupied, I departed home and summoned her and bringing wine I drank and made her drink... until sleep overcame me until the morning".[1]

Intellectually, then, Baghdad during Ma'mún's reign was at its most brilliant. But signs were not wanting that the best days of the Caliphate were over, with a consequent decline in the material prosperity of the capital. Ṭáhir "Ambidexter", once Ma'mún's trusted lieutenant, in A.D. 820 declared himself independent in Khurásán, of which he had been appointed governor by the Caliph. There were risings too in other parts of Persia to point the demands for reduced taxation; and in addition to campaigns against Byzantium there were long-drawn-out efforts—with inevitably heavy expenditure and insecurity of trade—to subdue the Heresiarch Bábak the Khurramí, who for more than twenty years kept the west and north-west of Persia in terror and defeated all the efforts of Ma'mún's armies to subdue him. He was finally captured in the reign of the Caliph Mu'taṣim in A.D. 838, five years after Ma'mún's death. During that time rumours of his successes kept Baghdad in a constant state of fear that he would attack the city.

There were other causes for disturbance also, nearer

home. It has been recorded how the usurping Caliph Ibrahím, son of Mahdí, escaped Ma'mún for six years. Early in A.D. 825 reports reached Ma'mún that some of the earlier supporters of Ibrahím were now conspiring to replace him on the throne. In fact preparations for the rising were complete when one of the parties to the secret disclosed it to Ma'mún, telling him that the first step was to be the cutting of one of the bridges for the purpose of delaying the despatch of troops when the insurrection was announced. The ringleaders, Ibrahím ibn 'Ayisha, Mohammed ibn Ibrahím, Malik ibn Sháhí, and one or two others, were immediately seized in their homes. Ma'mún gave orders that Ibrahím ibn 'Ayisha was to be bound and left standing in the sun at the gate of the royal palace for three whole days—the time being the end of June. He was then scourged and flung into prison. Malik ibn Sháhí and his companions were beaten with whips and cast into the same gaol. There they accused a number of notables in the city of being concerned in the plot, but whether from diplomatic motives or otherwise, Ma'mún took no steps against the men denounced. Those who were in the prison meantime found an opportunity of meeting and concocted a plan to break out of the gaol. They were betrayed, however, by their action in barricading the prison gates from within, and at the time arranged for the escape, Ma'mún in person was on the spot with a body of troops ready to receive them. Their fate led them to be seized and crucified on the lower bridge across the Tigris.

At the same time orders were issued that Ibrahím

was to be taken at all costs. The story of his capture is a romantic one and the historians all give it with a varying amount of detail, Ṭabarí's account being the simplest. According to him, Ibrahím, disguised as a woman, was out walking during the night, accompanied by two women, when he was challenged by a negro sentry who asked who they were and where they were going at that late hour. Ibrahím in a panic offered the man a valuable signet ring as a bribe to let them go and ask no questions. The sentry seems to have been intelligent as well as loyal. Noticing that the ring was a man's his suspicions were aroused, and he took the party of three to the chief of the watch, who told them to uncover their faces. On Ibrahím's refusing to obey, his veil was pulled aside by the officer of the watch, thus disclosing the disguised man's beard. There was nothing for it now but to take him to the officer in command of the bridge, who recognized him and marched him to the gate of Ma'mún's palace, where orders were given that the prisoner was to be kept within the gates. The next morning members of the Abbasid family, army chieftains and others who had known Ibrahím, were admitted to behold the spectacle of the quondam Caliph with the woman's veil which had been part of his disguise still round his neck, and the woman's cloak, with which he had been covered, round his body.[1] Ma'mún seems to have realized that the man's power for danger was at an end. He was pardoned and spent the rest of his days as a professional singer.

A different cause of unrest was Ma'mún's persecution of men who differed from him in their beliefs.

In spite of the general latitude of thought which he permitted there were certain doctrines which he held very strongly, in common with the school of Mu'tazila, or "Seceders". One of these was that the Koran was created by Allah and was not, as the orthodox believed, something co-eternal and co-existent with Allah. In order to ascertain whether this and other favourite doctrines of his were being professed by the cadis and others responsible for the spiritual welfare of Baghdad, he instituted an inquisition in which a number of the religious leaders of the city were questioned on their views. Most of them gave satisfactory replies, but one, Aḥmad ibn Ḥanbal—the most eminent of them all and the founder of one of the four Sunní, or orthodox, schools of theology—insisted on the orthodox view that the Koran was uncreate. He would undoubtedly have been put to death if Ma'mún himself had not died during the course of the inquiry.

CHAPTER VII

Baghdad without a Caliph

The new Caliph, Mu'taṣim, was left a legacy of war. In north-western Persia, Bábak, the Khurramite, the heretic who was claiming to be a god, brought terror not only into the lands he infested, but into Baghdad itself. From the neighbourhood of Baṣra another danger threatened. There the Zuṭṭ,[a] a confederacy of wild tribes who dwelt in the marshes, had assumed authority and threatened to march on Baghdad. A campaign of nine months' duration was necessary before they were subdued, and in token of victory five hundred Zuṭṭ heads were sent to Baghdad to adorn Mu'taṣim's gates and to restore equanimity in the capital. After them came a great multitude of survivors carried in triumph to the city by the victorious general 'Ujayf. The long string of barges, with 27,000 captives on board—men, women and children, all blowing horns—were passed in review by the Caliph himself from his own vessel. After three days in Baghdad the prisoners

[a] They appear to have been of Indian origin, probably the descendants of Jat warriors whom Yezdigird III, the last Sassanian king of Persia, had induced to come to his aid against the Mohammedan Arabs. Both the present-day gypsies and the Marsh Arabs, the *ma'dán*, seem to be their descendants. See de Goeje, "Mémoire sur les migrations des Tsiganes à travers l'Asie", and my "Note on the Marsh Arabs of Lower Iraq", *Journal of the American Oriental Society*, XLIV, 130 ff.

were sent on a weary march northwards through Persia, and were lost to sight.

The expeditions sent against Bábak remained unsuccessful for three years more, but meantime events of importance were taking place in Baghdad. Mu'taṣim, who was the son of a Turkish mother, had conceived a violent hatred of the Persians and the Arabs, and having, like most of his line, an inordinate fear of violence to his person, he had formed his bodyguard of mercenaries from Turkestan and North Africa. Gradually he had been increasing their numbers until they exceeded 70,000 men, so that although the Persians continued to be the viziers and administrators of the empire the Turks now formed the greater part of the army of which their generals took entire control. The Arab amírs who had been in command were ousted, and the Turks took possession of the city, whose inhabitants were put to the unpleasant necessity of finding accommodation for the foreign troops. Being subject to no control but that of their own generals, who cared little for what their men did out of their sight, the mercenaries showed their contempt for the Caliph and the citizens of Baghdad by their outrageous conduct. They made a practice of galloping in companies through the narrow streets, trampling underfoot women, children and anyone else not nimble enough to leap out of their way. It was natural that reprisals came to be common. Foreign troopers who had been rash enough to venture out alone were found murdered in the streets, and the discovery of their corpses was an incentive to retaliation to such an extent that there appeared to be every likelihood of civil war between the citizens and the Caliph's troops if adequate measures were not soon taken to prevent the conflict.

Mu'taṣim determined on the decisive step of moving the seat of government from Baghdad to Samarra on the Tigris, about eighty miles north of the capital. The place was at that time a Christian village possessing a large monastery, whose land he purchased. In the year A.D. 836 the Caliph left Baghdad, and never again returned to it. Of Samarra he tried to make a city that would rival Baghdad in splendour. He built fine palaces and mosques, barracks for his Turkish and Berber troops, and hundreds of houses for his courtiers and servants, but it did not succeed in rivalling the older city. It became rather a kind of early Versailles situated somewhat distantly from its Paris. Its name was flatteringly derived from the Arabic phrase *surra man rá'a*, which means "He that saw it was gladdened"; though a Baghdad interpretation of the phrase ran: "Whosoever saw it (with the Turks settled there) rejoiced (at Baghdad's being rid of them)".

Numerous compositions are extant in prose and verse intended to flatter the new capital and to express sycophantic approval of the Caliph's choice of it. Some are cautious in their flattery, managing to praise Baghdad while by implication calling Samarra better. One such effusion reads:

It [Baghdad] is the mother of the world and the mistress of cities.... Men of understanding have said Baghdad is the garden of the earth and the City of Peace, the Dome of Islam and the Gathering-place of the Helpers (of the Prophet);

chiefest of cities, meeting-place of all good qualities and source of all things of beauty and grace. In it are the great masters of every art and the unique ones of the age in every faculty.

There follows a euphuistic catalogue of the ways in which Baghdad was defective:

Allah has roused them that inhabit it to rebellion and has caused its walls to tumble down. Despair speaks within it and the cord of hope is there cut short. It is as though its prosperity went anhungered and its ruins were scattered broadcast.... [But as for Samarra] its star is wakeful and its air is clear; its day is always as the early morn and its night as the dawning. Unlike your city [Baghdad] of the unclean skies and of suffocating climate, whose air is dust and whose terrain consists of dunghills, whose water is dirt, its walls a sore trial, and its October a July. How many a one is burnt up in its sunshine and drowned in its shade! Its inhabitants are wolves and their speech nought but defamation....Their stream is barren, their wealth sealed up...their walls are built of reeds and their houses are mere birdcages.[1]

This latter composition bears upon it all the marks of the "boasting-matches" in which the Arabs delighted, and it was obviously designed to reconcile the Caliph to his exile from Baghdad. But there seems to be visible in it also an indication that during Amín's reign the capital had lost some of the magnificence of Hárún's day. Yet it was still firmly established as the centre of a widespread commerce, and it retained that position in spite of the removal of the Caliph's court. If life was less splendid now for those whose interests had lain about the royal personage, it was much more peaceful for the ordinary citizen and his family, who could go about their business without danger from a "brutal and licentious soldiery". Nor did Baghdad by the removal of the seat of government lose its place as the greatest and richest city of the empire. As such it had to be taken into account by anyone with the ambition to be master of the Caliphate, which indeed stood in great danger—during the twenty years or so that followed the transfer to Samarra—of being subordinated to the continually growing power of the Turkish generals. With each Caliph now they contrived to arrogate increasing authority to themselves, and, since few of the successors of Mu'taṣim were capable enough to keep control of the reins of office, the Turks gradually assumed virtual command of the government.

The Caliph Wáthiq, son and successor of Mu'taṣim, was a debauchee who died after a reign of less than six years. His physical excesses had not prevented his holding decided views on questions of faith and inflicting them upon his subjects. Like Ma'mún, he was a Mu'tazilí or Freethinker. He too insisted on the doctrine that the Koran was created and was ready to punish anyone who held the contrary view. In spite of the permanent inquisition that he instituted, there were some inhabitants of Baghdad who were not afraid to expound the orthodox doctrine which opposed his. Amongst them was Aḥmad ibn Naṣr al-Khuzá'í, whose family was of some standing in the city and who had himself been one of the "puritan" leaders during the lawless period before the coming of Ma'mún established order. Wáthiq's governor in the city was zealous in carrying out his master's orders, until his measures brought on revolt. Two of Aḥmad's most influential supporters planned a rising. By intensive propaganda and the liberal distribution of money they persuaded a number of enthusiasts to be ready for action on a particular night and to assemble at the beat of a drum, which was to be the signal. The rising was to take place simultaneously on the east and west sides of the city. Unfortunately for themselves, the leaders had left the distribution of some of the money which was to be used for bribes to agents not sufficiently discriminating in their choice of likely revolutionaries. A number of the recipients gathered together for a carousal on the night before the one appointed for the rising, and, as the wine began to take effect, they were seized with the desire to begin action immediately and proceeded to beat their drums. The rest of the conspirators however were unprepared for this precipitate action and none of them stirred. But the noise of the carousal and the drumming led to inquiries, which disclosed the whole plot. The ringleaders were arrested and sent before the Caliph, who set up an inquisition into the views of all the persons concerned in the conspiracy. Aḥmad was questioned by the sovereign himself on the point of the creation of the Koran, and receiving unsatisfactory replies Wáthiq called for the famous sword "Ṣamṣáma", and himself struck off Aḥmad's head. It was sent afterwards to Baghdad and displayed for a time on both sides of the river. Of those associated with Aḥmad about twenty were tracked down and cast into dark dungeons where they were shut off from receiving the alms which were commonly given to prisoners, heavy weights were fastened upon them and they were forbidden to see any visitors.[1]

It may incidentally be mentioned that Wáthiq's zeal for the doctrine of a created Koran was such that when on one occasion there was an interchange of Moslem and Roman prisoners, he made sure that the Moslems who were coming over to him held the right views before he would accept them in exchange.

Orthodoxy resumed its sway with the next Caliph, Mutawakkil, whose reign meant for Baghdad a period of turmoil and misery. He had a mania for building, and practised extortion on his subjects to satisfy his craving for architectural monstrosities. This passion he combined with a cruelty and bigotry equal to the worst in the history of Islam. It may be put down in part to the influence of the Turkish commanders who had ousted the Persian courtiers and scholars from their place of importance at the court. Whatever the reason, Mutawakkil, in complete contrast with the comparatively liberal policy of his immediate predecessors, insisted on the strictest adherence to the letter of authority as it was laid down by the Sunní, or traditionalist, doctors. An early manifestation of his views was an edict against Christians and other "protected" peoples, who were all compelled

to wear honey-coloured robes and girdles. They were to ride on saddles with wooden stirrups; on the back of their saddles they were to affix two globes. Those who wore tall conical hats were to affix two buttons on them and the hats themselves were to be of a different colour from those worn by Moslems. They were to affix on a prominent part of the clothes of their slaves two patches, which were to contrast in colour with any clothes that were showing; one of the patches to be in front and the other behind, and each to be the size of four fingers and the colour of honey. If any [of such non-believers] wore a turban it was to be of the colour of honey; such of their women as went out of doors were not to appear in public except dressed in a honey-coloured outer wrapper. He also commanded that their slaves were compelled to wear plain girdles [of the kind ordinarily worn by the "protected" peoples] and were forbidden to wear the embroidered belts donned by free Moslems. He also commanded that the newer buildings amongst their places of worship were to be demolished, that a tenth of their dwellings was to be seized; where there was sufficient room in the churches or synagogues they were to be turned into mosques, otherwise the space they had occupied was to be left vacant. He further commanded that wooden figures of devils were to be affixed with nails to the doors of their dwellings in order to distinguish them from the houses of Moslems. Moreover he forbade the employment of non-believers in any ministry or in any office of the government in which they would be in authority over Moslems; he also forbade their children to be taught in Moslem schools, nor was any Moslem to teach them, nor were they [the Christians] to display a cross on Palm Sunday, nor were they [the Jews] to cry out their *Shema'* ("Hear, O Israel," etc.[1]). Lastly he commanded that their graves were to be level with the ground in order not to resemble the graves of the Moslems.[2]

The edict was promulgated in A.H. 235 (=A.D. 849–50). In the next year Mutawakkil carried his zeal for orthodoxy and his hatred for the 'Alids so far as to destroy the tomb of the Prophet's martyred grandson Husain son of 'Alí, at Kerbela, which had by that time become a place of pilgrimage; the buildings around the tomb were to be demolished and the site of the tomb was to be ploughed over and sown with seed and no visits to it were to be permitted. Whether this order was ever put into effect is a matter for doubt, since the shrine at Kerbela to this day attracts hundreds of thousands of pilgrims from all over the Shí'a world.

In Baghdad the Caliph's "post"-agent was busy. A man reported by him, on dubious evidence, as having reviled Abú Bakr and Omar the "orthodox" Caliphs and also 'Á'isha and Ḥafṣa, the wives of the Prophet, was ordered by Mutawakkil to be beaten to death with whips; his body to be thrown into the Tigris without any prayers said over it, and not to be handed over to his kinsfolk for burial. This order was duly carried out in the public gaze.[1] Another victim of the Caliph's bigotry was the Christian doctor Bukht Yishú', who had once been Hárún al-Rashíd's physician and who was now condemned for some offence to 120 lashes and imprisonment.

Mutawakkil's repressive measures gained him the favour of the orthodox. In Baghdad the rigid and literalist sect of the Ḥanbalís (followers of the jurist Aḥmad ibn Ḥanbal) carried out a house-to-house visitation in the city and dragged out for punishment anyone whom they considered opposed to their views. In reliance upon their support Mutawakkil made an attempt at asserting his authority over the Turkish bodyguard, and for a time he was successful in giving the Caliphate a revival of prestige. Unfortunately for himself he employed his renewed power in satisfying his lust for cruelty, until at last his own son entered into a conspiracy with the Turkish guards to assassinate him.

The matter of the succession at once became the subject of fierce quarrels amongst the Turkish generals, who wrangled over possession of the new Caliph. Even if he personally no longer meant very much to the outside world, in his official capacity he still commanded the respect and prayers of all pious Moslems, and any attempt to wield his authority against his consent would have roused the whole of the empire that was still loyal to the Caliphate. In the choice of a Caliph the claims of heredity could not be entirely set aside, but each of the rival Turkish pretorians strove to have his own nominee appointed. Matters came to a head in A.D. 862, when, on the death of the Caliph Muntaṣir, a section of the Turks decided to disregard Mu'tazz, the legitimate heir, and to appoint Musta'ín, an Abbasid of their own choosing, to be Caliph. The people of Samarra however, in loyalty to the Prophet Mohammed's family, gathered in force to oppose the candidate of the Turks and to enforce the claims of Mu'tazz. Fierce battles broke out in the streets, report of them spreading to Baghdad, where shortly afterwards matters of even greater importance came to complicate the situation.

In the long-drawn-out war between the Caliphate and Byzantium it happened at about this time (A.D. 863) that a Moslem army was defeated with the loss of two popular generals. News of the misfortune put the finishing touches to the hatred and resentment which the citizens of Baghdad already felt for the Turkish guard that misruled the affairs of the Caliphate, and even dared to make and unmake Caliphs without reference to other Moslems. There was a wild outburst of rioting in the city. Prisons were opened, one of the two boat-bridges was cut and the other set on fire, the office of the prison records was looted and the registers cut up and thrown into the water, and the houses of the Christian officials were raided and robbed. By various means also money was got together to aid in the campaign against Byzantium and national feeling was thoroughly aroused. However, the riots ended as suddenly as they had begun, when the governor succeeded in persuading the citizens that the irregularly appointed Caliph would make a more worthy sovereign than the legitimate claimant to the throne.[1]

At Samarra a two years' struggle ended in the recognition of the rightful prince Mu'tazz as Caliph. Musta'ín the usurper fled to Baghdad, where the governor received him loyally and, with the agreement of the section of the Turkish troops who were in the city, he was declared Caliph in the old capital. The party of Mu'tazz had 50,000 troops at their disposal and were ready to fight in support of his claims. At Musta'ín's suggestion, therefore, Baghdad was put into a state of readiness to withstand a siege. The export of food to Samarra was prohibited, the double walls of the city both on the east and west banks were heightened and strengthened, extra shelters also being built along them to protect the defending troops from the weather. Outside the walls the moats were cleaned out and deepened while the gateways were strongly garrisoned and equipped with heavy catapults. At the outer gate of the Shammásiya gateway, at the northern point of the east bank, five engines of war lay across the breadth of the roadway, and at the inner gate a very heavy door, covered with sheets of iron, seems to have been suspended by ropes from the top of the wall, in such a manner that it could be let down suddenly to crush anyone who attempted to force the gateway. Outside the city all canal bridges were destroyed and the dykes cut so as to flood the country and hamper the enemy as much as possible.

Before the final measure was taken Musta'ín wrote to the revenue officials in each city that all income was to be brought to Baghdad and not to Samarra, and he further sent to the Turkish troops and others in Samarra ordering them to cast off allegiance to Mu'tazz and to return to their former allegiance to himself. Mu'tazz, at Samarra, had in the meantime taken similar proceedings and both Caliphs bid for the support of the troops who lay further afield, in Syria and elsewhere. In the neighbourhood of Baghdad the inhabitants of the villages, through fear of the Turks, fled into the city, leaving behind them their crops and movable property and thus increasing the difficulty of maintaining supplies. The enemy also were not without allies in the city. Of one amongst their agents, who obtained admission on a specious plea, it was reported—after his departure—that he had plotted to set fire to the roofs of the bazaars on both sides of the city. As a measure of precaution the bazaar roofs were then removed, for a fire in the besieged city would have meant catastrophe.

Towards the end of March A.D. 865 the Turkish advance guards came within sight of the Shammásiya gate and halted there, but were driven off by a party that sallied out. On the next day the commander of the city sent out a strong body of troops with a number of the religious leaders and cadis of the city for the double purpose firstly, of overawing the enemy and of recalling them to their loyalty to Musta'ín, and, secondly, if they failed to respond, to warn them to be prepared for battle. The expedition failed to have effect, and in the subsequent battle the first blow was struck by the Turkish troops, who attacked the Shammásiya gate but were driven off, though not without heavy losses in killed and wounded to the defenders. Several days later a force of Turkish and other troops, said to be 4000 strong, marched down with Mu'tazz from Samarra and encamped on the west bank of the river, threatening the older part of Baghdad. This time a sallying party from the city inflicted heavy losses on them; hundreds of heads were taken to adorn the two city bridges, and much plunder was carried off. Those who had distinguished themselves in the fight were decorated with bracelets, and everyone who brought a Turkish or Maghribí head to the house of the city commander was given a present of fifty dirhems.

The fierceness of the last battle had shown that the besiegers were in earnest. Further steps were at once taken to increase the defences of the city. In front of the Shammásiya gate houses and gardens had hitherto been left untouched. These were now levelled to give the mangonels a clear field against future attack. The preparations did not come too soon, for as soon as they were completed an attack was launched by the Turks and Maghribís. The Turks used burning oil in an attempt to set alight the war engines at the gateway, but they were unsuccessful in this and were driven off by the fire of mangonels that were stationed on floats in the river and could enfilade them. The simultaneous attack by the Maghribís was directed against part of the Shammásiya wall. One of the attackers, we are told, managed to scale it by means of a grappling hook. He was allowed to reach the top. There he was set upon and decapitated, his head being afterwards thrown with a catapult into the Maghribí camp.

Amongst the incidents of that day was one in which an excited defender of the wall was moved by his feelings to cry out aloud the name of the Caliph for whom he was fighting. In the confusion of the moment he cried out, "O Mu'tazz, Victorious One", by error for "O Musta'ín", and was promptly beheaded by his outraged comrades. Another event was the arrival of ten sea-going ships of war from Baṣra. Each vessel had on board a captain, three napthamen, a carpenter, a baker and thirty-nine oarsmen and warriors. The fleet advanced to a station on the river opposite the Shammásiya gate and attacked the Turks there with flames.

During the months that followed, the minor victories gained by the defenders in the neighbourhood were definitely wiped out further afield by a series of overwhelming disasters which disheartened a number of the principal citizens and sent them over to the party of Mu'tazz. A further display of dissatisfaction came when in August A.D. 865 a group of the Háshimite family of the Abbasids met in angry protest at the hardships they had been made to suffer with the rest of the inhabitants. They threatened Musta'ín and the governor of the city that if proper supplies were not forthcoming they would open the city gates and admit the Turks. When an emissary of the governor was sent to parley with them, they refused either to listen to him or to accept the governor's offer of a month's supplies, and departed raging to their homes without any agreement having been reached.

In view of the very serious dissatisfaction in the city, it became imperative for the governor to take some immediate step that would bring public opinion round to him. He decided on a surprise attack. At a given signal all the city gates on both sides of the river were flung open, the mangonels from the gates and the barges on the river opened fire on the besiegers, and the city troops rushed out *en masse*. After some fighting, which concentrated for the most part round the Shammásiya gate on the north of the city, the Turks were routed, their red standards captured and their camps looted. A body of the citizens pursued the flying enemy, and might have followed them to Samarra had they not been warned to turn back. Flushed with victory and roused by a promise of reward for the head of every enemy Turk they brought in, they returned to cut off Turkish heads on the battlefield. While they were so employed a wind sprang up from the south, raising a cloud of dust and carrying the smoke from the burning Turkish tents across the troop of citizens engaged in their gruesome task. Suddenly one of them, resting from his labours, caught sight of a red Turkish banner flying in the midst of the dust and smoke. Not knowing that it was a captured trophy, he raised the alarm that the Turks had returned, and fled in a panic into the city followed by his fellow-citizens.

The Turks soon found that the pursuit had ceased, and, cautiously returning to what was left of their camp, they discovered the mistake that had been made. The besieged were now in worse straits than ever. Discouraged by real reverses and terribly disappointed to find their potential victory turned into a defeat, the citizens turned upon the governor, demanding food and the raising of the siege. The only course open to Ibn Ṭáhir, the governor, was to communicate with the enemy to arrange terms of peace, which included secretly offering to depose Musta'ín, who was living in his house, and acknowledge Mu'tazz as the Caliph. The mass of the people were given to understand that the peace arranged included the continuance of Musta'ín in the Caliphate and the appointment of Mu'tazz as the heir apparent. It was only when the Turkish envoy came to the gates and called out that "The Commander of the Faithful and Abú Aḥmad" (the leader of the Samarra party) were dictating the terms of peace, that the citizens awoke to the fact that Ibn Ṭáhir's plan was not what they had imagined. Hundreds strong, they made their way to the governor's house and demanded an explanation. They were kept waiting for hours shouting out threats, and at last Musta'ín appeared at an upper floor with Ibn Ṭáhir at his side and assured the mob that he was being well treated by Ibn Ṭáhir and had received no harm from him. After numerous conferences in the weeks that followed,

Ibn Ṭáhir was empowered to sue for peace by Musta'ín, who agreed to abdicate. At the beginning of the year A.D. 866 peace was proclaimed, and Mu'tazz was acknowledged Caliph in the pulpits of the two great mosques on the east and west sides of the city. Musta'ín at the same time left the city with a promise of safe-conduct; in spite of which covenant he was murdered by a Turkish soldier not long afterwards.

The second siege of Baghdad had lasted for over a year. Hundreds of its citizens had been killed in battle or by famine, and the eastern parts of the city, particularly in the northern quarters of Shammásiya, Ruṣáfa and Mukharrim, had suffered damage so great that they were never afterwards put right. The new Caliph did not remain in the city but moved to Samarra amongst his old supporters. They repaid his confidence by murdering him in the most brutal fashion (A.D. 869).

The historians who deal with the events of the twenty years that follow do not often mention Baghdad, while the references that do occur are no record of peace and prosperity. Plague, flood and riot within, combined with threatened danger from rebels abroad, make up the sum of them. The external danger was the most serious. Relying on the disturbed condition of affairs at the capital of the empire, in September, A.D. 869, there arose a certain pretender whose name was 'Alí son of Mohammed. He gave himself out to be a descendant of the great Caliph 'Alí, the cousin of the Prophet and the man to whom the Shí'a or schismatic section of Islam owed a veneration exceeded only, if at all, by that paid to the Prophet himself. In his search for supporters the pretender found the material he required amongst the Zanj, or negro, slaves labouring in the saltpetre works that were situated in the great Tigris-Euphrates marshes to the north of the Persian Gulf. To them "he represented...how badly they were being treated, and promised them, if they joined him, freedom, wealth, and—slaves".[1]

They gathered to him in vast numbers, gang after gang, most of them ignorant of Arabic but all of them loyal to the leader who not only promised rich material prosperity but was able, from his religious pre-eminence, to offer spiritual blessings in addition. The first attacks were directed against the city of Baṣra, and the capital felt the pinch when its supply of dates, the staple article of diet, began to be restricted. The government in successive years despatched more than one army against the rebel negroes, who swept them aside and advanced slowly but surely northwards. Muwaffaq, the brother of the reigning Caliph Mu'tamid, in A.D. 872 himself led an army into the marshes, which took an even greater toll of casualties than the black enemy himself. Three years later, when the war had been dragging on for over five years without any decisive result, the negro leader was unexpectedly helped by a rising against the capital from a different quarter. This was the rebellion in Persia under Ya'qúb son of Layth the Coppersmith, who had already taken possession of the eastern province of Khurásán and was advancing through the provinces of Pars and Khuzistan upon Baghdad. There was nothing to stay his advance, and he succeeded in capturing Wásiṭ on the lower Tigris with little loss.

By this time the Caliph's troops had been diverted from the Zanj rebels to face this newer and apparently greater danger. Mu'tamid himself, with all the men he could muster, marched down from Samarra in "the mantle of the Prophet, and with the Prophet's staff in his hand", in a holy war against the godless rebel. About fifty miles below Baghdad the armies faced one another. And now Muwaffaq took command, with excellent results. Ya'qúb was defeated, his troops were dispersed and his camp, with rich booty, fell into the hands of the government forces (A.D. 876).

The Zanj took advantage of Ya'qúb's advance to move upstream from their marsh territory. It took them two years more however to capture Wásiṭ, which the Persian rebel had held. From there they advanced to within seventy miles of the capital, which would inevitably have fallen if Ya'qúb had not opportunely died, and so set free a number of defensive troops. With the danger from Persia to some extent lessened, the Caliph's regent, Muwaffaq, could devote himself to the Zanj peril, which was now very great owing to the opportunities the negro army had had for growth during the years when the Caliph's troops had been engaged in another quarter.

With ten years elapsed since the beginning of the war, Muwaffaq had by bitter experience learned something of the strategy to be employed against this particular foe. Towards the end of A.D. 879 he despatched his son Abú 'l-'Abbás (afterwards the Caliph Mu'taḍid) with a fleet of vessels—all of which, small and great, had to be propelled by manual labour—to deal with his amphibious enemy. His operations were in part successful and the Zanj were compelled to retreat down the Tigris. About a year later Muwaffaq himself appeared with an army to push forward the advance, but he now began to combine diplomacy with his military methods, by which he contrived to get numbers of the Zanj leaders to desert to him. They were followed by a great many of the common troops, who were attracted by promises of amnesty and reward. The final operations were protracted over a space of three years, but on Saturday, November 23rd, A.D. 883, Abú 'l-'Abbás was able to appear in procession in Baghdad with the head of the Zanj king displayed on a pole. In honour of the victory "the streets were decorated and the shops shut".[1]

Less than a year after the declaration of peace an unexpected calamity overwhelmed the west side of the city. The 'Isá canal, which connected with the Euphrates, overflowed its banks and submerged several of the city quarters. About 7000 houses collapsed, and, seeing that most of the buildings in Baghdad were of mud or mud bricks, there is every probability that their destruction was complete.

To add to the general discomfort in the city, there were periodical outbreaks of the Turkish and Berber mercenaries, of whom rival sections either fought each other in the streets for supremacy, with frequent bloodshed, or else united in demonstrations of violence to enforce payment of the arrears of their hire. At Samarra matters were even worse, though the Caliph Mu'tamid was able to escape the terrors of the foreign guard through the efforts of Muwaffaq, who held the Turkish and Berber troops in check until the sovereign found an opportunity in A.D. 892 of escaping to Baghdad and so restoring it to its old position of supremacy. Between him and Mu'taṣim, who had originally transferred the royal residence from Baghdad, six Caliphs had reigned in the short space of thirty-six years. On his arrival he expressed a wish to live in the once famous Barmecide Palace known as the Ma'múní or Ḥasaní, in which the widow of the Caliph Ma'mún was still living. Another residence was promised to the old queen, who asked for a little delay in which she might put her belongings in order and prepare them for transportation. This was granted, but instead of doing what she had said, she used the time at her disposal in putting the palace into a state of perfect repair. She ordered the walls to be hung with carpets woven of gold thread, the floors covered with reed mats, and the storerooms filled with everything that even the most exacting prince might require. Mu'tamid did not long enjoy the comforts of his new residence, for he died in it six months after his arrival.

CHAPTER VIII

Baghdad Restored

It was long since Baghdad had deserved its title of the "City of Peace". Almost from its foundation the history of the city had been one of struggle and turmoil; and therein perhaps lies part of its interest. Alarms from the outside of the city were not less in the reign of Mu'taḍid, the next Caliph. Actually they were more serious than ever, but the new monarch was a person of different calibre from his more immediate predecessors, desirous and capable of holding the power of the realm in his own grasp and of keeping order. In the capital almost immediately after his accession he set about the work of restoration, at any rate so far as his own residences were concerned, and he began the construction of a palace that would be more in accordance with his tastes than those already existing in Baghdad. With that end in view, he acquired a large tract of land round the Ma'múní or Ḥasaní Palace, and demolished all the buildings that stood on it. He then greatly enlarged the house and enclosed a piece of the desert for the purposes of a parade ground. On the completion of that work Mu'taḍid laid the foundations of a new palace a little lower down on the Tigris. The new construction was interrupted for a time by a rebellion in Upper Mesopotamia, to quell which the Caliph himself led an expedition from Baghdad. On his return he noticed that smoke from the city was carried across the site of his new building, which he accordingly abandoned, choosing another site, this time at a distance of two Arab miles from the river and on the Músá canal. There he erected a magnificent house which became known as the "Palace of the Pleiades", and he surrounded it with beautiful gardens that inspired more than one poet to verse. Between it and the Ma'múní Palace the Caliph constructed an underground passage along which the women of his household could go backward and forward without being subjected to vulgar curiosity. It was in existence for nearly two centuries, being finally destroyed by an inundation of the Tigris.

This did not complete Mu'taḍid's building activities, for he built yet a third royal residence on the river bank above the Ma'múní. Little is known of it beyond its name which was *Qaṣr al-Firdaws*, or "Paradise Castle". The three new palaces, with the gardens surrounding them, lay some distance downstream of the "Round City" and on the opposite side of the river. The older part of the "Round City" was by now crumbling—Mu'taḍid himself having demolished part of the walls[1]—and the great structures like the Khuld Palace were falling into ruins, the natural processes of decay being aided by the brittle nature of the mud bricks and other materials used in the construction. New buildings however were now being erected, though they do not seem to have reached the size or the magnificence of the older ones. The main bazaars of the city had been transferred to the east bank, where they stretched from the head of the main bridge for some distance along the Khurásán highway. The population was more than ever inclined to cluster round the new palaces, and the mosques and houses that they built for their needs formed the nucleus of entirely new suburbs, which grew into modern Baghdad. Indeed the wall which later surrounded the suburbs covered substantially the same ground as the city wall of to-day.

If the various assaults on the city had from time to time brought about architectural changes in it, they had not materially altered the habits and customs of its inhabitants. Undisturbed by wars and rumours of wars the various classes of Baghdad society had followed their own ways of life modified by the slow development that inevitably came with the passage of time. The class that has a special interest for us is that of the numerous men of letters, even if it be only because, being the most articulate, they have provided a more easily accessible picture than the rest of the times in which they lived. The historians of the period however concern themselves almost exclusively with the Caliphate and the political happenings which they considered important. But glimpses are occasionally to be obtained of the ordinary life of the people—which the historians took for granted—from biographers and from authors either of text-books written for the use of the public of their day or of story-books compiled for its delectation. One such text-book, composed probably about the end of the ninth century of our era, is the *Kitáb al-Muwashshá*[1] of Abú 'l-Taiyyih Muḥammad ibn Isḥáq who lived somewhere between A.D. 860 and

A.D. 936. He was of Beduin extraction and by profession a grammarian. For a time he taught in an elementary school intended for children of the lower classes in Baghdad, but he appears also to have given lectures in the palace of the Caliph Mu'tamid. In writing his book, which is the only one preserved out of many that he compiled, the author proposed to give an exposition of the qualities commendable in a man of polite education. A considerable part of the book is devoted to describing the moral characteristics of what we should call a gentleman, the qualities of *adab*, polite behaviour, and *muruwwa*, manly honour. The larger part of the work, however, is nothing more than a "book of etiquette", which describes the laws of love and love-making (according to the ideas of his day), of dress, of the table, etc. The general principle of the book is that *adab* must be accompanied by *muruwwa*, but that the latter may be sufficient in itself. In the ideal man both are present. Together with honourable conduct, the keeping of covenants, telling the truth, the guarding of secrets, and so on, polite breeding demands silence as a desirable quality in a man. It is better than speech, which, employed to excess, lowers a man's dignity. Even worse than excessive speech are jesting and frivolity, which a man of learning must at all costs avoid. However, pleasantness and affability are not thereby excluded.

In his costume the man of polite education and the man of letters should confine themselves to the best qualities of linen, dyed in pure (? sober) colours. Clothes of impure (? gaudy) colours such as yellow or amber are only suited for women, singing-girls or serving-maids; yet they may be worn when one is being bled or is undergoing medical treatment. At drinking-parties and at times of relaxation, clothes of variegated colours may be worn, musky cloaks, yellow shirts and amber-coloured drawers. It would be wrong to appear in the streets in such garb. Equally unfitting would it be for a man of breeding to appear in clothes of which some were soiled and others laundered, or some laundered and others new, or some linen and others silk. All should be of the same kind and should match. The book lays down the kinds and colours of the shoes that may be worn—stout or light, black with red or yellow with black—what stones are suitable in a signet ring and what perfumes are permissible.

Women of polite education may suitably wear outer robes of silk, etc., in various hues, black veils of certain qualities of material, and white, skirted pantaloons. They may not wear girdles threaded through their clothes and so concealed, nor cloaks of white linen—except where the material contains contrasting patterns in it, for that material is confined to men. Nor are the colours yellow, black, green, rose or red always suitable, except in particular stuffs, for some of these colours are characteristic of the clothes worn by Nabaṭean women or serving-maids, while white is also the colour of repudiated women, and blue is worn by widows.

At table it is recommended that all morsels taken should be small; the tender part only of the meat should be attempted, gristle, tendons and offal such as spleen or lung are to be avoided; nor should a polite man develop a liking for fat, or indulge in too many vegetables. If he desires to suck out a marrowbone he should choose a small one and not a large, coarse one; but if by chance he has taken one that is over-large he should rest it on the back of his fingers when dealing with it and put it to one side of the common tray when he has finished. He should not keep changing his seat, or lick his fingers, or over-fill his mouth, or dip pieces of bread into the dish; and he is particularly warned against salted foods, beloved of women. One meal in the daytime is considered sufficient and it should be eaten in very leisurely fashion; though while the food is still before them men of breeding will not indulge in overmuch laughter or conversation.

When offering food to visitors, care and discretion must be used not to offend, for there are certain things which have a hidden and unfortunate significance; for example the orange, of which the inside is different from the outside. Its exterior is comely but it is sour within; it is pleasant to the smell, but quite the contrary in taste.

In company a polite man does not stretch out his legs, or scratch himself, or touch his nose, or interlock his fingers, or sit in a sprawling fashion. In the street he does not walk too quickly, with his eyes fixed on the road to his goal, nor does he walk back the way he set out. He does not drink water from the *ḥubb* [the large, porous, earthenware jar which acts as a kind of reservoir to a smaller jar below used as a drinking-vessel], nor in a wine shop, or in a mosque, or at the roadside. He will not enter a cookshop, or eat anything bought in the bazaar; nor will he eat in the middle of the highway, or in the mosque, or in the bazaar.

To the baths he should go alone, and when there should not stare at anyone else, or hang his clothes on the common peg, or put his foot into the well by which the water runs away; that is what the vulgar do. He should not rub his hands with a rag, or roll in the hot earth of the bathhouse. For him, it is necessary to enter the bathhouse dressed in a short garment; to sit alone and to one side, and not to squat upon his heel as though ready in a moment to depart; to do that is an insult to breeding. He should always be properly dressed and never be seen in dirty or torn clothes; his nails should not be long, nor his hair too abundant; his nose should not run, nor his hands be black.

Not all these admirable rules were always carried out to the letter. There was a certain Ibrahím ibn Isḥáq al-Ḥarbí who did not bother overmuch with externals and took things as they came, summing up his philosophy of life in the following words:

> A man who does not flow along with destiny does not enjoy life. My shirt was ever clean, but my loincloth could be exceedingly dirty. It did not occur to me that they ought to be alike. One of my heels was worn down, but the other was good, and though I walked all over Baghdad, this side and that, it did not occur to me to mend them, and I complained neither to my mother, nor my sister nor my wife nor my daughters. He only is a man who keeps his woes to himself and does not trouble his family with them....For ten years I could see out of one eye only and I told no one of it. I spent thirty years of my life content with a single loaf of bread a day and only that when my family brought it to me. If they omitted to bring it, I went

hungry till the next night. Nowadays I eat half a loaf of bread a day with fourteen dates if they are of the *barní* or *naif* variety, and twenty if they are of the *daqal* [a very poor] variety. When my daughter was ill my wife remained with her a whole month and my meals during that time came to a dirhem and two and a half dániqs in all [about sevenpence altogether]; and I went to the baths and bought soap costing two dániqs.

Once when I was in great need my wife said to me: "You and I can bear hunger, but what of our two daughters? Give me some of your books and let me sell or pledge them". But I clung to my books and told her to borrow something for the girls and wait another day. That night there was a knock at the door, and when I called out to ask who was there a man replied: "One of your neighbours". I bade him enter and he replied that he would come in if I put out the lamp. So I threw something over the lamp and again asked him to come in. He entered, put something down at my side and departed. When I uncovered the lamp and examined what he had brought, I saw a kerchief of some value containing several kinds of eatables and also a paper containing 500 dirhems.

Ibrahím died in A.D. 898 and was buried in the Street of the Anbár Gate, "and", says the biographer, "there was a great concourse at the funeral".[1]

In his book called the *Prairies of Gold* Mas'údí, who was a kind of Baghdadí Herodotus, tells us something of the palace life of the period. He speaks of beautiful gardens and pleasaunces and of luxurious quarters inhabited by the Caliph's women; but he also describes vaulted underground torture chambers in which the Caliph took his horrible delight. The wealth of the capital was still enormous in spite of defaulting provinces, and Persia still continued to send tribute. Mu'taḍid on his accession had wisely reappointed 'Amr ibn Layth to the governorship of Khurásán and in A.D. 896 there arrived from him a present of a hundred blood camels, a great number of dromedaries, many chests full of precious stuffs and four million dirhems of silver. Amongst the gifts there was also sent, as a very valuable trophy, an Indian idol of yellow copper [? i.e. brass] in the form of a woman with four arms, having round its middle two girdles of silver encrusted with red and white precious stones. Borne on a carriage in front of it were a number of smaller images having hands and faces inlaid with gold and set with jewels. These were set up for public exhibition in the police headquarters of the city and for three days drew marvelling crowds.[1]

Mas'údí further shows how the Caliph maintained law and order in the capital. In one case, which is given at length, his methods may be said to anticipate those of "the Third Degree". The occasion was when ten bags of coin, which the Caliph had sent to his army paymaster for the hire of troops, were stolen by someone who in the night obtained access to the treasurer's house by breaking through a wall. The robbery was discovered the next morning, and after investigation the chief of the guard was told that he would be held responsible for the recovery of the money. The Caliph himself summoned his special agents, who were known as "repentants", that is ex-thieves who could generally be relied upon to know the authors of any particular burglary, and often, says the author, "shared the proceeds of a robbery with the culprits themselves". These "repentants" were told what had happened and were sent out in search. "They scattered amongst the streets, bazaars, inns and taverns, searched upper chambers and back chambers, the shops of offal sellers and houses where gaming was carried on." Soon they brought back a miserable looking wretch, thin, feeble and ill-clad, whom they all denounced as the thief. The chief of the guard began questioning him, asking particularly who his confederates were, since he could not have carried off all ten bags alone. The fellow denied all knowledge of the theft, even though he was promised a pension and an establishment if he confessed, and was threatened with the most terrible maltreatment if he persisted in being stubborn.

The Caliph had at last to be informed that a suspect had been taken but that no chastisement could make him speak. Mu'taḍid, in a rage at the clumsy methods which might have killed the man before he had told where the money was, had the suspect brought before him and promised him a full pardon if he would disclose where he had hidden the bags of gold. But the Caliph was no more successful than his officers, and at last he summoned his physicians and told them to take the man away and subject him to the most careful treatment, feeding him well and nourishing him until he had been restored to perfect soundness of body. He was taken away and treated with the utmost indulgence until the doctors finally pronounced him well. Again he was brought before the Caliph, who inquired after his health and received a blessing in reply. "And now," said the Caliph, "where is the money?" But threats and promises were of no more use now than on the previous occasions; the man denied all knowledge of the theft. It was then that the Caliph put into action a new method which he had contrived for making the man speak. He ordered thirty negro slaves to be brought in and gave them strict orders that the suspect was to be kept continuously in a sitting position on one spot. He was not to be allowed to change his position in the slightest; either to lean his elbow on the ground or to lie down or even to let his head droop. If he tried to sleep he was to be roused by a violent blow. After a couple of days of this treatment the fellow dropped to the ground incapable of movement, and in that condition was carried before the Caliph, who bade him swear by all he held sacred that he had not taken the money. The man did so, and Mu'taḍid, turning to those who stood by, said: "My heart affirms that the man is innocent and that we have behaved culpably towards him". He then ordered a table to be laid with food and refreshing drink and ordered the man to set to. When he could eat and drink no more, perfumes were brought in and lastly a feather-bed, on which he was told to lie down. But he was no sooner asleep than he was violently aroused and hurried, heavy with sleep, to the Caliph. "Speak," said the prince, "how did you contrive this theft? How did you make the hole? How did you get out? Who was with you and where did you go with the money?" He replied: "I was alone. I came out by the hole by which I entered. Near it is a *ḥammám* [bath house], which has a pile of brushwood in front of it for heating the bath. The money is hidden under that brushwood".

The thief was allowed to go back to his bed and the bags of gold were discovered in the place he had described. Needless to speak of the culprit's fate when he woke from his slumbers![1]

There were times when the Caliph met his match. Thus the saintly Abú 'l-Ḥusain al-Núrí happened to see a vessel on the Tigris laden with thirty jars belonging to the Caliph. Suspecting they contained wine, he asked the boatmen about them, and on finding his conjecture was right he took a boat pole and smashed all the jars but one before he could be stopped. He was brought before the Caliph to answer for his misdemeanour, and when asked, "Who made thee the *muḥtasib* [inspector]?" he boldly answered, "Who made thee Caliph?" and was pardoned.[2]

The skill which was effective in home affairs was also applied to the government of the empire. In Persia, Mu'taḍid's policy was as strong and cunning as his predecessor's had been weak and vacillating. When 'Amr ibn Layth, the Coppersmith, asked permission to add Transoxiana to his possessions, Mu'taḍid determined to be rid of him and induced Isma'íl the Sámánid, the semi-independent governor of Transoxiana, to attack him. In A.D. 900 (A.H. 287), 'Amr was routed in battle and taken prisoner, being sent to Baghdad a year later.

The mighty ruler, whose presents and trophies four short years before had been the finest spectacle that could be furnished to the mob of Baghdad, was now paraded before that mob in procession, as customary at the arrest of great State offenders or heretical princes....The one-eyed, sun-burnt captive sat upon a great caparisoned two-bunched camel—one of the animals that he himself had sent as a present on the occasion just alluded to—clothed in a rich silken robe, and with a tall cap upon his head. The sight touched the very mob in the street, and they refrained from the customary reproaches and curses.[1]

In A.D. 912 'Amr was murdered, and in the same year the Caliph died in the Ma'múní Palace, by poison it was said, and was buried on the west bank in the castle of the old Ṭáhirid governor of Baghdad. This castle was known as the "Marble House", and was at times used as a royal residence, though it came to be used more often as a place of sanctuary for the relatives of those Caliphs who were suspected of being partial to assassination as a means of safeguarding their thrones.

Under the *régime* of the Caliph 'Alí Muktafí, who succeeded his father Mu'taḍid, Baghdad saw the completion of the *Táj* or "Crown" Palace, that was to become a famous royal residence. Part of the materials for it were taken from a castle known as *al-Kámil*, or "The Perfect", of which no more than the name is known, while a great part of the rest of the required building supplies were torn from the ruins of the great palace of the Khosroes at Ctesiphon. The façade of the new building, which fronted on the Tigris, seems to have been especially impressive, if one may judge from the accounts of it. Its lowest storey in particular was considered worthy of frequent description. It consisted of a series of five arches, springing from piers that were built up of four marble columns and each having another supporting column in the centre. Upon the first storey rested another one of almost equal grandeur and the whole formed a suitable frontage for the magnificent building that stretched far behind. The special feature of this was the "Hall of the Sultanate", a great chamber having a particularly ornate window, at which each new Caliph sat at his accession in order to receive the homage of his subjects assembled in the vast court below. In front of the palace a long buttress was pushed out from the foundations into the Tigris. It was so constructed as to form a mole or pier through which the water was allowed to flow, and which provided easy access to a large stretch of gardens on the bank opposite the palace.

Amongst the buildings constructed hard by was the "Dome of the Ass", so called because it could be climbed on donkey-back by a ramp which ascended it, while another, within the grounds of the Ma'múní Palace, was the *Jámi' al-Qaṣr* or "Palace Mosque". Its special claim to notice is that it has left one of the few surviving monuments of the Abbasid period in Baghdad, in the crumbling minaret standing in the quarter of the city known as *Súq al-Ghazl* ("The Thread Bazaar"), which lies to the east of New Street, or Khalíl Páshá Street as it is sometimes called, and not far from the present Latin church. The mosque itself has long disappeared, but it was originally built on the site of the vaulted chambers in which the Caliph Mu'taḍid kept his prisoners and which his successor destroyed before building the mosque. At first the new place of worship was intended for the residents of the palace, but the general public were also admitted, and it soon became one of the most frequented mosques in Baghdad. It remained so until the Mongol conqueror Húlágú destroyed it in the sack of the city in A.D. 1258.

There were times during Muktafí's reign when the process of rebeautifying Baghdad was threatened by a foe vastly more formidable than either the Zanj or the rebels of Persia had been. The new danger came from the Carmathians, a body of sectaries whose doctrines connected them with the Isma'ílís, of whom another section acquired horrible fame as the Assassins. Qarmaṭ, their leader and the originator of the heresy which made them detestable to other Moslems, had, at the time of the Zanj advance on Baghdad, met the negro general with a proposal to join forces. It was not accepted and the Carmathians went their own way. A series of victories that enabled them to subdue Syria brought them within measurable distance of Baghdad, whose inhabitants were terrified by reports that the Carmathians had slaughtered the greater part of the inhabitants of Ba'albek and put to the sword every living thing—man, woman, child and beast—in the town of Salamya. Rumours of all kinds were afloat, and every tale brought from the enemy camp was eagerly seized upon and circulated. Thus, a doctor who lived in the Báb al-Muhawwal quarter reported that one day a woman had come to him and asked for treatment for a wound in her shoulder. He told her that as he was an eye doctor he could do nothing, but that there was a woman coming who attended to women and treated wounds, and he asked the patient to wait. As she seemed to be in great trouble and was weeping, he questioned her about herself and asked what had caused the wound. In reply she told him that she had a son who had run away from home, leaving her destitute. After a time she had followed him and found him in the Carmathian camp, then at Raqqa, where she discovered to her horror that he had cast off allegiance to his old beliefs and become a Carmathian. While in the camp she was persuaded to do a service to a woman in childbirth, who said that she had been carried off by five Carmathians and did not know which was the father of the child. All five claimed the honour, and as a reward for the Baghdad woman's services one of them helped her to make her way back to her home. On the way out of the camp she was overtaken by her son, who accused her of wishing to degrade his sisters by bringing them to the camp and struck her with his sword, thus causing the wound. The woman ended her story by saying that when the Commander of the Faithful returned to Baghdad with Carmathian prisoners she saw her son amongst them as they walked in the triumphal procession, and she cursed him, saying: "May Allah not lighten your woes nor redeem you".[1]

The triumphal procession mentioned by the woman came as the result of an isolated victory against the Carmathians in Muktafí's reign. The terror which they had excited in the citizens of Baghdad was avenged by a horrible display of cruelty towards the captives. They were brought into the city through the Anbár gate on elephants and imprisoned until preparations could be made for their execution. For this, a platform ten cubits high was erected in the courtyard of the old mosque on the east side of the city. There the prisoners were taken up one after another, their arms and legs were cut off and thrown to the huge crowd of spectators standing below, and only then were the victims decapitated. The leader himself was put to death with inhuman tortures. What struck Ṭabarí, who describes the scene, most particularly, was that none of the prisoners made any sound or denied that they were Carmathians.

That was by no means the end of these heretics, for it was not until the middle of the tenth century that their activities ceased. During Muktafí's reign they made several attacks upon pilgrim trains returning from Mecca, in one of which they are said to have left 20,000 dead on the field. In A.D. 929 they invaded Mecca itself and carried off the sacred Black Stone which they kept for twenty years, and ten years after that they were reported to be still levying blackmail on pilgrim caravans.

In the reign of the Caliph Muqtadir, who succeeded Muktafí, Baghdad was brought into political contact with the western world in a way unknown since the days of Charlemagne. Tired of the long struggle with the Caliphate, which had continued intermittently since the early days of the Abbasids, the Empress Zoe, acting as regent for the infant Emperor Constantine VII of Byzantium, sent an embassy to Baghdad to negotiate peace. The Baghdad historian al-Khaṭíb describes the coming of the delegation and gives us a picture of the magnificence of the Caliph's court and of the crowds of the citizens of Baghdad, ever ready to flock to a spectacle. He says:

In the days of Muḳtadir ambassadors from the Byzantine emperor arrived, so the servants spread magnificent carpets in the Palace, ornamenting it further with sumptuous furniture; and the Chamberlains with their Deputies were stationed according to their degrees, and the Courtiers stood at the gates and the porticoes, and along the passages and corridors, also in the courts and halls. The troops, in splendid apparel, mounted on their chargers, with saddles of gold and silver, formed a double line, while in front of them were held their led horses similarly caparisoned, whom all might see. The numbers present under arms of various kinds were very great and they extended from above the gate (at the northern end of East Baghdad) which is called the Shammásiya, down to the palace of the Caliph. After the troops, and leading to the very presence of the Caliph, came the pages of the Privy Chamber, also the eunuchs of the inner and outer palace in gorgeous raiment, with their swords and ornamented girdles.

Now the markets of Eastern Baghdad, with the roads, and the house tops and the streets, were all filled with people who had come sight-seeing, and every shop and high balcony had been let for many dirhems. On the Tigris there were skiffs and wherries, barques, barges and other boats, all magnificently ornamented, duly arranged and disposed....[1]

Another account of the event reads:

Then it was commanded that the ambassadors should be taken round the palace....The envoys, being brought in by the Hall of the Great [Public Gate] were taken first to the Khán al-Khayl [the Cavalry House]. This was a palace that was for the most part built with porticoes of marble columns. On the right side of the house stood five hundred mares caparisoned each with a saddle of gold or silver, while on the left side stood five hundred mares with brocade saddle cloths and long head covers;

also every mare was held in hand by a groom magnificently dressed. From this palace the ambassadors passed through corridors and halls opening one into the other until they entered the Park of the Wild Beasts. This was a palace with various kinds of wild animals therein, which entered the same from the Park, herding together and coming up close to the visitors, sniffing them, and eating from their hands. Next the envoys went out to the palace where stood four elephants caparisoned in peacock-silk brocade, and on the back of each were eight men of Sind, and javelin men with fire, and the sight of these caused much terror to the Greeks. Then they came to a palace where there were one hundred lions, fifty to the right hand and fifty to the left, every lion being held in by the hand of its keeper, and about its head and neck were iron chains.[1]

Near the main buildings of the palace stood the "New Kiosk", whose courtyard contained an object very greatly admired by the inhabitants of Baghdad. This was a large rectangular tank of polished tin fed by a conduit of the same bright metal. Surrounding it were set artificially dwarfed palms that by skilled cultivation were induced to bear eatable dates out of the proper season. A further curiosity was contained in the "Palace of the Tree", which took its name from an artificial tree that stood in the courtyard of the building. Its leaves were of gold and silver, and in its branches were lodged birds of the same precious metals, so constructed that they piped when the wind blew.

Altogether the envoys from Byzantium were shown twenty-three, or perhaps more, palaces, the majority of which had been paid for at some time or another with money extorted from the unfortunate inhabitants of the "City of Peace".

If the Caliph impressed his visitors by his display of wealth and power, his subjects were more capable of judging his real position. He had been put on the throne as a lad of thirteen by his predecessor's vizier, 'Abbás ibn Ḥasan, who had consulted various officials before making the appointment. One of these officials, Ibn al-Furát, who himself afterwards became vizier, when asked for his advice had said:

For God's sake do not appoint to the post a man who knows the house of one, the fortune of another, the gardens of a third, the slave girl of a fourth, the estate of a fifth, and the horse of a sixth; but one who has mixed with people, has had experience of affairs, has gone through his apprenticeship and made calculations of people's fortunes.[1]

The year after Muqtadir's succession a number of the notables of the city formed a conspiracy to depose him, and to assassinate him if that became necessary. In his place their choice fell upon 'Abdulláh ibn Mu'tazz, who would consent to accept office only on the condition that there would be no bloodshed. The plan which the ringleader in the conspiracy had formed was to isolate Muqtadir from his attendants as he went to the mosque and to fall on him unawares. That part of the plot failed however and the Caliph was able to reach his own palace unharmed. When an attack was led against the royal building, his servants and eunuchs, who numbered over 11,000 Greeks or negroes (if *al-Fakhrí* is to be believed), proved unexpectedly loyal and repelled the attackers. Discouraged by this check the conspirators drew off, and were attacked in their turn by a number of the servants led by Múnis the eunuch, who had embarked in boats on the Tigris and made for the house which ʿAbdulláh ibn Muʿtazz and the more influential of his supporters were occupying. The counter-attack ended in the utter rout of the conspirators, some of whom were able to escape from the city while others were caught and put to death, amongst them being ʿAbdulláh himself, whose Caliphate had lasted only one day. Ibn al-Furát supplied a further example of his cynical wisdom after this affair when he advised the Caliph to destroy the rolls containing the names of the conspirators if he wished to procure peace. The lists were accordingly sunk in the Tigris and the conspiracy allowed to sink gradually into oblivion.

The peculiar character of Ibn al-Furát displayed itself in various ways during his three terms of office as vizier. Money, of which he made and lost large sums, was the mainspring of action to him, and for it he debauched both his own office and other important departments of the State. It was he who first sold the office of cadi. On one occasion, when in flight between two periods of office, he took refuge in the house of a haberdasher named Abú Umayya al-Akhwas at Baṣra.

While enjoying this refuge, he said to his host: "If I should be made vizier, what would you like me to do for you?" The man said he would like to have some government appointment. Ibn al-Furát replied: "Unfortunately you cannot be made into a minister, or a governor, or a chief of police, or a secretary of state, or a general: so what post can I offer you?" "I leave it to you", said the host. Ibn al-Furát then suggested a judgeship, and he consented.[1]

As Commander of the Faithful, Muqtadir was to

some extent the recipient of the loyalty of the citizens of the capital. Occasionally he justified his position as head of Islam by re-enacting old repressive laws against non-Moslems. But in character he was a weakling, and as he grew older he was much influenced by the women of his harem, who wielded great power. In A.D. 918 the supreme authority fell into the hands of the Caliph's mother, who reigned as queen regent, holding audience to redress wrongs and looking into the petitions of the people each Friday. It was she and not the Caliph that held public audience, to which she summoned cadis and nobles, and she herself signed and issued State edicts. It cannot be said that her reign was without benefit to the city. Through her influence, for example, hospitals were opened for the free use of the citizens, for whom a good deal of public-spirited work seems to have been carried out during the reign. Several of the hospitals were in the charge of Sinán ibn Thábit ibn Qurra, a notable physician belonging to a famous Ṣábian family which had long practised in the city. Muqtadir was himself interested in the physical welfare of the inhabitants. When in A.D. 931 it was reported that a patient had died in consequence of a physician's blunder—which must have been a very egregious one to attract attention—the Caliph immediately issued an order to his *muḥtasib* that no doctor was to be permitted to practise unless he passed an examination conducted by Sinán. After the test the examiner was to specify to each candidate what branch of the art of medicine he could practise. The number of candidates who were successful, on both sides of the city, came to 860 odd, not counting those whose skill in practice was too well known to require testing. But the standard of the qualifications demanded does not appear to have been high if we may judge from the record of one of the men who presented himself for examination. He was an old man of venerable appearance, whose test was to spend a day in Sinán's consulting room dealing with the patients who arrived. At the end of the day, the examiner, with amazement at the man's ignorance and yet with great politeness, asked him who his teacher of medicine had been. In reply, the old man produced from his sleeve a paper containing some gold dínárs. He laid it before Sinán, and said: "I can neither read nor write. I have never read a word. I have a family and my income covers a wide circle. I beg of you not to deprive me of it". Sinán laughed, and said: "On condition that you never treat a patient for anything you do not understand, nor advise any bleeding or purgative except for the simplest ailments". The old man replied: "That has always been my practice, for I have never prescribed anything beyond oxymel and julep", with which words he departed.[1]

Though treatment in the hospitals was not entirely without discrimination against non-Moslems, yet the medical policy of the time on the whole can bear comparison with what was current in the West at a much later period. When 'Alí ibn 'Ísá was vizier it happened that epidemics broke out in the city and the country round it. The vizier wrote to Sinán asking him to appoint doctors whose business it would be to make daily visits to the prisons, where the inmates, because of their numbers, could not fail to be smitten by any plague that was rife, and were in addition prevented by their incarceration from consulting doctors. In the Sawád district, in the neighbourhood of Baghdad, Sinán was to appoint physicians to travel about amongst the rural population with medicines and potions, staying for a period in each district to treat cases. He did as he was directed, and sent out a number of his colleagues who travelled from place to place. In the course of their tour, coming to Súrá, a town whose inhabitants were mainly Jews, and the seat of one of the two great Jewish academies of Babylonia, they wrote to Sinán informing him of the preponderance of Jews in the place. He sent on the information to the vizier, adding that the physicians wished to know whether they were to remain and give the Súráns treatment or to depart elsewhere. To indicate his own feelings in the matter he reminded the vizier that in the royal hospital treatment was given both to Moslems and "protected" non-Moslems. The vizier replied to the effect that he agreed with Sinán that treatment both of "protected" non-Moslems and of animals was lawful, but that in the matter of medical treatment human beings must take precedence of animals and Moslems of non-Moslems, and that when the Moslems had been attended to, the next class might receive treatment.[1]

The luxury of the palace in Muqtadir's day was in greater contrast than normally with the general poverty of the city, for there were occasions when food was so dear there as to cause widespread want, with consequent rioting. The poorer members of the population, knowing nothing and certainly caring nothing about the laws of supply and demand, were insistent only that bread should be cheap. When it was not, as happened in A.D. 921, they looked about for a cause and a victim. They found one in a certain Ḥámid ibn ʻAbbás, whom they accused of preventing supplies from entering the city. A mob gathered round his house, and after looting it proceeded to open the prison gates and to rob the house of the city's chief of police. Only when a number of the looters had been killed in a charge by armed troops was the crowd persuaded to disperse. A subsequent attempt by the governor of the city to fix prices succeeded only in increasing the hardships of the poorer inhabitants, and matters were not adjusted until a new harvest increased supplies.

In the dramatic monologue composed by ʻAbd al-Muṭahhar[1] there is a hint that, in spite of the occasional scarcity of food, the lighter side of life was not neglected during the reign of Muqtadir. The speaker of the monologue, a fictitious character called Abú ʼl-Qásim of Baghdad, is pictured as a light-hearted rogue boasting before an assembled company of the various amenities of his city. In the course of his speech he talks of popular songs and singers, of whom he says:

> If I were to mention all the various tunes popular with listeners and the songs current amongst men and boys, and girls both slaves and freeborn, it would be a lengthy and tedious process....In my own time—while I am on this subject—in the year 306 [A.D. 918–19], I and a company of my friends from the Karkh counted four hundred and sixty slave-girl singers performing in the two parts of the city, as well as ten freeborn

women singers and seventy-five boys, "full moons", all of whom combined in themselves beauty, technique and virtuosity that surpass the limits of description. And that is not counting those to whom we had no access because of their lofty station, or because they were closely guarded, and it is in addition to those who laid no claim to professional skill in singing or music and only performed on occasions when they were in good spirits or when they were intoxicated and threw off restraint.

This is evidence that the citizens could be amused by unlawful means and were not averse to treating their religion lightly when it suited their pleasure. On the other hand, they had a stern way with anyone whom they suspected of heretical views. Their fanaticism was disagreeably shown at the death of the historian Ṭabarí, whose *Chronicle* has been so often quoted in these pages. He died in A.D. 923, and, according to the historian Ibn al-Athír (†1232–3),

he was buried by night in his house, because the mob assembled and prevented him from being buried by day, declaring that he was a Ráfiḍí (Shí'ite) and even a heretic. And 'Alí ibn 'Ísá used to say, 'By Allah, were these people to be questioned as to what was meant by a Ráfiḍí or a heretic, they would neither know nor be capable of understanding!' Thus Ibn Miskawayh, the author of the *Tajáribu 'l-umam*, who defends this great leader of thought (*Imám*) from these charges. Now as to what he says concerning the fanaticism of the mob, the matter was not so; only some of the Ḥanbalites, inspired with a fanatical hatred of him, attacked him and they were followed by others. And for this there was a reason, which was that Ṭabarí compiled a book, the like of which had never been composed, wherein he mentioned the differences of opinion of the theologians, but omitted all reference to Aḥmad b. Hanbal. And when he was taken to task about this, he said: 'He was not a theologian, but only a traditionist'; and this annoyed the Ḥanbalites, who were innumerable in Baghdad; so they stirred up mischief against him, and said what they pleased.[1]

The year before that event there had been a gross example of official persecution when Ḥusayn ibn Manṣúr al-Ḥalláj, the mystic, was arrested and put to the torture. The charge against him was that in an outburst of ecstasy he had cried out: "I am the Truth" (i.e. God). The Ṣúfís looked upon this as simply an intensified statement of the central idea of mysticism, whereas the orthodox regarded it as sheer blasphemy. The historian 'Aríb, who continued Ṭabarí's *Chronicle*, makes him out a rank impostor, playing on the credulity of his fellow-men for his own advantage: "To the Sunní he showed himself a member of the Sunna sect, a Shí'ite to those of the Shí'a belief, and a Mu'tazilite to those of the Mu'tazilí faith". It was not difficult to mislead a people which with its fanaticism combined an amazing amount of superstition and simple-mindedness of a kind that is often illustrated by the historians. An example given by Ibn Miskawayhi displays it to perfection:

"In the summer season [of A.D. 916]", he says, "the common people were alarmed by a creature which they call *zabzab*, and professed to see it at night on the roofs of their houses, and which they said devoured their small children. Indeed it would bite off the hand of a sleeping man or the breast of a sleeping woman and devour it. They would keep guard against it the whole night and take care not to sleep; and they would beat mugs, cups or mortars to frighten it. Baghdad was in a state of terror in consequence until the Sultan got hold of a strange white beast like a sea-hound, which he declared was the *zabzab* and had been caught. This was suspended on an 'ostrich' [a kind of wooden framework] upon the Upper Bridge, and left there till it died. This made little impression till the moon waxed and the people could see that there was no reality about what they had imagined. Then they were appeased; only meanwhile the thieves had found their chance when the people were occupied with watching on their roofs, and there were many burglaries."[1]

It was easy therefore for a clever charlatan to find a following. *Al-Fakhrí* says that al-Ḥalláj

propounded a mixture of good and evil doctrines, passing from one site to another and seeking to lead people astray by deliberate resort to trickery. Thus he would dig a hole in the ground and hide a skin of water there; in another place he would hide food and so forth. Then he would pass by these places accompanied by his disciples, one of whom would ask for water to drink or perform his ablutions. Thereupon al-Ḥalláj would take a pointed stick and dig in a place he knew of till he drew water.[2]

In the end he aroused the suspicions of the vizier Ibn al-Furát and the cadis. They put him to a test of his religious beliefs, which were not found satisfactory, and he was brutally done to death. After his execution the booksellers of the city were summoned and made to swear on oath that they would neither buy nor sell any of the numerous works he had composed.[3]

In spite of the official view of him al-Ḥalláj continued to be regarded as a saint. His tomb in West Baghdad became a sacred place of pilgrimage to Ṣúfís, attracting thousands of visitors each year. It was in existence until a few years ago, when it was destroyed in one of the periodic inundations that sweep the lower parts of Baghdad.

The vizier, Ibn al-Furát, if he showed himself a fanatic on this occasion, seems normally to have tempered his religious zeal with a taste for letters and luxurious hospitality. It was said of him that except in winter no person left his house without a drink of iced sherbet. If it was dark, a servant bearing a torch of fine wax was sent to light the guest on his way home. In the vizier's house there was kept a room stocked with writing-materials to which his guests were at liberty to help themselves. The fact that the price of candles, ice and writing-paper was noticeably raised in the Baghdad bazaar during Ibn al-Furát's periods of office, indicates not only that his guests were numerous, but that literary composition was a fashionable pursuit. It seems to have remained so in spite of the unrest of the period, which became feverish when report came, in A.D. 924, that the dreaded Carmathians were on their way to the city. The news was brought by pilgrims from Mecca and at once the city was in an uproar. "On both sides of the river, Baghdad and its streets were in a ferment. Women came out barefoot, with dishevelled hair, beating their faces till they were black, and shrieking in the roads."[1] The mob, who detested Ibn al-Furát, fixed upon him as the arch-Carmathian and assaulted him with brickbats as he sat in his boat on the Tigris. As a direct result of these popular demonstrations the Caliph al-Muqtadir was forced, against his will, to deprive Ibn al-Furát of office, and it was only by the efforts of Múnis the eunuch that the vizier escaped death at the hands of the infuriated crowd.

Ibn al-Furát's son, Muḥassin, whose arrest had been

ordered at the same time, contrived to escape to the house of his mother-in-law. She hoodwinked the search parties that were sent after him by dressing him in women's clothes and spending the day with him in one of the city cemeteries, returning at night to the house of one or other of his numerous friends. It happened once that darkness fell when they were still at a considerable distance from the house in West Baghdad at which they had planned to spend the night. Possible danger from guards or robbers put them in a panic, until a woman who was with them suggested spending the night at a house close by that belonged to an acquaintance of hers. All might have been well if a slave girl had not happened to enter a room in which Muḥassin had been put to change his clothes. She gave the alarm, and he was arrested and put to the torture.

There seems to have been no period during the dominance of Baghdad by the Turkish and Berber troops when their abominable conduct did not disturb the peace of the city. They had no scruples about resorting to and encouraging open vice in the streets, and no woman—and scarcely a man—was safe from attack. Such violence and crude immorality were bound sooner or later to have their effect on those of the community that prided themselves on their piety and adherence to the laws of the faith. Under the surface of orderly life carried on by the mass of the citizens also there was dissatisfaction simmering which might at any time break out in riot and murder. The revolt came from the puritan and ascetic party of the Ḥanbalís, followers of the great Baghdad jurist Aḥmad ibn Ḥanbal. Throughout the period of turmoil they had attempted to enforce conformity with their own rigorous standards and beliefs, and were able, as has been seen, to prevent the customary rites of burial when the great Persian theologian and historian Ṭabarí, of whose views they disapproved, died in Baghdad in A.D. 923. As the disturbances continued the Ḥanbalís formed themselves into a reforming committee. Numbers of the sect paraded the streets, entering houses in which they suspected violation of the principles of Islam, and inflicting summary justice whenever they found an offender. In Gibbon's version[1]—after the original derived from Ibn al-Athír[2]—they "invaded the pleasures of domestic life, burst into the houses of plebeians and princes, spilt the wine, broke the instruments, beat the musicians and dishonoured with infamous suspicions the associates of every handsome youth". Not religious offenders alone suffered at their hands, but even members of rival Moslem sects differing from their own merely in minor points of doctrine. Thus Sháfi'ís were beaten with sticks almost to the point of death whenever they were encountered, until the reform at last became a greater evil than the original malpractices, leading the Caliph al-Ráḍí to issue a manifesto against the Ḥanbalís to the following effect:

You assert that your ugly faces are after the likeness of the Lord of the Universe and your vile exteriors are fashioned after His, and you speak of His hands and fingers and legs. . . . Then also there are your attacks upon the most excellent of the Imáms and your imputations of unbelief and error against a section of the people of Mohammed....Now therefore the Commander of the Faithful swears by Allah...that if you do not put an end to your detestable beliefs and your perverse tenets... he will set sword to your necks and fire to your houses and dwellings.[1]

The threat seems to have had but little effect. The years following have left such a record of confusion that it is impossible with the sources available to obtain any clear picture of what was happening in the city. Yet it can be said with certainty that by comparison with what followed the reign of Rádí was a peaceful one. The murder of the Caliph himself by Múnis, the captain of his guard, is merely an incident in the degradation of the Caliphate. Temporal power had for long been dissociated from the office, and yet it continued to have a spiritual significance amongst Moslems which could be made an immensely strong lever in the hands of anyone desirous of power, provided he could manipulate the authority which loyalty placed in the Caliph's hands. For that reason there continued the bitter competition between rival Turkish officers for possession of the person of the Commander of the Faithful, a contest which ultimately defeated its own ends.

At intervals Baghdad underwent siege from one or other of the rival generals, and the confusion at the capital gave the provinces the opportunity they were always waiting for to cast off authority, or at any rate to cease the payment of taxes. With the reduction of trade and revenue the capital became so miserably poor that even the mercenaries of various nationality found it difficult at times to squeeze any money out of the miserable inhabitants. But they were not without resourcefulness, and one method of raising funds—one not unknown in that neighbourhood in quite recent times—consisted in their granting permission to carry on a system of brigandage in return for a fixed fee. A certain Ḥamdí, who had become famous as a highwayman in this reign, was accorded a license to rob on payment of a monthly toll of 25,000 dínárs. His method was to make attacks on houses in the night by the light of torches, and carry off any property he could lay his hands on.[1]

During a large part of the period of unrest there was no recognized and absolute governor of Baghdad. The Turkish generals held authority in turn when one or other of them was able to gain the upper hand for a brief period, but as a rule they attempted to govern and issued their licenses in rivalry at one and the same time. As for the citizens, they had by now accustomed themselves to go their own way without reference to any government, and their daily life was not unduly disturbed except on occasion. This happened when lack of orderly conditions brought on a disorganization of commerce or a dislocation of transport serious enough to diminish the city's food supplies. The famine that broke out in Baghdad in A.D. 944 was only the gravest of a series. It came at a time when many of the private houses, mosques, baths and palaces of the city had been allowed to fall into ruins through lack of means to repair them. Those of the original occupants who had not abandoned them roamed the streets in search of scraps of food, while men who were able to depart to cities where food was more plentiful did so, leaving the weaker members of their families to their fate. Generally it was a grim one, for very often bands of young girls--many of them of gentle upbringing, and even members of the Caliph's harem—were to be seen wandering about the streets crying, "Hunger, Hunger!"[1]

The scarcity of food was the culmination of an intolerable state of affairs. But Baghdad's feebleness was itself to be the cause of a release from misery for it attracted the attention of Persia, where in A.D. 945 the general Buwayh, the newest of the long series of Persian warrior families to assert their independence in the Caliph's provinces, had carved out an empire for themselves by the sword. Aḥmad, the youngest of them, extended his own realm into Iraq and his road led inevitably to Baghdad.

If the Sunnite citizens of the metropolis had had any power or inclination to affect the course of their own government they might have opposed the advance of the Buwayhids, who were fanatically Shí'ite in faith and hence likely to prove troublesome rulers in a city whose population was mainly Sunnite. To those in authority however the fact that the Buwayhids were likely to have spiritual as well as physical objections to the Turkish troops, was, if anything, an inducement to encourage the Buwayhid advance. In January A.D. 946 the force under Aḥmad, after meeting considerable opposition on the way, encamped outside the Shammásiya gate of the city. He was received by the Caliph Mustakfí, to whom he swore a solemn oath of allegiance, being rewarded in return with a robe of honour and the office of *Amír al-Umará* or "Commander in Chief". In addition he received the personal title of *Mu'izz al-Dawla* ("Strengthener of the State"), while his brothers were honoured by titles respectively of *'Imád al-Dawla* ("Support of the State") and *Rukn al-Dawla* ("Pillar of the State"). At Aḥmad's advance the Turkish garrison had fled, in justifiable apprehension that he was not likely to tolerate any rivals, and dispersed to Mosul and elsewhere in Iraq. Meantime he himself, having billeted his troops on the citizens, much to their disgust, settled down in the palace of the famous Múnis the eunuch to survey his new province.

CHAPTER IX

Baghdad under Persian Masters

The new commander of Baghdad was not left for long in contemplation, nor could he immediately fulfil the hopes of those citizens who were anxious for peace. Soon after his entry into the city he had to stand a siege from Náṣir al-Dawla, father-in-law of the Caliph Muttaqí and the governor of Mosul, who had himself, not so long before, been the *Amír al-Umará*. The aggressor, from his headquarters at Mosul, could command the whole of northern Mesopotamia with the large force at his disposal. It was decidedly in his favour also that in any attempt on Baghdad he could rely on the active sympathy of those of the scattered Turkish soldiery who had remained in the city, ever ready to take advantage of a chance of regaining the perquisites which they had lost to the Buwayhids. His campaign might very well have succeeded. He did in fact seize the eastern part of Baghdad and he was able to deal a blow at the Buwayhid trade by a very shrewd step. The Persians had set up as Caliph a prince whose official title of *al-Muti'* was inscribed on a new set of coins. Náṣir al-Dawla forbade his followers to use this coinage as currency and substituted coins which he minted bearing the name of his son-in-law the earlier Caliph al-Muttaqí, who could be regarded as neutral. All was going well and the Buwayhid general had made up his mind to retire—was in fact preparing to return to

Ahwáz, whence he had come to Baghdad—when it occurred to him to attempt a surprise attack on the enemy. His plan succeeded to perfection. The troops that he sent across the river in a night attack caught Náṣir al-Dawla utterly unprepared, and being no match for the Persian soldiery in strategy, the governor of Mosul was driven out of his position and only with difficulty escaped to a neighbouring village, from which he sued for peace. The Persian soldiers followed up their victory by looting any houses in the city that promised plunder, without stopping to ask whether the owners were in political sympathy with them or not. Only when the Sultan Mu'izz al-Dawla himself rode through the streets at the head of a body of troops, killing and dispersing looters, were the citizens given any respite, though even then supplies of food continued for some time to be scanty.

Under the strong rule of the Buwayhid governor, life in the city gradually assumed an aspect less closely resembling that of an armed camp, and some of the arts and amenities of peace resumed their places. Apart from a destructive fire which burnt down a large part of the old *Súq al-Thaláthá* ("the Tuesday Market") in A.D. 951–2, the historians report no calamitous occurrences, until A.D. 955–6, when Mu'izz al-Dawla fell seriously ill. At once report was spread that he was dying, and the turbulent part of the population, which had been kept in order too long for its taste, proceeded to make demonstrations in the streets in the hope of upsetting the government, or at any rate of creating circumstances favourable to looting and general lawlessness. They were reckoning without the courage of the governor. When news of the rioting was brought to him he raised himself from his sick-bed, mounted his horse and rode through the streets to show he could still be reckoned with. The demonstrators took the hint and the rioting ceased.

If Mu'izz al-Dawla kept the peace of the city, he did not lighten its financial burdens. In the matter of taxation he was no more lenient than his predecessors and he squeezed the population as much as he was able. Sometimes his methods were indirect, as when he sold the office of the chief justiceship at Baghdad to 'Abdulláh ibn Ḥasan ibn Abí Shawárib for an annual sum of 200,000 dirhems,[1] leaving it to the judge to recoup himself from litigants or culprits who were brought before him. At other times it was direct pressure on merchants and others who could stand it that brought in the necessary revenues.

The outstanding figure in Baghdad in the reign of this prince was his vizier al-Muhallabí, who set a fashion in the patronage of letters by throwing his house open to scholars and scientists. Amongst his clients was Abú 'l-Faraj of Isfahan, who achieved fame by compiling the encyclopaedic *Kitáb al-Aghání* or *Book of Songs*, a great thesaurus of poetry and a storehouse of information about the lives, manners and habits of the poets and singers who had flourished from pre-Islamic times down to the compiler's own day. The work represents colossal labour and might well form the basis of a study of Islamic humanism. Its value was clear to the literary men who followed him, but it is an interesting fact that not all his contemporaries were favourably disposed towards it. A younger contemporary of his, Tanúkhí, criticized his methods and accused him of great dishonesty on the ground that he copied directly from books when he should have used oral traditions supported by the proper chains of authorities. "He used to go into the bazaar of the booksellers, when it was flourishing and the shops were filled with books, and he would buy numbers of volumes which he would carry home. And all his narratives were derived from them."[1]

Another client of the vizier, a celebrity in his own day but not often mentioned by the biographers, was Aḥmad ibn Ibrahím Abú Riyásh, a man of vast learning but of unpolished company manners. When he was invited out to dinner he would pick a large piece of meat out of the tray provided for all and put the piece back into the middle of the tray after he had taken a bite. When his habits came to be known, a separate tray was generally provided for him. He was once dining with al-Muhallabí, and during the meal he kept on blowing his nose on the napkin that was passed round for the guests to wipe their hands. Also his method of eating olives was to squeeze them in his hands until the stone shot out. On one occasion a stone hit the vizier in the face. "Yet", says the biographer Yáqút, "he was tolerated for his great learning."[2]

Much of what we know of the topography of Baghdad in the early days of the Buwayhid domination is derived from the work of Iṣṭakhrí, a Persian geographer contemporary with Mu'izz al-Dawla. In A.D. 951 he completed his *Masálik al-Mamálik*, "The Roads of the Kingdoms", a route book designed to be a guide for wayfarers travelling on business of State. A part of the plan of the work is to give succinct descriptions of various parts of the Moslem empire. In his account of Baghdad the author tells us that the eastern side was occupied entirely by the royal *Ḥarím* (the Caliph's Apartments) which, together with other palaces and a chain of gardens, extended along the river bank as far as the Bín canal, two parasangs below the city. Up-stream of the royal palace a line of buildings rising straight above the water gave Baghdad's water front a total length of five Arab miles. The eastern part of the city at that day was called the "Side of the Arch", from a great arched gateway that stood at the entrance to the main bazaar. This was in addition to the names "Ruṣáfa" and "Mahdí's Camp". The western side of the city was known by the old name of the "Karkh", a name which it still has.

Three "Friday" mosques, those in which the special weekly prayers, including that for the Caliph, were offered up, are mentioned by the geographer. One stood in Manṣúr's "Round City", another in Ruṣáfa and the third in the Royal Precincts. There was still another Friday mosque at Kalwádhá, in a bend of the river on the east bank, below the city. Iṣṭakhrí is careful to point out that the canals which watered the river were fed from the Nahrawán canal and the Támarrá (Diyálá) river, only a very little water being raised directly from the Tigris by waterwheels or other mechanical means. On the west side water was brought by the 'Ísá canal from the Euphrates. This canal was big enough to allow quite large river boats to come directly to the city from the Euphrates.

Of the inhabitants of the city we gain almost no information and the description of the place itself is very brief. The author gives the obvious reason for his reticence in the concluding sentence of his account, which says: "We will not enlarge our description of Baghdad, for it is known to all and we need not prolong our discourse."[1]

In A.D. 962 the fanatical Shí'ism characteristic of the Buwayhid princes displayed itself in a manner calculated to rouse the most furious dissension. For some reason which the historians do not explain, Mu'izz al-Dawla induced his followers to cover the doors and walls of every mosque in the city with insults and curses upon Mu'áwiya, Abú Bekr, Othman and Omar, all of whom, according to the Shí'a, had been usurpers of the Caliphate. The opprobrious legends were erased during the night, but Mu'izz al-Dawla insisted on having them restored. On the advice of his vizier al-Muhallabí, however, only Mu'áwiya was specifically mentioned, the rest being reviled collectively as "the doers of wrong against the family of the Prophet of Allah". The next year, on the 10th day of the month of Muḥarram, the anniversary of the death on the field of Kerbelá of Ḥusain, the Prophet's grandson, the amír issued an edict that in mourning for the tragic event the shops in the bazaars were to be closed and all buying and selling was to be suspended. Proprietors of cookshops were forbidden to cook, the butchers to slaughter and water carriers to draw water. Further the population were to array themselves in robes of mourning, while the women were to appear with hair in disorder and blackened faces and, in grief for the martyrdom of Ḥusain, were to rend their garments and parade the streets beating their breasts.[1] If the Shí'a had not had the support of the authorities, it is hinted in the histories that Sunnite opposition to this enactment might have been considerable. As it was, the orthodox inhabitants apparently permitted it to be carried out without any visible protest that year. Two years later, however, when the same behests were made, there was fighting between Shí'a and Sunnís near the graves of the Quraysh, though it cannot have been very serious, no deaths being reported in the annals and only a little wounding and looting. The celebration of the anniversary is reported regularly thereafter during the domination of Mu'izz al-Dawla and of his son 'Izz al-Dawla, who succeeded him in A.D. 966 and who had few concerns beyond women, music and juggling.[2]

Under the *régime* of that degenerate amír, Byzantine armies were able to penetrate far into the Moslem empire, and the Hamdánid prince Abú Taghlib of Mosul, who ought to have been the bulwark of the State, bought off the invaders with gold. News of the destruction wrought by the enemy under John Zimisces in A.D. 972 threw Baghdad into such a panic that in that year the '*Ashúrá* (the 10th of Muḥarram) mourning celebrations were omitted. Instead, the mob expressed its anger at the damage done by the Byzantines in outbursts of rioting, in fighting between Shí'a and Sunnís,

UPPER BRIDGE AT BAGHDAD, LOOKING EAST

in looting and burning. The conflagration destroyed most of the quarter of the Karkh which was inhabited exclusively by Shí'ites and contained many warehouses full of merchandise. Thirty mosques were burnt down and many people lost their lives in the fire, which was said to have been started by an order from the vizier Abú 'l-Faḍl after a police magistrate had been killed in a brawl. The vizier had ordered "inflammable water" from the coppersmiths' quarter to be thrown on to that of the fishmongers, who seem to have borne a character for quarrelsomeness not unknown further afield, and the fire, once started, could not be confined to its allotted area.

It was after these outbursts that 'Izz al-Dawla demanded from the Caliph al-Mutí' the wherewithal to defend the city against the invaders. He was told by the Caliph in reply that "his revenues and his provinces had been torn from his hands and that he was ready to abdicate a dignity which he could no longer support".

The ultimate retreat of the Greeks calmed the fears of Baghdad, but the damage caused by the internal disturbances took considerable time to repair. One of its consequences was the enmity that arose between the vizier and the *naqíb* or "overseer", an official who now came into prominence for the first time.[1] His office was created by the Buwayhids in order to avoid a difficulty in which they found themselves in relationship to the Caliph who, though he no longer possessed any temporal power and was a Sunní, was yet acknowledged as chief by all Moslems. This acknowledgment was irksome to the Buwayhids' Shí'a fanaticism, and the *naqíb* was appointed to administer their special religious forms and to provide a way of escape from Sunní authority in matters of faith.

Though the general effect conveyed by the reign of Mu'izz al-Dawla is one of turmoil and unrest, it was not devoid of constructive effort. It has been seen that scholarship received some encouragement. Architecture too was practised. The amír for his own occupation built a palace in the neighbourhood of the Christian community house and church, the Dár al-Rúm, on the east bank of the Tigris. For the gates of his residence Mu'izz purloined those that belonged to the municipal gateways of Ruṣáfa and the "Round City", and others also that the Caliphs had built into their palaces at Samarra. The foundations of the palace were sunk thirty-six cubits deep and were strengthened with lime and baked bricks. The whole cost amounted to 13,000,000 dirhems—nearly half a million sterling—but it was all extracted from the pocket of the amír's friends. "This palace", says the historian Ibn al-Jawzí, writing about A.D. 1250, "has now been effaced and there remains no trace of it. The Tigris washes the site of it and the wild beasts have their lairs in it; but the church still stands as it was."[1]

Al-Mutí' also, the incompetent ruling Caliph, devoted such energies as he possessed to erecting palaces. Of these he put up three, known respectively as the Palace of the Peacocks, the Octagonal Palace and the Square Palace. Details about them have not been preserved but they must have been of considerable size. In the century following, together with the remains of the old palace of the "Táj" in the grounds of which they were constructed, they were said to have taken up about a third of the total area of East Baghdad.

No further change of note took place in the general appearance of Baghdad until the new Buwayhid prince 'Aḍud al-Dawla succeeded to the office of *Amír al-Umará* in Iraq. Under this distinguished monarch the Buwayhid power reached its zenith, extending over an empire that approached in size that of Hárún al-Rashíd. He kept court as *Sháhinsháh* or "King of Kings" at Shiraz, but he was fully aware of the great value of Baghdad and made particular efforts to replace some of the prosperity which the city had lost. As the Persian historian Mirkhwánd puts it:

In the year A.H. 368 [=A.D. 978] 'Aḍudu 'l-Dawla, having turned the ray of his attention towards the ruined palaces of Baghdad, put the mosque into a state of repair, allotted offices to *imáms* [leaders of prayer in the mosques] and *mu'ezzins* [officers of the mosque who call the Faithful to prayer], sought out the orphaned, the poor and the feeble, and provided for them. He brought prosperity to the bazaars, compelled the owners of dilapidated property to put it into repair, and, wherever there was a dried-up canal he caused water to flow again in it...and from Baghdad to Mecca wherever a well had fallen in he restored it....To learned doctors, preachers, travellers, grammarians, poets, physicians, mathematicians and engineers he allotted regular provision. To his vizier Naṣr ibn Hárún, the Christian, he gave permission to rebuild the Christian churches.[1]

Under 'Aḍud al-Dawla the inhabitants of the city celebrated traditional occasions without much hindrance. We hear of a celebration at the Mu'taḍidí New Year's Day (June 11th) when people put decorated dolls "the size of a boy" on the roofs of their houses and brought them out "splendidly arrayed with ornaments like those of a bride and before which they flourish(ed) drums and plates and light(ed) fires".[1] Other ways of celebrating the Caliph's New Year were the bringing of gifts, splashing in the water and strewing dust about.[2]

The amír made room for his new buildings by demolishing the spacious mansions put up by his predecessors. He left standing the "Palace of the Sixty", the special feature of which was a cloistered court joined by a cloistered passage to a chamber of curious construction and roofed with numerous domes. Near this building he planned to lay out a magnificent garden that was to connect with the others lying along the river bank below the main bridge. There were buildings on the proposed site already. These were acquired at great expense and demolished, elephants being then used—to the continuous wonderment and delight of the Baghdadís—for trampling down and levelling the ground. Nearly 5,000,000 dirhems were spent on the scheme but it was never fully carried out.

'Aḍud al-Dawla's greatest claim to notice in connection with Baghdad, is his building of the famous hospital that came to be called after him the *Bímáristáni 'Aḍudí* ("The 'Aḍudí Infirmary") or the *Máristán*, for short. He erected it near the site of the old Khuld Palace—perhaps partly on the ground once occupied by the palace[3]—and endowed it with the sum of 100,000 dínárs (nearly 50,000 pounds) per annum. For the staff of the hospital he sought out twenty-four physicians known for their skill without distinction of faith or country, and put in charge Abú 'l-Ḥasan Thábit ibn Sinán, a member of a famous Ṣábian family of physicians and scholars. The staff, in course of time, formed a medical school, to which students came to learn their art and at which the chief physicians in the city held teaching posts.

For centuries the hospital remained a place of refuge for the sick of Baghdad, who were there cared for and fed according to the most enlightened ideas of the day. About two hundred years after its foundation, the Moorish traveller Ibn Jubayr visited it when he came to the city after a pilgrimage from Granada to Mecca. The *Máristán* was then situated in the Bazaar of the Hospital, one of the lesser quarters of the city close to the river. The buildings consisted of a large main portion "like a palace", with numbers of separate wards and smaller houses built along the river bank. Regular days, Mondays and Thursdays being favourite ones, were allotted by the physicians for their visits to attend to the sick. A special staff was maintained to supply prescribed diets and medicines,[1] of which a list is preserved in a manuscript now in the British Museum.[2]

An early senior physician at the hospital was Hibatulláh ibn Ṣá'id, who was chief of the Christian doctors and head of the Christian community at Baghdad. He was a man of parts, knowing Persian, Greek and Syriac as well as Arabic. Also he was fond of music and was a patron of musicians. For a long time he was physician to the Abbasid Caliphs, and as an old man attended on the Caliph Muqtafí. Yáqút, in his *Dictionary of Learned Men*,[3] says that Hibatulláh owned the bottle factory in Baghdad and that when Yaḥyá ibn Hubayra became vizier he appropriated the factory, which apparently was a profitable concern. At the conclusion of his next visit to the Caliph, the doctor found difficulty in rising to depart. "You are getting old", remarked the Caliph. "Yes," replied Hibatulláh, "and my bottles are broken." The cryptic remark led to inquiries and the factory was restored to him. This factory, it may incidentally be said, was the nucleus of a large and flourishing industry, so that in the twelfth century the fame of Baghdad glass was spread far and wide. The poet Kháqání, in order to praise Isfahan, depreciates Baghdad which to him "is the place merely of the makers of bottles to hold the rose-water that is the joy of Isfahan's households".[1]

The Buwayhid amír himself found time from occupations of State to indulge in serious study, and used even to read Aristotle in his spare time.[2] It was a strange form of relaxation for a man whose system of government was to inspire dread in the hearts of his subjects, and who commanded a proper reverence and awe in those who attended his ceremonial audiences by such barbaric methods as having wild beasts chained to either side of the platform on which his throne stood. In his processions through the streets, lions, tigers and elephants figured with the same purpose of inculcating a due reverence for the Amír al-Umará.

'Aḍud al-Dawla died at Baghdad in A.D. 983, about a year after the completion of his hospital, and promptly the succession became a matter of dispute. The notables at Baghdad elected his son Ṣamṣám al-Dawla, who remained in office for about a year but was then ousted by his brother Sharaf al-Dawla, who did not enjoy the sovereignty for long. Yet during his short reign the arts of peace made some progress. In the year A.D. 988 he ordered the construction of an observatory in imitation of the one built by Ma'mún, in order that the "seven stars" might be watched in their course through the stations of the Zodiac.[1]

The wranglings of the Buwayhid amírs were complicated by the rivalries of the Turkish and Dailemite soldiers and, not for the first time, the streets of Baghdad assumed the character of a battlefield on which foreigners fought for possession of the city, while its rightful owners and inhabitants seemed content to look on almost as disinterested spectators. When not so engaged they took advantage of the absence of the governor of the city, not for the obvious purpose of joining forces against the common enemies, but to fight out their own religious animosities, so that Shí'ites struggled for mastery with fellow-citizens who were Sunnites, while brigands and professional soldiers took advantage of their preoccupation to rob both parties, to ravish and burn. So strong were sectarian hatreds that in the year A.D. 1001, during a fight between Turkish soldiers and the Shí'a inhabitants of the Karkh quarter, the Sunnite citizens went to the help, not of their fellow-citizens, but of their Turkish fellow-Sunnites.

It may be that the Sunnites had reason to grasp at any opportunity for asserting themselves, for the government had remained consistently sympathetic with the

Shí'ites. In the year A.H. 402 (A.D. 1011–12) the reigning Buwayhid prince Bahá al-Dawla[1] permitted the residents of Karkh to celebrate the 10th day of Muḥarram as a day of mourning. The bazaars were closed, men and women wore mourning garments and marched through the streets in procession. But it must be admitted that the prince himself, at the orthodox Festival of Sacrifice,[2] distributed clothes, wheat, dates and money amongst the poor. He rode to prayers at the various Friday mosques, where he delivered the statutory addresses. Afterwards he set free prisoners and pardoned debtors who owed less than ten dínárs. Where it was more he accepted assurances that the money would be paid.[3]

In the next year there was an anti-Christian outbreak which arose in a peculiar fashion when the wife of the Christian Abú Naṣr ibn Isrá'íl, who was a court official, died. Her funeral took place in the daytime, and accompanying the body were mourning-women, drummers, singers, bearers of crucifixes and candles, and a number of monks. The elaborateness of the procession roused the anger of a certain Háshimite, a member of the Caliph's family, who expressed his displeasure by throwing stones at the corpse and cursing it. It happened that one of the slaves of Abú 'l-Munáṣib, Abú Naṣr's employer, was in the procession. He promptly turned on the Háshimite and thrashed him, drawing blood, and when a crowd gathered at his cries the Christians were forced to take refuge with the corpse in the church in the Dár al-Rúm. There they were followed by the Moslem crowd, who pillaged the church and many of the Christian houses in the neighbourhood, and set afoot a bout of general rioting during which the bazaars and mosques had to be closed. Soon copies of the Koran were being raised aloft on poles—a favourite trick—and the mob was marching to the house of the Caliph (al-Qádir) to make complaint. Abú 'l-Munáṣib, the employer of the Christian secretary, was summoned for explanations, his house having meanwhile been plundered, and the Christian Ibn Isrá'íl himself was arrested, while various unfortunate Christians were crucified by the mob. So great were the disturbances that the Friday services in the mosques were suspended that week. Inevitably therefore the repressive measures against the *Dhimmís* (the Christians and Jews) were put into force again with increased harshness.[1]

It cannot be said that the Buwayhid rule of Baghdad was at any time primarily for the benefit of its citizens. To very few oriental monarchs, it may be presumed, did it ever occur that government meant something more than the opportunity for filling their treasuries. And yet under one or other of the amírs there had been periods during which the whole of the city gave the appearance of peace and men were able to carry on their ordinary avocations without disturbance. Some of the Buwayhids and their officers, as has been seen, had even been beneficent, according to their lights. The Hospital of 'Aḍud al-Dawla has been noticed as one famous establishment erected for the public benefit. Another was the Academy built by Shápúr ibn Ardashír, the vizier of Bahá al-Dawla. It was founded in the Karkh in the quarter "Between the Two Walls" in the year A.D. 991 and had a library containing over 10,000 volumes, many of them autographs. In A.H. 451 (A.D. 1059) a great fire in the quarter destroyed the library with much other property. In his account of that year, Ibn al-Athír the historian says that amongst the books were 100 copies of the Koran in the writing of the famous scribes the Banú Muqla, and that the crowd looted a great many volumes.[1] Shápúr generously endowed the Academy, which was much frequented by literary men. "Its members seem to have enjoyed pretty much the same privileges as belong to the Fellows of an Oxford or Cambridge college."[2] The blind poet Abú 'l-'Alá al-Ma'arrí was included in the membership for a while and found it a congenial resort and Baghdad the true centre of learning.[3]

Such buildings and institutions were tributes to Baghdad's position of importance in the Moslem world. Yet its pre-eminence was gone. It now shared honours with Cairo and Cordova, with Ghazna and Shiraz, to which men of ambition gravitated in search of fortune and, incidentally, of fame. Since the coming of the Buwayhids Iraq had been governed as a mere province of Fars, and on one occasion in A.D. 1058 a Buwayhid underling went so far as to gather a crowd in Baghdad and declare publicly in the mosque of the Caliph Manṣúr that he and they owed allegiance to the schismatic al-Mustanṣir, the Fáṭimid ruler of Egypt. That was when the Buwayhid power was at its ebb, but even before that time arrived the Persian overlords had reason to wonder whether the Abbasid capital was worth the anxiety it caused them. The constant unrest with which they had to deal, the rioting of troops clamorous for arrears of pay, the struggles of rival bodies of mercenaries and the internecine religious bickerings of the citizens themselves sorely tried the patience of the rulers. In the year A.D. 1018 Sulṭán al-Dawla declared that "the government of Iraq needs a man who is a tyrant and a brute".[1] He appointed to the task one Ibn Sahlán, who must have been a man of the right calibre, for promptly on his arrival men who had been gaining a rich livelihood by robbery and brigandage betook themselves elsewhere.

The reputation to which their going paid tribute was enhanced by Ibn Sahlán's efforts to get at the root of the city's troubles. As a first step he banished numerous members of the Háshimite clan, a discontented body of Sunnites who claimed kinship with Mohammed. To balance their expulsion he sent out of the city the fanatical Abú 'Abdulláh, one of the religious heads of the Shí'a, and then as a final measure, with great impartiality, he surrounded with his Dailemite mercenaries both the Karkh quarter, the stronghold of Shí'ism, and the Báb al-Baṣra quarter, the centre of Sunnite fanaticism.

With power in their hands and the certainty that their officers would never call them to account for anything they did, the Dailemites proceeded to amuse themselves in their own way at the expense of the citizens. Thus in Ramaḍán drunken soldiers would meet citizens anxious to celebrate the fast, and compel them to drink wine.[2] And they did not stop at grosser jests. Ibn Sahlán himself harried the Turks and the population generally, and when the inevitable complaints began to pour in to the amír, the "tyrant and brute" was compelled to flee for his life. Several years later brigands and robbers are reported to have been carrying on their trade more briskly than ever, slaying, looting and burning[1]; while the miserable Turkish troops, now leaderless and utterly without provision, were almost of necessity driven to brigandage and practised extortion on the various quarters of the city, particularly on the Karkh, in which many merchants had their stores.

The proceeds of these depredations cannot have been very great—doubtless experience had taught the wealthier citizens the art of concealment—for in A.D. 1027 we find the Turks petitioning that some commander be appointed over them to take charge of their affairs. The man they themselves chose was apparently not agreeable to those in authority, but we find the Turks acquiescing in the election by the Caliph of the Buwayhid viceroy Jalál al-Dawla, to whom they promised their loyalty. On June 22nd, A.D. 1027, proclamation was made of his investiture and on meeting the Caliph he behaved with great deference towards him. Drums were beaten and trumpets blown at the gates of the "Government House", and the ceremony was completed by the mention of Jalál al-Dawla as *Sulṭán* in the statutory Friday oration in the Great Mosque.[2]

The appointment seems to have given both Turks and citizens some measure of confidence, which induced some slackness in the vigilance that each normally exercised. In the records of the year after the appointment we read of an epidemic of horse-stealing for which the Kurds are blamed. The only resource which the Turkish ex-soldiers could think of was to keep their horses in their own houses, and even Jalál al-Dawla, if the records are to be believed, thought it expedient to keep his horses in a building inside the "Government House". With this lack of courage and resourcefulness it is not surprising that the hopes in the new leader did not find fulfilment, but dissatisfaction was temporarily stilled by the distribution of largess and by some looting, that was made possible in a serious riot between the Shí'ites and Sunnites. On this occasion Jews also were involved, because they were accused of having helped the Shí'ites. It was an affray serious enough to make the authorities cut the main bridge in order to separate the combatants.

The authority gained for himself by Jalál al-Dawla was of short duration. In A.D. 1032 the Turks, disappointed in their hopes of regular pay, attacked his house, looted it, and even stripped the clothes off the backs of his clerks and servants. The Sultan fled, but he was brought back and reinstated in office by the Turks when they found it impossible to get a new chief. His incapacity showed itself again in the next year with the appearance of a picturesque brigand who went by the name of al-Burjumí and who terrified the citizens of Baghdad, entirely outdoing the efforts of the Turks. As a base of operations he took up a position on the east bank of the river, where, in the middle of a marshy region with patches of deep water, he had discovered a mound that he turned into a stronghold. From it he raided the city, keeping the richer members of the community in such a state of terror for their persons and property that they transferred their treasures, as a desperate measure, to the safe-keeping of the "House of the Caliphate". Mention of "the brigand" was avoided as much as possible, and when there was occasion to talk of him at all he was called "The Chief, Abú 'Alí". His fame increased to such an extent that a section of the inhabitants were for mentioning him in the *khuṭba*. It was in his favour that he never attacked or robbed a woman, and that he used his powers quite impartially against Turk and citizen alike. When one of the Turkish chiefs wished to celebrate the circumcision of his son he did not venture to begin the festivities before he had sent a present of camels, fruits and wine to al-Burjumí, who tapped all possible sources of revenue systematically. Caravanserais where travellers congregated were regularly visited for tribute, singing-girls were made to pay a part of their earnings, and even the Sultan had to surrender some of his revenues. In the streets, the robber band flaunted gilded banners as a mark of their prestige and insisted on being addressed as "generals".

Success in the end made al-Burjumí careless, though not before the business of the city on both sides had been thoroughly disorganized; and it was then that the Sultan laid an ambush for him and, having succeeded in capturing him, promptly drowned him, although the rogue had offered a huge sum of money to be released.[1]

That an individual without any considerable backing

of troops could for so long have terrorized the metropolis must be taken as evidence—supported also by other indications—that the Buwayhid power was definitely reaching its end. It was made more obvious than ever in the next few years when Beduin raiders from without joined their attacks to those of the brigands and Turks inside the city. They blockaded the roads and waylaid travellers; and even inside the city walls they laid whole streets near the mosque of Manṣúr under regular tribute and were able with impunity to rob the women visiting the graves in the burial grounds. At times they kidnapped people coming out of the city gates and sold them "as though they were Greek prisoners".[1]

The Caliph made a feeble attempt on one occasion to assert his vanished authority when a slave broke into the palace gardens and, after eating some of the royal fruit, disappeared. In a pious fury the monarch wrote to the Buwayhid viceroy, bidding him find the wretch who had inflicted this indignity upon a royal dwelling. But though a search was made the culprit could not be discovered, "because", says the historian Ibn al-Jawzí, "of the absence of any respect for law and order". On this subject and that of the general disregard of religion the Caliph now approached the cadis and the ecclesiastical lawyers. He ordered that no marriages were to be performed, the doors of all mosques were to be locked and preparations were made for him to leave the godless city. Whether through these measures or not, the slave was caught, but was released again after an hour's detention.

Among the special burdens laid on the citizens by the brigands at this time are mentioned the tribute extracted from certain quarters for permission to draw water from the river, a tax on the incomes of the *ráwís* or public storytellers, and fines levied on any citizens who broke the fast of Ramaḍán, drank wine, or in other ways transgressed the laws of religion.[1]

Even in these circumstances the pleasures of life were not forgotten and the chronicles continue to recount those events which then, as now, had a "news value". Thus we are told that in A.H. 431 (A.D. 1039–40), when conditions in the city were disagreeable in the extreme, a son was born to the Caliph al-Qá'ím, and people celebrated the event by public rejoicings and by decorating the city on both banks.[2]

In A.H. 445 (A.D. 1043) Jalál al-Dawla, one of the last reigning Buwayhids, and one who had ruled independently of Fars, died in Baghdad, and was succeeded in office by a prince as helpless for good or ill as the Caliph himself, so that the chief authority was again transferred entirely to the Persian province. Of the events accounted remarkable thereafter was the union in A.H. 442 (A.D. 1050–1) of Shí'ites and Sunnites against a common foe, Abú Muḥammad al-Nasawí, who had been appointed head of the security force in the city and had by his conduct aroused the fury of the population. So great was the sudden friendliness of the ancient enemies that the mu'ezzins in the Karkh—the dominant Shí'a quarter—used a Sunnite formula[3] when calling the faithful to prayer, and the mu'ezzins in the Báb al-Baṣra—the fanatically Sunnite quarter—

returned the compliment with the Shí'ite formula, "Come to the best of deeds". Moreover Shí'ite and Sunnite, Dailem and Turk joined in the pilgrimage to the Shí'a shrines, the tombs of the imáms, at Káẓimayn and elsewhere, visits never made by Sunnites in ordinary circumstances.[1]

The concord disappeared in the next year when offensively Shí'ite "slogans" were written up on prominent buildings in the city in letters of gold. Efforts were made to have the offending words removed, but the Shí'ites insisted on their retention, with the result that the ancient hatred broke out with redoubled violence. In the riots that followed, a member of the Sunnite clan of the Háshimites was killed and his body carried round the various Sunnite quarters with the purpose of inflaming public opinion. After the funeral the next day, crowds of Sunnites gathered with hostile intent round the great shrine of the imáms at Káẓimayn, which they had visited with at least outward reverence the year before. Finding the gates locked they broke in, pillaged the sacred building and desecrated tombs and vaults by burning them. The tombs of the imáms themselves did not escape the general destruction, whilst amongst others destroyed were those of the Buwayhids Mu'izz al-Dawla and Jalál al-Dawla. On the next day the Sunnites came again and dug up the graves of the two imáms, Músá al-Káẓim and Muḥammad ibn 'Alí, with the intention of transferring the bodies to the tomb of the great Sunnite doctor Aḥmad ibn Ḥanbal. This step however was not approved by the important Sunnite families, the Háshimites and

Abbasids, who claimed relationship with the imáms, and the project was abandoned. During this time the inhabitants of the Karkh had not been idle, and on their own, the west, side of the river, had plundered and burned the college of the Ḥanifite doctors and killed one of them. They then turned their attentions to the east bank the inhabitants of which seem to have satisfied their pugnacious desires.

This depressing record of strife is to some extent lightened by certain indications—not offered by the regular historians—that beneath the stormy surface life in the city continued to possess qualities less rough and brutal. To the lurid picture of turmoil there can be added the details of everyday doings and ordinary thought which are necessary to the truth of the composition and tone down its crudenesses. Account must be taken, for example, of such details as are to be obtained from the dramatic monologue, already quoted, composed by Abú 'l-Muṭahhar,[1] who seems to have written just before the close of the period. The name of the hero of the monologue is Abú 'l-Qásim of Baghdad, a genial "rogue and vagabond", who tells the adventures that he experienced during a day in the metropolis. He is described by the author as "an elderly man whose white beard gleamed from a face so ruddy that red wine came near to dripping from it, and whose eyes seemed to peer out of green glass and to be revolving in quick-silver". In pursuit of his disreputable avocation

it was his practice to enter some rich man's house, pretending to be half dead and ready for any asceticism. He would be dressed in a Persian cloak, of which one corner would be thrown over his forehead, concealing half his face.

He would seat himself in any company that was present, and after reciting passages from the Koran would greet the room, reserving special blessings for the master of the house. There he would sit for a long time reading the Koran in a low voice, and, after indulging in various expressions of humility and self-abasement, he would catch the eye of one of the company, who would recognize his kind and smile. Promptly he would tune his lyre to a coarser note and, addressing each member of the company in Rabelaisian verse, would describe the characteristics of each city "type". His least obscene remarks are reserved for the cadger, who goes about from door to door with a nose as keen as a fly's for savoury odours from the kitchens, and who, finding a wedding or a circumcision being celebrated, is by no fear of a thrashing from a porter kept long hesitating on the threshold, though sometimes he is turned back with a curt request to loosen his purse-strings if he is hungry.[1]

On one occasion when he is invited to a house, he addresses one of the assembly who has not spoken to him in a flow of coarse humour: "O you shaped mandrake root, why don't you speak? you face on a wall! Are you a clod or an animal? You, who being present are yet absent". When this amusement begins to be tedious, one of the company suggests that the fine weather be celebrated in a bumper, and drinks to the health of Isfahan. This leads to a boasting match on the relative merits of that city and Baghdad. Through the exasperating bombast and distortion it is possible to catch a glimpse of the real Baghdad. Abú 'l-Qásim is made to sing the praises of the city and, challenging the champion of Isfahan, he says:

> In your town do I see a river like the Tigris, covered with ships and boats, flanked by palaces and kiosks, amongst which there resound the strains of song, the throbbing melodies of reed pipes and water wheels, the cries of sailors and the calls of the mu'ezzins...? Here you shall see beauty from whichever side you approach, and everywhere you shall be astonished. Do I see in your city the masters of all crafts and skilled trades such as may be seen in Baghdad? Here are paper-makers, calligraphers, tailors, wood-turners, makers of coats of mail, gilders, cooks, musicians and other craftsmen of marvellous skill and without number.[1]

He speaks appreciatively of the fine, rich, outdoor clothes worn by the Baghdadís. "Silken robes embroidered with spun gold and mingled amber, or with beautiful patterns woven as though of the flowers of spring, or cloaks of Chinese gauze, fine as air or as a mirage."[2] He has something also to say of the expensive decorative details of Baghdad architecture: "Roofs covered with teak wood, staircases inlaid with ebony and ivory, fine porticoes and verandas".[3] And he is not to be kept on the outside of these splendid mansions. In a manner perfectly possible in Islamic lands, where religion and the laws of hospitality diminish social differences, he is able to penetrate into the houses of the rich, in which he sees a taste for "imported" luxuries which can be compared with that of the most recent civilization: "Audience chambers, in which the floors are spread with Maghribí carpets and Kharshaní mats, with long Andalusian and Cordovan rugs, Armenian 'throw-downs', Greek coverlets of velvet, divans from Tustar and gilt leather dining-carpets from Maghrib".[1] When food is brought it is on a table standing on "legs made of Khurasan *khalanj*[a] wood, without joint or flaw in it, red with white, like a tray of gillyflowers, and having a crystal inlay and covered with an embroidered cloth that distracts a man's attention from the food laid out on it".[2]

The rogue's palate is sufficiently educated to understand what food to recommend, and he knows what the standard of table service should be in a good house. On the table which he describes there are spread out amongst less recognizable dishes, wheaten bread

> like morsels of guinea gold,...sharp Dínawarí cheese, which breaks up the appetite and sets the stomach in motion,...Greek cheese, toasted, as though all the fatness of kine were allotted to it, and of a sharpness which makes the eye of the consumer to water as though he were parting from his loved ones,... and peeled fresh white walnuts, which when eaten with the Dínawarí or Greek cheese is sweeter than health to the body; turnips, white and red...cucumber in vinegar, asafoetida root, egg-plant pickled and dressed with the juice of pomegranate seeds.

There is also an "infusion of *daqal* dates without any contaminating *harakan* dates whose sourness makes the birds drop from the vaults of heaven". For condiment there is salt, "white and pure as molten silver". The more solid dishes are roasts of duck, veal, fat turkey, suckling lamb, "round, one in length and

[a] A sweet-smelling wood which shows two colours when polished.

breadth," and fatted pullets. They should rest on a bed of mince or rice mingled with soured milk and saffron and powdered with sugar. Further, there are young pigeons and various kinds of partridge and goose and other waterfowl as well as common yellow sparrows stuffed with peeled almonds, Khurásán raisins, Jurján grapes, and Ḥulwán figs, and decorated with citron leaf.[1]

When the time comes for the food to be removed "there enters a butler of jovial countenance and cleanly garbed, of excellent training and unobtrusive breath. He carries *sulṭání* toothpicks properly straightened,...or *mámúní* toothpicks perfumed....After them he brings *mahlab* plums, scented and perfumed from the shop of the spicers' company".[2]

He knows of many more vintages than one, "clearer than water from heaven...more delicate than a zephyr".[3] He likes a man of presentable appearance to recite about "a girl, a cup, a hunt or a frolic",[4] and for a singer he prefers

> a minstrel of clear speech poetically endowed and clothed in true music...for whose song the veil of the ear is raised; such song as captures the heart in all assemblies, mingling with every particle of the soul; song which stirs every spirit, makes heads dance, brings a thirst for the cup, fills all ears with joy and lights a fire in every heart; so that he brings health with his song and exaltation with his melody.[5]

He has a great contempt for singers who "kill" melodies by singing out of time or tune, whose teeth are over large, or who bellow and bray like asses.[6] One of his counts against Isfahan is that he sees there no good girl singers, or negress tambourine-players, or (white) dancers or players on the lute, who walk upon delicate feet, with plump thighs like two papyrus stalks which they move quickly like a partridge or a *rá'ibí* pigeon.[1] And these public performers of the Baghdad commonalty are but the "threshold" compared with the girl singers in the possession of Baghdad's princes.

Then comes the story of one Ibn Ghaylán, a draper, who heard one of these girls sing and was so overcome by the beauty of what he had heard that he fainted and had to be restored with camphor and rose-water, and the recitation into his ear of verses from the Koran.[2]

CHAPTER X

The Greater Seljúqs and Baghdad

Towards the middle of the eleventh century events were happening in Persia that were for the second time in history to change the politics of Baghdad for well over a century. The ruin of the empire of the Caliphs and the dissensions amongst the Buwayhids, which had split up Persia into a number of small principalities, presented opportunities to the vigorous Turkoman tribes of the Ghuzz, who were then advancing to power over the ruins of the Ghaznawid and Buwayhid empires.

Above the din of strife at Baghdad distant rumours of the victorious advance of Tughril Beg, chief of the Seljúq tribe of the Ghuzz, had been heard by the Caliph, who sent him friendly greetings and received in return rich presents and messages of loyalty and regard. In A.H. 444 (A.D. 1052) some warriors of the Ghuzz raided Fars, and though they were driven off from Shiraz, the capital, the enfeebled Buwayhids must have seen in the attack the end of their own rule. That same year a section of the Ghuzz reached Ḥulwán on the borders of Iraq, but Tughril Beg, who was in command, forbade any advance to the capital.[1] The reason given for the failure to advance is a dubious one, but there is no doubt that the Seljúq chieftain was steadily, though slowly, conquering the provinces surrounding Iraq. After he had subdued Rayy (Rhages) in A.H. 447 (A.D. 1055), he determined upon a pilgrimage to Mecca, which was to be combined with an expedition to Egypt, by way of Hamadán, Kirmánsháhán, Ḥulwán and Baghdad. On his arrival at Ḥulwán substance was given to the reports of his progress by the appearance of his advance guards marching along the Khurásán highway towards the capital. People on the east bank were thrown into a panic and moved across the river, while the Turks transferred their tents outside the city walls in preparation for flight.

In advance of himself, Tughril Beg, who was a Sunnite, sent messages to the Caliph, who had for long had to deal with heretic Shí'ites, assuring him of his loyalty and obedience and asking for permission to enter the city. The reply was flattering in the extreme. The Ghuzz prince was proclaimed Sultan, superseding the Buwayhid in the *khuṭba* in every mosque of the city, and the chief officers of the state came out a day's march as far as Nahrawán to give him the welcome demanded by ceremony. On Monday, December 18th, A.D. 1055, the new sovereign entered the city of the Caliphs.

An unfortunate incident marked the very beginning of the Seljúq *régime*. A troop of Tughril's horse who wished to buy fodder, stopped a man in the Báb al-Azaj quarter and asked him where they could find what they needed. Misunderstanding both their language and their gestures he became alarmed and cried out that he was being attacked. The crowd that gathered began throwing stones, and the rumour went abroad that al-Malik al-Raḥím, the last Buwayhid amír, with such troops as he had, was trying to oppose Tughril's entry. For some reason, perhaps only because he was a familiar evil or because there was a large Shí'a element in the city, popular support rallied to the Buwayhid, and there was an attack on the Seljúq troops which might have had very serious consequences if the inhabitants of the Karkh, who were Persians and therefore understood the language of the foreign soldiers, had not come to their help and so saved the situation and earned Tughril's thanks. Nevertheless many of the citizens were not content until they had seen the troop of Seljúq horse ride outside the walls, back to the main body.

If the Buwayhid had made use of his opportunity it is possible that he might have continued in power for some time to come. As it was, he and his retinue went quietly to the government house and awaited their fate, thinking that it would be a fortunate one. However Tughril wasted no compassion on al-Malik al-Raḥím, whom he seized in spite of the Caliph's protests, and sent to Rayy to be put to death. The Seljúq army also, in rage at the inhospitable treatment of the Baghdadís, attacked any citizens that ventured outside the walls and looted several of the quarters on the right bank, so that citizens in possession of valuables fled with them to the mosques and the guardposts. At the same time Tughril gave orders that any property belonging to the Dailem troops who had fought for the Buwayhids or to the Turkish soldiery was to be seized.[1] These mercenaries were now left in Baghdad without any resources, and those that did not find employment elsewhere turned into beggars or thieves.

The Ghuzz troops did not confine their plunderings

to Baghdad. All the villages in the rich agricultural district which supplied the city were looted and the crops and cattle seized, with the consequence of an enormous rise of food prices in the Baghdad markets. When finally the Ghuzz army continued their march to Baṣra they left the countryside waste. But in the capital Tughril had the government buildings repaired and enlarged, though he ill repaid the services of the Shí'ite inhabitants of the Karkh quarter by insisting that their mu'ezzins were to dilute their own call to prayer with Sunnite phrases.[1]

During Tughril's absence from the city for about a year the unfortunate events of his first visit seem to have been forgotten. He was received on his return with most elaborate ceremony. At the Raqqa gate, to which he had come by the river, a cavalcade of notables was waiting to accompany him "into the courtyard of al-Salám and the fortress of Islám".[2] The procession, with the amírs riding in front and conspicuously bearing no weapons, advanced through a great concourse of people towards the place where the Caliph sat on a raised platform behind a curtain. It was lifted at Tughril's approach and the Caliph was disclosed wearing his insignia—the Prophet's robe and ring. At a sign from him the Turkish prince was seated upon another platform alongside his. Arab Caliph and Turkish prince, communicating through an interpreter—for the one knew no Turkish, the other no Arabic—then assured each other of mutual loyalty and friendship, and the Captain of the Guard explained to Tughril that he was appointed regent of the realm.

"The Commander of the Faithful", Ibn al-Athír makes the officer say, "thanks you for your efforts, lauds what you have done, and has pleasure to have you by him. He has given you charge of all the territories which Allah has bestowed on him and has transferred to you the care of his servants. Therefore be God-fearing in what he has entrusted to you; acknowledge the favours of Allah, strive to spread justice abroad, to prevent wrong-doing and to prosper the subjects of the Caliph."[1]

Tughril was then invested with a robe of honour, a collar and bracelets, and also with a scented gold-embroidered turban, symbolizing the combination of the Arab and non-Arab crowns. The Caliph also gave him two swords and addressed him as "King of East and West". Tughril, in token of servitude, kissed the sovereign's hand and laid it upon his eyes.[2]

The new Sultan was not content to remain idle in Baghdad. Using it as a centre for his campaign, he subdued southern Iraq and returned again to Persia, where he became involved in difficulties owing to the rivalry of his brother Ibrahím Yannál. Now Tughril had not long been gone out of the city when the ex-general of the Buwayhids, Basásírí, who had laid siege to Mosul and captured it before Tughril Beg could march against him, contrived by evading the Seljúq's pursuit to descend on Baghdad. At the rumours which preceded the pretender, as he came marching down the Euphrates, the Caliph decided on flight and moved from the west bank to the east, where the way lay open towards Persia. When the enemy actually arrived he was accompanied by a force of only four hundred men, and they were in a state of collapse from hunger and fatigue. But he was offered very little opposition, even though, almost on his arrival, he boldly marched into the great mosque of Manṣúr and publicly declared his allegiance to the Shí'ite prince of Egypt, Mustanṣir the Fáṭimid, and on the first following Friday did the same in the mosque at Ruṣáfa on the east side of the city. As a token of the change of allegiance, moreover, he ordered that the colour of clothes was to be changed from the Abbasid black to the white of the Fáṭimids.[1]

In this peculiar situation the officers left in charge of the city, together with the notables who wished in every circumstance to stand well with those in power, were in a dilemma. The greater portion of the population favoured the rebel: the Shí'a because he was of their way of belief, the Sunnites because they were furious at the Seljúq outrages. For the authorities the way out lay in a policy of waiting and non-intervention, and they left it to the Seljúq Sultan to settle the difficulty as best he could. There was indeed an independent attempt by a warlike cadi, followed by members of the Háshimite clan (who as members of the Prophet's family considered themselves the champions of Sunnism), to attack Basásírí, but their attempt proved abortive and they were driven off with considerable loss in dead and wounded. The rebel followed up his victory by looting the royal quarters, though the Caliph had first been rescued by friends and carried off to the Euphrates.

Basásírí could now play the prince. On the Festival of Sacrifice he crossed to the great mosque on the east bank, with the Egyptian standard over his head, distributed largess and generally tried to convey the impression that here at last was a tolerant and liberal ruler. He belied the promise in one respect. He had taken prisoner the Caliph's officer known as the *ra'ís al-ru'asá*, the "head chieftain", and to provide a spectacle for the mob he had the prisoner brought out in chains, dressed in a woollen cloak with a red *turtur*, or criminal's cap of red felt, on his head, and round his neck a collar of camel skin. He seated the wretched man on a camel and drove him thus attired through the streets, making him recite the verse of the Koran: "Say, O God, Lord of kingly power, thou dost grant kingship to whom thou desirest and removest it from whom thou desirest".[1] As the prisoner went by, the Shí'ite crowd from the Karkh spat in his face in expression of their disapproval of his past fanatical conduct towards them. When he had gone the full length of the road he was brought back to Basásírí's camp. There he was dressed in an ox-hide with the horns fixed above his head, and was put to death by crucifixion.[2]

From Baghdad Basásírí marched to Wásiṭ and Baṣra, and continuing his march after taking these cities he came to Ahwaz. But Tughril Beg had by this time regained his full power and influence by killing his brother Ibrahím in battle in Persia, and since he was now able to assist his supporters—one of whom was the ruler of Ahwaz— Basásírí was compelled to retrace his steps along the Tigris without having achieved all he wanted. Moreover the Seljúq monarch was now free to march down to Iraq again. His ostensible purpose was no more than to see that the Caliph, to whom he owed allegiance, was installed once more in his palace at Baghdad. Accordingly he sent messengers to inform Basásírí that he would be content not to march on Iraq on the conditions that the Caliph was allowed to return home, that he, Tughril, was acknowledged as suzerain in the *khuṭba*, and that his name appeared on the coinage. When Basásírí by his silence indicated defiance, Tughril set his army in motion. By the time he reached Qaṣri Shírín on the Persian frontier, the Shí'ites of the Karkh quarter were in a panic and moved their families out of the city downstream. There many of them fell into the clutches of the tribesmen, then, as now, ever on the watch for loot. The departure of the inhabitants of the Karkh was a signal to their bitter Sunní rivals of the Báb al-Baṣra quarter to spoil such parts of the deserted streets as remained unprotected. They were not content to rob but burnt Saffron Street, which, according to Ibn al-Athír, was the finest and best built thoroughfare in the city.[1]

At Nahrawán, between Qaṣri Shírín and Baghdad, the Caliph joined the Sultan, and the two came into the capital together, the Sultan humbly leading the Caliph's horse. There was no ceremony at this entry. Basásírí was still popular and most of the important supporters of the Seljúq prince and of the Caliph had fled the city, leaving only one to receive the Commander of the Faithful.

In the neighbourhood of Kúfa meanwhile, the Sultan's troops and those of his allies were fighting Basásírí, whose end came in battle when, an arrow having brought down his horse, he fell on his face to the ground, unable to escape. One of the wounded men of his own side pointed him out to the enemy, who cut off his head and sent it to Baghdad, to be exposed in triumph there at one of the city gates.

When Tughril Beg died in A.D. 1063 he was succeeded, after some delay, by his nephew Sultan Alp Arslán, who in a short reign of nine years was able by hard fighting and tremendous effort to expand the empire to which he succeeded until it included all the land from the Mediterranean Sea to the confines of eastern Persia. To him directly Baghdad does not owe very much, but his mighty vizier, who is generally known by his honorific title of the *Niẓám al-Mulk*, "The Ordering of the Kingdom", for a time renewed some of the departed glories of the city. This famous minister, who is associated in legend with Omar Khayyam and the "Old Man of the Mountains", chief of the Isma'ílí Assassins, served Alp Arslan and his successor Maliksh※áh for a period of thirty years. Being primarily soldiers they left the administration of their empire during that time to the skill of the Niẓám al-Mulk, whose powers were practically absolute and who worked with an honesty of purpose that is rare in oriental history.

The result of his efforts was an era of prosperity of a kind which Baghdad had not known for a long time. In A.H. 457 (A.D. 1065) the building was begun of the famous college, known after the vizier as the *Madrasat al-Niẓámiya*, or Niẓámí College. It was one of three great schools which he founded and endowed, and it became the most famous of them all. The

Persian geographer Qazwíní, in his dictionary of geography which he called *Áthár al-Bilád* or "Monuments of the Countries (of the World)",[1] relates how the schools came to be built:

> There is a story that the Sultan Alp Arslán, going into the town of Naisábúr one day, happened to pass by the gate of a mosque and saw a number of scholars gathered there. Their clothes were in tatters, they made no obeisance to him as he passed, and called down no blessing on him.... The Sultan in surprise asked the Niẓám al-Mulk (who accompanied him) who they were. He replied that they were seekers after knowledge, in spirit the noblest of men; that they took no pleasure in things of the world, and that they testified to their poverty by their garb. Perceiving that the Sultan's heart was softened towards them, he continued: "If the Sultan would grant me leave, I would build them an abode and provide them with an endowment, so that they could occupy themselves in the search for knowledge and pray for blessings on the Sultan's majesty". The Sultan gave permission and the Niẓám al-Mulk gave orders for colleges to be built in various parts of the Sultan's empire. He further ordained that one-tenth of the royal revenue allotted to him as vizier should be set aside for expenditure on the building.

These *madrasas* were not the first to be built, but it is probable that the Niẓám al-Mulk was the first to make provision for the physical needs of the students.[2]

The building of the *madrasa*, which lay on the east bank, was completed in September, A.D. 1067, and lectures seem to have begun at once. The influence of the school stretched beyond the limits of Baghdad. Indeed some of the details of its organization appear to have been copied by the early universities in Europe. It was founded officially as a theological school, being recognized both by the religious leaders of Islam and by the State, i.e. the Caliph, who provided its revenues, though by indirect means. The University of Paris in the same way derived its standing by the authority both of Church and State.[1]

The Caliph's intimate connection with the *madrasa* made his permission necessary before any teacher could take up duties there. For not having obtained this permission the *mudarris* (or professor) Yúsuf al-Dimishqí was excluded from the Friday assembly in the Caliph's mosque and even the substitute sent by Sultan Mas'úd was refused permission to teach until the prince himself had interceded with the Caliph.[2]

At the outset the school by no means obtained everyone's approval. The land upon which it was built had been seized without compensation to the expropriated owners and a number of houses were removed to make room for it.[3] This led to a difficulty at the opening ceremony. The first principal or professor while on his way to the *madrasa* was stopped in the street by a youth who asked him how he, a man of piety, could teach in a school standing on ground unlawfully seized. The professor promptly returned home, in spite of the fact that a large number of people were waiting to hear his lecture and indeed waited for him for nearly the whole day. He was finally persuaded to take up his duties after twenty days' debate, during which time a substitute teacher acted for him.[4]

The Niẓám al-Mulk had intended that the main function of the school was to teach the rigidly orthodox system of theology propounded by al-Ash'arí,[5] who fixed the tenets of the Sunní faith for all time. The system was by no means universally accepted. Twenty years before the school's foundation the adherents of al-Ash'arí had been officially cursed from the pulpit, with all other "heretics", by the 'Amíd al-Mulk, the Sultan Tughril Beg's vizier, and the cursing was continued until the Niẓám al-Mulk himself abolished the practice.[1] The most famous adherent of the Ash'arí system was the theologian and mystic al-Ghazálí, renowned in the annals of Islam not only as the greatest of its dogmatic theologians but as the most saintly of its mystics. In A.D. 1091 he was given a professorship at the Niẓámiya college, and remained there for four years, during which hundreds attended his lectures although even he was not free from attack. Thus amongst his pupils was a fanatic named Mohammed ibn Tumart, who spent the major part of his life in North Africa. He violently criticized the professor for wearing good clothes and particularly for donning an especially handsome academic robe for his lectures in the *madrasa*.[2] A sudden impulse towards the unworldly life of a Ṣúfí made him cast off his professorial robes and don the patched cloak of a wandering dervish.

Each new appointment to the post of *mudarris* or professor is noted by the historians for many years after the foundation of the college, and it may be assumed therefore that the position was one of considerable importance. Also it would seem that only one *mudarris* was elected at a time, and great difficulty was caused when, in A.H. 483 (A.D. 1090), two eminent scholars arrived in Baghdad, both armed with diplomas of appointment from the Niẓám al-Mulk. An arrangement by which the two professors lectured on alternate days seems to have been the only way out of an embarrassing situation.[1] There was no restriction on the number of *faqíhs*[2] (lecturers), or *mu'ids* ("répétiteurs").[3] Easily the most famous in after life of those who taught in a subordinate capacity at the *madrasa* was the poet Sa'dí of Shiraz. Of his life at the school he tells us that he thoroughly earned his salary, for he was engaged day and night—almost like Charles Lamb's schoolmaster—"in a perpetual cycle of teaching and repetition."[4] Another teacher was Bahá al-Dín (Bohadin) the biographer of Saladin.[5] He kept the manners and customs of the Baghdad court all his days both in his living and his way of dress. His was a rigid system of etiquette, and officials who came to visit him at Mosul in his audience chamber always took the place regularly assigned to them, without venturing in his presence to move to a higher one.[6] Some of his reminiscences are reported in Ibn Khallikán's biography of him. One of them is that some of the students[7] of the Niẓámiya once ate the kernels of the *baládur*[8] to sharpen their wits and memory. The effect was to drive them mad, and one appeared in the college and listened gravely to discussions, though he was entirely nude except for a cap.[9]

The *faqíhs* in course of time acquired a strong corporate feeling which showed itself as occasion demanded, as for example in A.H. 547 (A.D. 1152) when Ya'qúb the Scribe died in the *madrasa* without leaving an heir. The Caliph's officer, whose business it was to take charge of the property of persons dying without heir, came into the *madrasa* to place his seal on the door of the small upper story chamber in which Ya'qúb had lived. The *faqíhs* resented the presence of the officer and assaulted him, and the porter on whom he called for assistance thrashed two of the presumptuous *faqíhs*. Thereupon the other students locked the college gates, threw the "Preacher's Chair" (pulpit) into the roadway and that night demonstrated on the flat roof of the college in a disorderly manner, asking others to join them in defiance of the authorities. The *mudarris* was able to still the demonstration, but had to make his apologies for the disorder to the Caliph himself whom he visited in the Táj Palace.[1]

The Moorish traveller Ibn Jubayr visited the *madrasa* in A.D. 1184 and attended a lecture given by the *faqíh* Raḍíy al-Dín al-Qazwíní. The lecture took place following the afternoon prayers on the Friday—the day after the traveller's arrival in Baghdad. When the class was assembled, the lecturer mounted a platform or pulpit, and the students, sitting on stools in front of him, read out, or rather intoned, the Koran. The shaikh then delivered an address, interpreting a section of the Koran with a wealth of learning and the application of pertinent traditions of the Prophet. The teacher was then assailed by showers of oral questions from all parts of the room, and, when he had answered them with great elaboration and facility, he received a number of written questions with which he dealt. By the time he had answered all these, evening prayers were due and the class dispersed.

The Niẓámiya *madrasa* was not the only public institution founded in the early Seljúq period; and at the same time older establishments were not forgotten. In A.D. 1068 there died a certain 'Abd al-Malik who had repaired and endowed the 'Aḍudí hospital afresh, also increasing its staff by twenty-eight physicians.[1]

In the same year that the building of the Niẓámiya was begun, Sharaf al-Mulk al Mustawfí ("The Treasurer") came to Baghdád and took advantage of his important office to emulate the vizier. He accordingly built a shrine over the tomb of Abú Ḥanífa at the "Gate of the Arch" to the north of the eastern part of the city, and in addition built a *madrasa* there for his friends. It was said of Sharaf al-Mulk that he had a complete suit of clothes for every day of the year, and always wore what was seasonable.[2]

Later on, one Khamartagín, a servant of the prince Táj al-Dawla Tutush, son of Alp Arslán, built a bazaar near the Niẓámiya college, a *madrasa* in the same neighbourhood for the Ḥanafite sect and a hospital in the Báb al-Azaj quarter. They were all called "Tutushí" after the prince.[3]

The new structures were erected after the great flood of A.H. 466 (A.D. 1073), the year following the succession of Malikshâh to the Seljúq Sultanate after his father Alp Arslán. In that year the Tigris, in high flood, submerged most of the town lying on the east bank and a good deal of that on the west bank. Only the Caliph's palace and the buildings protected by its dykes escaped catastrophe. The water also rose in the subterranean conduits and wells on the east bank and drowned a number of people. In the night a high wind drove a huge volume of the flood water right up to the upper stories of the buildings; and it is especially noted by the chroniclers that water poured in at the windows of the 'Aḍudí hospital. No vessel of any kind would venture out, and the majority lay tied up under the lee of the Táj Palace on the left bank. The dislocation of traffic which this caused was so great that the vizier summoned the ferrymen and ordered them, on pain of death, to resume their work, and in spite of the perilous crossing they were forbidden to charge passengers more than the regular fare.

During the space of over twenty years following the disaster there came steady recuperation and a prosperity which showed itself in an exceptional plenitude and cheapness of food. When the Sultan Malikshâh paid the city one of his rare visits, in A.D. 1087, his main object was to find relaxation after strenuous campaigning. Apart from a state visit to the Caliph, his most serious business was polo and after that gazelle-hunting. The Niẓám al-Mulk, who came with him, inspected the great *madrasa* and gave his attention to matters that needed it.[1] Great headway was made during the period with the rebuilding of the parts of the city which the floods had destroyed. In addition there were considerable extensions of the eastern half of Baghdad, now the more important side of the city.[2] In A.D. 1095, in the reign of the Caliph Mustaẓhir, a wall was built round the *Ḥarím*, or Royal Precincts, which took in a large part of East Baghdad.[3] From its northern gate, to-day known as the Mu'aẓẓam Gate, a road led to the Sultan's palace, to which was added, several years later, the third of the city's great Friday mosques. The wall was extended in A.H. 517 (A.D. 1123) by the Caliph al-Mustarshid, who proposed to pay for it by a tax on all exports from the city passing through its gates. The measure proved very unpopular, and had to be discontinued after a large sum of money had been collected by its means. Ibn al-Athír reports that the money was returned to the citizens, though he does not explain how the delicate process of redistribution was carried out. However that may be, the citizens "increased their prayers" for their sovereign and volunteered their labour, each city quarter in turn contributing its share, and working to the music of drums and flutes. The cost of the wall was in the end made up by a gift from the vizier Aḥmad, son of the Niẓám al-Mulk, added to the proceeds of a forced levy on the city notables.[1]

The comparative peace and relaxation of pressure from the outside that had given the people an opportunity of restoring their city, also provided them with leisure to consider and renew their ancient internal animosities and to inquire into each other's religious and moral peculiarities. Doctrinal dissensions became violent and were not confined to those between Shí'a and Sunnites. It can hardly ever be said that the conflict was due to incitement by the Seljúq Sultans or their officers. Their conduct in this respect differed notably from that of the Shí'ite Buwayhids, who, more than once, as has been seen, outraged Sunní opinion by forcing their own sectarian practices upon a community of whom more than half found them detestable. Indeed it occurred more than once that Sultan combined with Caliph to quell disorder with its consequent harm to the city. Occasionally, as in A.H. 502 (A.D. 1108–9), their efforts were successful and both sects were able to visit their own particular shrines without molestation, even when the pilgrimage involved passing through a hostile quarter.[1]

Nevertheless there was a chronic condition of religious unrest, especially marked at this time in the internecine quarrels of Sunnite sects which blazed out afresh almost annually. In A.H. 469 (A.D. 1076–7) there were violent scenes at the Niẓámiya *madrasa* when the Hanbalites in their hundreds with noisy interruptions tried to drown the lectures of the learned al-Qushayrí who held Ash'arite views. Again in the next year the inhabitants of the Súq al-Madrasa quarter and those of the Súq al-Thaláthá fought on matters of doctrine. On both occasions numbers of the participants were killed in the dispute. The disturbances had a political sequel in the dismissal of the Caliph's vizier Fakhr al-Dawla, who had failed to prevent the attacks on the *madrasa* although the Nizám al-Mulk's own son had been there on the first occasion. Further, a new governor was appointed over Iraq by the Niẓám al-Mulk, who had been informed of the conflict in a poem which was sent to him, beginning:

O Order of the Kingdom (Niẓám al-Mulk),
Order is dissolved in Baghdad,
And he that dwells in it remains despised and outraged.[2]

Abú Shujá', the Caliph's new vizier, was a pious man

over-inclined to charitableness. He shut his eyes to the rioting between Sunnis and Shí'a until the Caliph Muqtadí warned him that his duties could not be carried out with such leniency and that his indulgence merely encouraged greater outrage. Only the destruction of the biggest and most important houses in each of the riotous quarters of the Karkh and Báb al-Baṣra would bring their quarrelsome inhabitants to their senses. In order to placate his sovereign, the vizier despatched the *muḥtasib* to carry out the disciplinary measures, but at the same time he gave the officer instructions to purchase the condemned properties at his expense in order to prevent hardship to any owner who might be innocent of offence.[1]

In A.D. 484 (A.D. 1091) the vizier's forbearance led to his dismissal on the count that he encouraged disrespect of the Sultan's officers. The incident which led to the charge was that a huckster had approached the Sultan's agent, the Jew Abú Sa'd ibn Simḥá, and on the pretence of offering him goods for sale had delivered him a blow which knocked his turban off. While the Sultan's governor and the Jewish agent were away at the Sultan's camp making their complaint, the Caliph issued an edict that all "protected" people, Christians and Jews, were forthwith to mark themselves with the special token and to garb themselves in the garments prescribed for them by the Caliph Omar. Many fled the city, while others found it advisable to become converts to Islam.[2] The reverberations of the affair continued for a number of years, and when, in A.H. 501 (A.D. 1107–8), the vizier Majd al-Dín was readmitted to office after a period during which he had been out of the Sultan's favour, one of the conditions of his reinstatement was that he was not to employ any "protected" Christians or Jews.[1]

Efforts were made during this period at the moral and physical cleansing of the city. For the first, in the year before the inundation of A.H. 466 (A.D. 1073), petitions had been sent by prominent citizens to the Caliph al-Qá'im complaining of the excess of wine-drinking and vice in the city and asking that places of ill-resort should be destroyed.[2] The Caliph's successor Muqtadí enacted several laws intended to safeguard the morals of the community. He banished singing-women and prostitutes from the city, ordering their houses to be sold; forbade anyone to enter the public baths without wearing a shirt, and he tore down various structures of reed and high towers used ostensibly for bird houses, but in reality for the unlawful purpose of spying on the private quarters of houses—an offence forbidden to this day under heavy penalties.[3] Lastly he forbade the ferrymen to carry men and women across together in their boats. Muqtadí's efforts were supported by some of his more ascetic cadis. In a particular case the chief cadi refused to accept the testimony of a witness on the ground that he was dressed in silk. When the complainant protested that on similar grounds the evidence of the Sultan and of the Niẓám al-Mulk would be discredited, the judge agreed with him and said he would not accept their testimony either.[4]

For the physical cleansing of Baghdad certain sanitary measures were introduced, the most important being to preserve the purity of the water supply. Thus, waste water from the public baths was no longer to be emptied directly into the Tigris but had to be received in pits dug for it. Further, the cleansing and curing of fish was forbidden in any place but the one specially allotted for the purpose.[1]

Towards the end of A.H. 484 (A.D. 1091) the Sultan Malikshâh paid the second visit of his reign to Baghdad. During his stay his birthday was celebrated with great magnificence and he marked his visit by building a new mosque, known as the "Sultan's Mosque", outside the palace of the Sultan.[2] At the same time also the Niẓám al-Mulk and other of the great officers of state built houses in the city in anticipation of frequent and lengthy visits to it. Fate, however, decided that both the Sultan and his vizier were to die within the year. "Their continuance after this was not long", says Ibn al-Athír in a moralizing tone that is rare with him. "They were after this all scattered by death and slaughter in battle and in other ways. Their armies did not avail them, nor did they accumulate anything. Praise be to the Ever-Continuous whose command never ceaseth."[3] At the end of the year the Niẓám al-Mulk fell sick "and treated himself, by giving alms". Some months later, after a quarrel with his master, he was dismissed from office, and shortly afterwards he was murdered—by Isma'ílí Assassins it is said. He was followed to the grave a few weeks later by the Sultan himself, who died at Baghdad.

CHAPTER XI

The Seljúq Decline

The death of Malikshāh was followed by a long struggle for the succession, in which Baghdad changed hands several times. Turkán Khátún, the Sultan's widow, made great efforts to secure the empire for her own son, who was an infant. The child died young, however, and Malikshāh's eldest son, Barkyáruq, was acknowledged Sultan at Baghdad in A.D. 1094,[1] only to be ousted in the same year by his uncle Tutush, who overcame a composite army of his rivals, including a detachment from Barkyáruq under the generalship of a Turkish adventurer named Karbúqá, who afterwards became lord of Mosul.[2] Barkyáruq contrived to regain mastery of Baghdad in the next year, but was again involved in an intermittent struggle to hold his sultanate, this time against his brother Mohammed. Each was successful in turn and at each change a new proclamation of allegiance was made in Baghdad, until for a short period in A.D. 1103, the responsible officers omitted the name of the Sultan entirely from the *khuṭba*,[3] being either too puzzled to know what Seljúq Sultan they were to acknowledge or perhaps feeling that in the circumstances it was safe to acknowledge no one, without fear of consequences. The struggle between the two brothers only ended in A.D. 1104 when Barkyáruq died.

Baghdad was now the capital only of Iraq, other members of the Seljúq family having possessed themselves of the other parts of the empire in Persia, Upper Mesopotamia and Syria. During the conflict the city had been to a large extent out of touch with the affairs of the rest of the world, and devoted itself to its own concerns. Reference has already been made to the Caliph's building of a wall round the *Ḥarím*, or Royal Precincts. It seems to have been of absorbing interest to the whole population, who entered with great joy into the task of building and treated it as if it were the most important thing in the world. They seem to have been almost entirely untouched even by reports of the advance of the Crusaders on Jerusalem, though, if the evidence is to be believed, in A.D. 1098 a number of captured deserters from the Christian army, besieged in Antioch by Karbúqá the Turk, were actually sent to Baghdad.[1] Even when a delegation came to seek help from the Caliph after the fall of Jerusalem, though sympathetic tears were shed, the interest of the city took no practical turn.

> In the audience chamber they [the delegates] let fall words which brought tears to every eye and grief to every heart. They stood in the mosque during the Friday assembly and demanded aid, weeping and causing all to weep at the mention of the calamities which Moslems had suffered in the noble and mighty city by the slaughter of men, the carrying off of women and the loss of possessions.[2]

It may have been that the piteous appeal touched the hearts of the great mass of the people; but Palestine had now for long been out of the hands of the Abbasid Caliphs, and formed part of the possessions of the Fáṭimid anti-Caliphs of Egypt, between whom and the Baghdad Caliphate there was bitter rivalry. It is possible further some private donations may have been sent to relieve the sufferings of Moslems ruined by the Crusade, but no help was given by the Caliph al-Mustaẓhir, who referred the delegation to the Seljúq Sultan Barkyáruq. At that time the Sultan was engaged in a struggle for life with his brother Mohammed, and there too the appeal came to nothing.

In A.H. 501 (A.D. 1108) a second appeal came, this time from Tripoli, which was beset by Raymund of Toulouse. The ruling chief of the besieged city, who in person headed the delegation, was received with great honour and consideration by both the Caliph and the Sultan Mohammed, who was now the reigning Seljúq. Troops were promised him and were detailed for service in Syria, but not a man from Iraq actually went to give battle to the enemy who had roused all other Moslem lands around the Mediterranean.

In spite of the city's detachment, there was one thing it shared with the whole of the Middle East. Ever since the murder of the Niẓám al-Mulk there had been universal terror of the Isma'ílí Assassins, whose mysterious methods of slaughter, together with the New Propaganda introduced by the Grand Master Ḥasan al-Sabbáḥ, had driven into every individual a fear for his own safety and a mistrust of every other man however closely related or of whatever exalted rank. To the unscrupulous this widespread fear and hatred of the Isma'ílís gave a weapon which they soon discovered to be of advantage in blackmailing operations or against enemies; for a man had only to be denounced as an Isma'ílí heretic to be seized and put to a terrible death.

In this way, in Sultan Mohammed's reign, the governor of Iṣfahan, one 'Abdulláh al-Khatíbí, had acquired power by insinuating himself into the Sultan's favour and pretending to a knowledge of all that was going on in the realm. It was the easier for him because the old Abbasid *baríd*, a system of combined espionage and express posts, had been abolished by Alp Arslán in spite of the protests of the Niẓám al-Mulk.

Al-Khatíbí was a man without any culture, yet extremely cunning, who had brought himself into notice by a piety and asceticism that were entirely false, all that he really had being "the outward show of a great coarse body and a thick, bushy beard".[1] His connection with the Sultan after a time brought him to Baghdad where he became "the touchstone of Islam" and the source of secret reports which sent many a man to his death.[2] His influence grew till he was able by devious ways to introduce a woman agent into the very household of the Caliph himself, where she found means of informing the Commander of the Faithful that his own brother Hárún was suspect. A huge bribe was sent to close the villain's mouth, and his power, instead of being brought to the sudden end which it deserved, was thereby actually increased. In the reign of terror that followed, no one was safe from his black-mailing operations, until the Sultan was induced to ask him one day how he explained the great increase of religious and moral laxity which he reported as existing amongst officials though it was apparently unheard of in the time of the Sultan's father and grandfather. Al-Khatíbí's cunning reply was that the officials of the earlier period were Persians of Khurásán and men of true faith, whereas the newer ones were Iráqís and hence heretics. The deluded Sultan was led by this lying insinuation to dismiss many Baghdadís and other men of Iraq from his employ, and to permit the men of Khurásán who were then in Iraq—an utterly contemptible body, riddled with Isma'ílism—to crowd into favour and office. It is not to be wondered at that al-Khatíbí's end came from an assassin's knife.[1]

"All things need intelligence except government",[2] quotes the vizier Anúshirwán *à propos* of this period of decadence and corruption. Amongst the Khurasanís who thus secured appointments on the score merely of their origin, was Mohammed al-Júzaqání, who became the '*amíd* (? deputy governor) of Baghdad. A fanatical adherence to the Ḥanafí school of Sunnism brought him to the notice of the Sultan. It went to such lengths that when a man in the street greeted him with *Salám* he would ask him to what sect of Islam he belonged before replying to his greeting. "He was a man of hideous looks, coarse intellect and bold face: like a finch for his diversity of colours, like a crow for his inconstancy and like a wolf for his depredations",[3] and he was able for a considerable time to tyrannize over the cowed city.

Another Seljúq official of this period was Abú Manṣúr al-Maybudí, "a mine of deceit and treachery", who owed his office to a woman. The fact was not unknown and blunt comment in prose and verse was not lacking,[4] both on it and on the contrast between his ponderous "coffin-full" of body and his "gossamer" intellect. When he leaned on his couch of state supported by a cushion "you would have thought there were two stuffed pillows".[1]

The shadow of the uneasiness cast by the Isma'ílís and of the uncertainty brought on by the Seljúq misgovernment in Baghdad was darkened by various reminders from Syria that the infidel Crusaders were pressing the believers hard. The city was at last definitely roused when in A.H. 504 (A.D. 1111) the Franks, after bringing numerous cities to terms, set upon and captured a large trading caravan from Egypt. The citizens of Aleppo, to whom apparently the goods were consigned, sent a body of delegates to Baghdad imploring assistance. They were joined by a good many of the learned scholars of the capital, anxious to uphold the prestige of Islam, and a great audience assembled in the Sultan's mosque. Then, as on previous occasions, the appeals seemed likely to be futile, but the zealous ones called attention to the urgency of their cause by the grave step of interrupting the Friday service and breaking the pulpit. The demonstration was effective in bringing a promise from the Sultan that he would send an army to fight the Holy War.

Remembering the former promise and sceptical of its fulfilment, the men of Aleppo and their supporters, on the Friday after their demonstration, went to the mosque in the Caliph's palace with a view to enforcing their appeal. They were followed by the citizens in a great crowd. The guardian of the gate who attempted to prevent their entry was swept aside, and the mob which poured into the sacred building tore down the grille surrounding the part of the mosque allotted to the Caliph's private use, broke the pulpit there too and caused the abandonment of the service. This time the Caliph (al-Mustaẓhir) added his appeals to those of the Syrians, and the Sultan sent to Mosul and to other cities within his sphere of influence commanding that the amírs were to prepare themselves to march in a Holy War against the Franks.[1] In the following year troops were actually despatched to help the harassed Moslems, though the effect was not as great as had been hoped.

Almost as soon as the disturbing elements had left, Baghdad settled down to its ordinary way of life again. For the marriage of the Caliph to the daughter of the Sultan Malikshāh the city was decorated and there was great rejoicing,[2] and when a son was born to the Caliph, drums were beaten and trumpets blown, and the vizier sat at the gate of the Firdús Palace in congratulation to his sovereign.[3] It happened about the same time that the Caliph's brother died. The beating of drums was discontinued for several days and the vizier sat at the Firdús gate in condolence.

The passion for building was scarcely interrupted. In A.H. 507 (A.D. 1113–4) a certain Kumashtigín founded a hospital in the city, and about eight years later the Mustawfí 'Azíz al-Dín built in the 'Attábiyyín quarter of Baghdad "a school for orphans, which he provided with a perpetual endowment by which the orphans, until they reached maturity, were assured of their expenditure, their clothing and their food. There they were taught their letters, learned the Koran by heart and acquired knowledge of what is lawful and unlawful".[1]

To the Mustawfí, incidentally, is ascribed what must be amongst the earliest of army field hospitals. It had instruments, medicaments and tents, and was staffed by a number of doctors and orderlies. Two hundred Bactrian camels were provided for the transport of the hospital.[2]

The reigning Sultan, when these public works were instituted, was Maḥmúd, nephew of Barkyáruq. His authority at Baghdad was intermittent, being challenged first by his uncle Sinjar, the ruler of Persia who was acknowledged as suzerain in Baghdad in A.D. 1119, and then by his own brother Mas'úd, who ruled at Mosul. This fraternal conflict was due to the intrigues of Dubays, son of the famous Ṣadaqa, who had founded a dynasty and built his capital at Hilla which lies near the Euphrates and about sixty miles south-west of Baghdad. Dubays turned the Sultan's pre-occupation to his own advantage by raiding Baghdad and harrying the surrounding districts. In spite of several expeditions against him and his allies he continued his hostile activities until, in A.D. 1123, the Caliph Mustarshid was roused to appeal for help to Bursuqí, the Seljúq governor of Mosul and Wásiṭ. The monarch himself prepared for war and went out to battle clothed in the black turban and cloak of the Abbasids and wearing the Prophet's mantle. Before he left the safety of the city walls he issued a proclamation that no soldier was on any pretext to remain behind, and that anyone of the citizens who desired to serve was to present himself to the authorities. A large number of men came forward for enlistment and were given money and arms,[1] while amongst the people in the city the excitement was intense. They gathered in huge crowds to watch the Caliph and his suite cross the Tigris to the west bank for the march towards the enemy's territory.

Dubays heightened his own men's eagerness for the battle by promising them the plunder of Baghdad and the choice of its women as the reward of victory. It is consistent with this incentive to valour that when the two armies faced one another, his troops leapt to the attack preceded by girls beating drums and by clowns of low character playing musical instruments. The Caliph's army, on the other hand, led by Bursuqí, waited soberly, reciting verses from the Koran and offering up prayers.[2] The first attack was launched at Bursuqí's right wing, which retired before it but recovered again. A second attack was no more successful, and this time the attacking troops were taken in the rear as they ran back to their own position. Their leaders were captured and many of the men were either taken prisoner or left dead on the field. Both sides now engaged and when the fighting was general, Bursuqí, who was watching from some rising ground, sent into the battle a party of 500 men that he had kept in concealment. Their arrival decided the day and Dubays' army retired in full flight, many of his men throwing themselves into the Tigris to evade capture.

Dubays himself escaped into the desert and after trying vainly to make terms with a nomad Nejdí tribe, he joined the Muntafiq confederation in the neighbourhood of the great marsh. With them he planned an attack on Baṣra, which was captured and plundered. When news of this exploit reached Baghdad the Caliph complained to Bursuqí for having permitted Dubays to continue his activities, and an expedition was fitted out to go downstream to put an end to them. But he escaped from Baṣra before the expedition had left Baghdad, having received information of what was afoot through his agents there, one of whom was the *naqíb* of the 'Alid community. This fact was discovered; the incumbent of the office of *naqíb* was removed and the office itself transferred to the *naqíb* of the Abbasids, thus bringing about its temporary extinction.[1]

The later history of Dubays is interesting. After leaving Baṣra he went to Syria, where he joined the Franks in the siege of Aleppo.[2] Later, in A.H. 519 (A.D. 1125), he returned to Iraq with a view to attacking Baghdad. The Caliph with an army marched to Daskara along the Khurásán highway, from the direction of which the attack was expected, but he allowed Dubays with a very small and desperate body of men to interrupt his communications and to intercept supplies sent out to the royal army from the city. This piece of incompetence gave rise to a report that Baghdad was in the enemy's hands, and on hearing it the Caliph's force, which according to Ibn al-Athír's figures was 12,000 strong, fled north-west to Nahrawan, leaving their heavy baggage behind on the road. "If Allah had not favoured them by the fever and consequent delay of Tughril (Sultan of Damascus and ally of Dubays) he would have annihilated the army and the Caliph too", for the roads were heavy with recent rains and a hundred men could have destroyed the whole of the Caliph's army. However, when Dubays came within sight of the royal standard he humbly kissed the ground, and declaring himself the servant of the Caliph he was forgiven, and peace was made.[1]

The relationships of Sultan and Caliph at this period had an important bearing on the fortunes of Baghdad. It has been indicated that the Caliph, Mustarshid, generally commanded the respect of the Sultan and others. This could scarcely be said of any other Caliph since the Buwayhids entered Baghdad and subdued the Caliphate to their own purposes almost two centuries before. Relying on the ancient powers of his office, Mustarshid now asserted himself in a fashion long in abeyance, while Sultan Maḥmúd opposed to him all the temporal forces left to his shrunken empire. The struggle that had long been brewing broke out openly in A.H. 520 (A.D. 1126) when the Caliph found himself involved in a quarrel between his deputy and the Seljúq governor of Baghdad. The latter, at a threat from the Caliph, left the city to make complaint to the Sultan, and to warn him that the Caliph's power was on the increase and that unless he (the Sultan) returned to Baghdad immediately the city would be lost to the Seljúqs.

Acting on this information, the Sultan began his journey to Iraq. He was met on the way by a messenger from the Caliph informing him that the country and its inhabitants were in an impoverished condition owing to the ravages of Dubays and that they could not possibly supply the needs of the company which the Sultan was bringing with him: he begged him therefore to postpone his journey to Baghdad until the land had been restored to some at least of its former prosperity, and promised him that no one should prevent his coming. The advice might have been honourably intended, but the Sultan would have none of it and only pressed on the harder.

At a report of the Sultan's rejection of his message, Mustarshid took steps to remove himself out of range of contact with the Seljúq, who still regarded himself as a vassal to the Caliph. With his womenfolk and children he left his palace on the east bank and, to the accompaniment of a great weeping from the citizens, crossed the river with a view to leaving the town altogether if the Sultan should persist in his purpose. To a message from the Sultan urging him to return he replied that he could not bear to be present and behold the sufferings that must come if the Seljúq army was imposed on Baghdad. In spite of further appeals for peace he remained on the west bank, giving orders that all the gates into the palace were to be closed with the exception of that of the Sentry Gate[1]. As a further precaution he gathered all the vessels on the river to his own side.

For a time the Sultan kept his army outside the city walls and except for the gibes and insults that flew backwards and forwards across the river no active steps were taken by either side. But either the Sultan's patience or his discipline suddenly failed and a number of his men, breaking into the royal palace, set about plundering it, though the main part of his army remained outside the walls. The looting of the royal house roused the citizens to a frenzy of anger and they gathered from all sides, some to repel the raiders and others with the less honourable motives of finding plunder for themselves. At sight of the gathering crowds the Caliph crossed the river and dug trenches during the night, presumably on a line between the city wall and the Sultan's army. But when the Caliph took the offensive and launched an attack which he hoped might be decisive, it failed through the desertion to the Sultan of a Kurdish chief and his men. At the same time large reinforcements reached the Sultan from Wásiṭ, and the Caliph, seeing it was time to make peace, sent overtures which were graciously accepted although there were not lacking counsellors of the Sultan who urged him to burn the city out of revenge. But he was content with an indemnity and, after a bout of illness, departed in A.D. 1127.[1]

A number of troubled years followed in which the Caliph Mustarshid's pugnacious spirit led him into a trial of strength with the Sultan Mas'úd and with the Atábeg Zangí of Mosul, famous for his efforts against the Crusaders. Zangí, having as his ally Dubays ibn Ṣadaqa of Hilla, in A.D. 1132, during an interval between two sieges in Syria, found time to remember that he was governor of Iraq and hence of Baghdad also, to which he came to assert his rights. The Caliph however would have none of it and routed Zangí and Dubays in battle.[2] He was not so successful with Mas'úd who, in a bloodless victory near Hamadan, captured the Caliph and ordered his army to return to Baghdad, forbidding them, on pain of death, to take refuge in Hamadan. Many of them lost the road home and died of their hardships. The Caliph himself was murdered in his tent in the Sultan's camp (A.H. 529=A.D. 1134–5), it is said by the hand of Isma'ílí Assassins.[1] But though most of the horrible crimes of the period were for convenience ascribed to these "Heretics", the people of Baghdad accused both Sultan Mas'úd and his uncle Sanjar as being guilty of the murder.[2]

CHAPTER XII

Two Sieges

The reek of turmoil arising from the death-throes of the Seljúqs was bound, while it lasted, to obscure everything else in Baghdad, and the annalists of the time are almost exclusively occupied with it. Yet it was but a stage in a long process. Since the days of the Caliph Ma'mún, Baghdad had been slowly but steadily losing the glories which had made it famous. At times it had recovered, but on the whole its story is one of decline. There now came a check to the process of decay, and one which may be explained by a temporary revival of the Caliphate at a time when the rapidly weakening Seljúq Sultans had to reckon with the usurpations of the Atábegs, once their servants. The Sultans did not even now yield their supremacy to the Caliphs without a struggle, which continued in desultory fashion until the Turkoman dynasty was finally extinguished in Iraq. When the conflict blazed out fiercely, as happened more than once, Baghdad prepared for, and suffered, the hardships of siege; in quiescent periods we find evidences that the ways of peace were still being trodden in the city.

One of the more lurid incidents in the long campaign came in A.H. 530 (A.D. 1136) when Sultan Mas'úd tried conclusions with the Caliph al-Ráshid B'illáh, the successor of Mustarshid. The Caliph had given refuge to a number of chieftains dissatisfied with the Sultan's overlordship, and in consequence Baghdad had, for the third time in its history, to stand a heavy siege. It was blockaded by Mas'úd for nearly two months without being stormed, although during that time the city was suffering as much from the depredations of brigands and other scoundrels within its gates as from the besiegers outside. At the end of the period the disheartened Sultan was actually on his way back to Persia, when, at Nahrawán, which lay on the great canal of the same name, he met reinforcements of troops and a number of ships from Wásiṭ which could sail up the Tigris and blockade the city from the river. He was induced at sight of them to turn back for another attempt, but the Caliph had abdicated and fled to Mosul, to 'Imád al-Dín Zangí, by the time Mas'úd reached Baghdad. On his arrival the city capitulated, but through the Sultan's vigorous efforts it did not suffer the looting and damage normally inseparable from the end of a siege.[1]

Mas'úd himself, after taking counsel with the late Caliph's vizier, agreed to the election of al-Muqtafí as the new Commander of the Faithful, a man who was to deal a hard blow to Seljúq power. Legend says that when the Sultan sent a messenger to the new Caliph confirming the income of his privy purse, he received a reply saying: "In this house there are eighty mules that bring water from the Tigris. Let the Sultan see to it that he who drinks this water has his needs supplied". It was a reply which led the Seljúq prince to express aloud the disturbing thought that he had placed too strong a man in the Caliphate.[2]

The Caliph's strength did not manifest itself for some little while and he seems to have devoted the interval to maturing plans for imperial aggrandizement, leaving his capital to take care of itself or be looked after by the Seljúq governor. When that official was absent from the city, and at times even when he was present, brigands roamed the streets and bazaars accosting prosperous citizens and openly transporting the collected loot on the heads of the porters who plied for public hire.[1] One such brigand, Ibn Bakrán, did not confine his operations to the city, and having amassed great wealth and influence, he proposed with a confederate to issue coins bearing their names from Anbár on the Euphrates; whereupon the governor of that district was addressed by the governor of Baghdad in a message offering him the alternatives of killing Ibn Bakrán or being himself killed. He made the obvious choice and Baghdad for a time found peace.

Yet there were times when nothing could be done by the governor or the citizens because persons of high rank would have been involved in ignominy. Thus the Greek governor Bihrúz (who at one time was a friend of Shádhí, Saladin's grandfather), was foiled in his efforts against the robbers because the son of the Sultan's vizier and the Sultan's own brother-in-law shared in the loot.[2]

At intervals, when the noise of the war drums became less obvious, the ordinary sounds of city life asserted themselves. Thus we hear in A.H. 541 (A.D. 1146) of a mission to the Caliph from Sultan Sanjar which included a preacher famous in his own day, al-'Abádí al-Muẓaffar ibn Ardashír. His efforts were not confined to persuasion of the Caliph, but a pulpit was set up for him on the bank of the Tigris in a place where the Sultan Mas'úd could hear him from a balcony in the palace, while the amír 'Abbás, master of Rayy, who was then in the city, moored his boat inshore to listen to the orator. He was surrounded by an enormous crowd from all ranks of society, many of them workmen who had dropped what they were doing and fought for places nearer him. The Caliph himself paid him the honour of inviting him to preach in the royal mosque.[1]

With the death of Sultan Mas'úd in A.H. 547 (A.D. 1152), the Caliph's latent determination to be sovereign in reality and not in name only, began to assert itself. The governor of Baghdad, the libertine Mas'úd al-Bilálí, fled, on news of his master's death, and the Caliph proceeded to ransack the houses of the Seljúq officials who had been stationed in the city.[2] He had, on his appointment, sworn an oath not to buy any Turkish slaves for the palace, and he now proceeded to banish from the city the "foreigners", meaning by that Turks and Persians who had had any connection with the Seljúq *régime*. Instead of them he appointed his Greek and Armenian mamelukes to be amírs in the various districts of Iraq,[3] and to his own vizier he gave the estates and office formerly held by the Sultan's minister. In anticipation of the challenge to his presumption he strengthened the walls of Baghdad, deepened its moats and dug out springs afresh. Also he kept his artificers busily engaged in manufacturing weapons of war, and, not content with defensive measures at home, he sent spies abroad with orders to report secretly any significant movements of the enemy.

The expected attack was delayed for nearly five years, during which time the rival Seljúq princes were far too occupied with their efforts against each other or holding back the Ghuzz invaders from the East to spare any attention elsewhere. At some time within the period of suspense, probably in A.H. 551 (A.D. 1157), the poet Kháqání, while on his way to Mecca on pilgrimage, visited Baghdad. To judge from his long poem *Tuḥfat al-'Iráqayn*, "The Gift of the Two Iraqs", he found it no mean city, for he begins by calling it "a city wide as sage's thought, clear above all existing things", and was greatly impressed by such of the citizens as he met. Yet a suspicion that it is only the professional panegyrist speaking is borne out by the fact that in another poem he finds it necessary to depreciate Baghdad in order to heighten his praises of Isfahan, which he had more recently adopted as his home. His disparagement is of greater historical value than his praise; for when he calls Baghdad the bottle factory for Isfahan's rose-water he indicates that the city's glass was still being manufactured and as famous as ever. If confirmation of this is needed it is to be found in the narrative of the Chinese traveller Chóu K'ü-feï, who visited Iraq probably in 1178,[1] about twenty years after the poet.

The long-deferred attack came in A.H. 551 (A.D. 1157), when Sultan Mohammed, son of Maḥmúd, commenced siege operations against the city on the pretext that the Caliph had refused to acknowledge him in the public prayers as lord of Iraq and of Baghdad. But Baghdad was full of men and supplies and the Caliph himself prepared to withstand blockade and attack. In order to lessen the area that it would be necessary for him to defend on the east bank, he had demolished a number of royal dwellings—probably by that time disused—such as the 'Ísá Palace, the Square Palace erected by his ancestor Mutí' about two centuries before, and several others. On the city walls mangonels were stationed to cover any approaches, and in order to make surprise attacks from the west more difficult the Tigris bridge was cut and all vessels in the river were ordered to moor under the walls of the Táj Palace. For the western side of the city little more could be done than to order the inhabitants to destroy any property that could not be moved and to transfer the rest, with themselves, to the defenced area. Most of the inhabitants obeyed, but the occupants of the Karkh and Báb al-Baṣra quarters, who were business men as well as fanatics, for once sank their differences and agreed that they could better safeguard their interests by deserting to the Seljúqs than by trusting to the efforts of the Caliph.

The attacking force divided itself into two, the Sultan himself being on the west bank, where he stationed mangonels to cover the important posts at the mouth of the Mu'allá canal on the opposite side. The rest of the besiegers encamped on the east bank, outside the Shammásiya Gate. For some reason or other, even when continual reinforcements of ships and men had supplied the Sultan with a formidable attacking force prepared for active service, he refrained for a long time from any movement beyond sending messages to the Caliph assuring him of his loyalty if only his own claims were acknowledged.

Some of the besiegers apparently had scruples about warring against the Caliph and the "Heart of Islam", and even when hostilities began, though there were daily battles between champions from both sides and ships fitted with mangonels exchanged shots, yet there was no general engagement for two months. There were a good many casualties from arrows, "burning bottles" and flaming naphtha thrown from mangonels, but the number of slain was very few. Within the city, compensation was paid for all wounds, until the vizier, whose business it was to inspect and assess the hurt done in each case, found himself perpetually in the middle of a crowd of warriors demanding attention, when he decided that the system must be discontinued if his patience and the royal treasury were not both to be exhausted. There appeared to be no lack of confidence however in the capacity of the exchequer, and the loyalty of the citizens was even further assured by the Caliph's ability, in spite of a comparatively strict blockade, to distribute full rations of grain and dates instead of having to resort to money payments in lieu of them.

Meantime the Caliph's vizier was using all the cunning he possessed to stave off attack as long as possible. At intervals he sent to the Sultan messages so worded as to make him believe that the gates would soon be opened to him, and the Sultan's officers kept receiving secret gifts of money accompanied by warnings that it was contrary to the teachings of Islam to rebel against the Caliph, or to attack Baghdad, which was his abode. To some extent the vizier's propaganda had its effect, but it did not prevent desultory assaults on the city; the most serious being from mangonels that launched missiles against the unwalled side along the river bank. But the advantage gained by this bombardment could never be followed up, the fierce resistance of the besieged making the landing of assault troops impossible.

When this irregular and indecisive warfare had dragged along for about two months, the attackers determined on stronger measures. A bridge was thrown across the river from the west bank to a point above the Seljúq palace, which lay on the east bank north of the defences. Bodies of troops with scaling ladders were sent across the bridge, but with such little effect that after several attempts on the walls the citizens opened their gates in mockery of the Sultan's efforts. He was never able to avail himself seriously of the ironical invitation. By the time he was ready to attack in earnest the diplomatic efforts of the Caliph and his vizier had persuaded Malikshāh and other claimants of the Seljúq throne to move hostile troops against the Sultan's base at Hamadan. On the day when news came to him of the danger nearer home he announced to his troops outside Baghdad that the siege would be raised and departure for Hamadan begun on the morrow. But his men had had enough of warfare and the blazing heat of the Babylonian summer. They broke as soon as the announcement was made, leaving tents, engines of war, food supplies and all else on the ground while they themselves crowded in hundreds on to the bridge that led homewards across the river. There was a high wind blowing at the time. The waves which it raised easily entered the now heavily overladen boats on which the bridge was laid and swamped a number of them, creating a confusion "like the Day of Resurrection".[1] Those in front, seeing what had happened, tried desperately to get back to their base from which they were now cut off, while those behind, eager to get away and unconscious of the disaster, pressed on with gathering impatience at the delay.

It was an opportunity which the men watching from the city walls could not resist. Seeing their late enemies entirely occupied with their own troubles, the Baghdadís rushed out in hundreds to the Seljúq palace, where they fell on the piled-up baggage already waiting for the march and carried off every article. Some of the besiegers had managed to cross the river and they, the Sultan amongst them, hastened along the Khurásán road towards Hamadan; the rest that escaped marched north along the river to Mosul under the city's governor, who had been an ally of the Sultan.[2] It was the end, the last effort which the Seljúq Sultans made to claim Baghdad as their own.[3]

CHAPTER XIII

An Indian Summer

The actual casualties of the siege had not been serious, but it was the cause, direct or indirect, of a plague that broke out almost with the departure of the enemy troops and carried off a fair proportion of the remaining inhabitants. It was followed three years later by high floods which washed away buildings, uncovered graveyards, and caused the collapse of innumerable walls by penetrating the cellars of houses. Perhaps the most serious result of the inundation for the peace of the city was that in every quarter boundaries were obliterated,[1] and, having to be restored by guesswork, were a cause of lasting friction between neighbours, and doubtless also of considerable litigation.

It was found impossible to rebuild everywhere. In some cases, probably, half-abandoned quarters were entirely deserted, while their inhabitants crowded into the more popular districts, thus leaving considerable parts of the city in ruins, to become the haunts of robbers and jackals. But in those quarters that were habitable there must have been a great deal of activity in repair and construction during the following years, for less than ten years afterwards the Jewish traveller Benjamin, of Tudela in Spain, passed through the city and found numerous splendid buildings within the *Ḥarim*, or Royal Precincts,[2] and twenty-eight synagogues "situated", as he says, "either in the city itself or in al-Karkh on the other side of the Tigris". His latter remark is significant as showing that the Karkh quarter had by that time become important enough to give its name to the whole of the western part of Baghdad.

Of the city as a whole Benjamin says that it was twenty miles in circumference and situated in the midst of palm groves and gardens. Amongst its inhabitants were philosophers skilled in every science, and wizards expert in magic of all kinds. Merchants from every land visited it with their goods[1] and pilgrims from distant countries halted there on their way to Mecca, in order to see the face of the Caliph. Amongst the public buildings on the west bank Benjamin mentions a hospital for the sick poor and another building—or perhaps a part of the same institution—in which demented people were kept chained until their reason was restored. The traveller's main concern, however, was with his own people,[2] who had ten academies in the city and whose head, "The Chief of the Captivity", was recognized as prince by all the Jews owing allegiance to the Baghdad Caliphate.

Benjamin's narrative contains a report of the events connected with the false prophet David Alroy, who at one period of his extraordinary career had been a student at one of the Baghdad academies. About A.D. 1160 he appeared at Amadia in Mesopotamia claiming miraculous powers as the destined deliverer of the Jews from the Gentile yoke. His activities attracted immense crowds of followers all over the country, but also drew the unfavourable attention of the authorities, Moslem as well as Jewish. But in spite of threats of physical punishment from the one and of excommunication from the other, his activities continued until his father-in-law murdered him in terror, or, as some say, for a bribe offered by Zayn al-Dín,[1] probably the Begtigínid Atábeg of Arbela who bore that name.[2]

Alroy's followers were not confined to the people of Amadia. According to the account of a contemporary, Samuel ibn 'Abbás,[3] who was a Moslem convert from Judaism, a large section of the Baghdad community was misled by Alroy. Their credulity was turned to account by two impostors who appeared in the city with letters purporting to be from the "prophet" and containing a declaration of the forthcoming deliverance of the people. It was proclaimed further, that on a certain night which was appointed they were all to fly to Jerusalem and that all were to be ready. In anticipation of this exodus a great many women were persuaded to bring money and valuables to the house of the two men for distribution as charity, and at the given time the flat roofs of the Jewish houses in the city were crowded with men, women and children in readiness for flight, much to the astonishment of the Moslem population who heard their excited cries. Morning brought disillusionment, but the year was for long afterwards known as "The Year of the Flying".[4]

Benjamin depicts the high status of the Jewish "Chief of the Captivity" in glowing colours, making a point of the fact that the whole population, of whatever faith, was bidden to pay him honour as he rode through the streets. The effect of the traveller's remarks is somewhat modified by his statement that every new "Chief of the Captivity" on his appointment was made to pay large sums to the Caliph and his ministers; a fact that would appear to be in keeping with what is known of the normal situation of the *Dhimmís*, or "protected peoples", at the time. Typical evidence for the generally inferior status of non-Moslems of the period is to be found in the biography of Hibatulláh Abú 'l-Barakát, a Jewish physician of Baghdad. He had gained such a high reputation for his skill that when one of the Seljúq princes fell ill in Persia, Hibatulláh was summoned from Baghdad to attend to him and after a time returned laden with honours and wealth. A certain haughtiness in his bearing after his return seems to have aroused the resentment of people with whom he had dealings, a feeling that expressed itself in scurrilous lampoons of which one was to the effect that his wanderings abroad were, after all, no more distinguished than the wanderings of his ancestors in the wilderness, and that he was a fool to hold himself so proudly when a dog was more esteemed. The effect of the satire was to make him resolve that he must become a Moslem in order to preserve his professional reputation. His daughters, however, being then grown up, refused to follow him in his change of faith and would as a consequence undoubtedly have forfeited their right to inherit from him if, before openly declaring his conversion, he had not obtained from the Caliph an edict assuring them of the succession to their father's property.[1]

A few years after Benjamin of Tudela, two other travellers followed in his footsteps, the Chinese Chóu

K'ü-feï and the Spanish Moslem Ibn Jubayr, both of whom wrote accounts of their wanderings, in which Baghdad and its inhabitants find an important place. The Chinese voyager found the city a place of wards and streets and "the general mart of the natives of the Western Heaven, the place where the foreign merchants of the Ta-shï assemble". Its inhabitants, he says, are tall and of a fine white complexion "somewhat like the Chinese", they trim their hair and wear embroidered gowns, and their food consists principally of cooked dishes, bread and meat. They do not drink wine. After their meals they wash their hands in bowls full of water. Chóu K'ü-feï's observations would seem to be accurate so far, but it is hard to believe that he is referring to the men of Baghdad when he says that they make use of vessels of gold and silver, helping themselves to the contents with ladles. Such references as we have point to a certain disapproval of gold and silver vessels, and food was as a general use eaten with the fingers.

There is a reference in the narrative to a "king", whose title in Chinese transliteration is given as *Ma-lo-fu*. This has been identified with the Aramaic *Mar-Aba*, a title of the Nestorian patriarch. Of him the narrative says that he went to divine service every seventh day, going to the place of worship from the palace in which he dwelt by an underground tunnel; and that if he went out he rode on horseback and had his face shaded by an umbrella. About the time of Chóu K'ü-feï's visit, or a little while before it (A.D. 1176), the patriarch Elias III was elected and ordained at the ancient seat at Ctesiphon and after his ordination went to take up his residence at Baghdad, about a day's journey to the north. The *Dár al-Rúm*, or "Christian Abode", in which his official residence lay, was amongst the parts of the city that had suffered from the siege and flood, and he set about rebuilding as much of it as possible, including the church and the residence or palace, to which the reference appears to be in the narrative.[1]

As an Arab and a Moslem Ibn Jubayr was naturally far more interested than the Chinese traveller in the city of the Caliphs though he also appears to have been very critical of it. He had been on a pilgrimage to Mecca and came to Baghdad via Hilla on the Euphrates. Between the two cities the road ran amongst prosperous villages with wide-stretching tracts of cultivated land, and the month being May A.H. 580 (A.D. 1184), the fields were covered with green, over which the eye ranged with delight. At one point of the journey he came in sight of the towering ruins of Ctesiphon which turned his thoughts in anticipation towards Baghdad, a day's journey away. "We had heard", he says, "that the air of Baghdad creates gladness in the heart, and gives ease and joy to the soul, and that you could scarcely find anyone there who was not gay and lively; even a stranger far from home".[2] He found reason for disappointment on his arrival the next day. True it was still the seat of the Caliph, but most of its impressiveness, he thought, had departed, and nothing remained but the glory of its name. For him it had no beauty to tempt his eye to linger except the Tigris, which ran "like a polished mirror"—a fanciful picture, if it be remembered that the Tigris in May is generally a turbid, muddy stream, considerably swollen by the melting snows of the Armenian mountains. For the ordinary inhabitants of the city he has nothing but contempt:

> You will find scarcely one of them who does not hypocritically fain humility, though internally he is full of pride and arrogance. They despise foreigners and display haughtiness and scorn towards those lower in station than themselves....Everyone of them in his own mind and imagination pictures entire creation as but a small thing compared with his own city. They hold in esteem no abode in the whole of the inhabited world but their own, as though they refused to believe that Allah had any countries or worshippers besides themselves. They trail their skirts frivolously and carelessly...thinking it the most sublime form of pride to trail their robes....Amongst themselves they sell loans for gold, and not one of them gives a good loan unto Allah. There is no obtaining of necessities in Baghdad except for money, even though you are compelled to borrow it; and you will spend it in the shop of a man who gives you short weight....The foreigner amongst them is given no hospitality; his expenditure doubled, he has to bargain for his keep....The ill nature of its inhabitants has spread to its climate and invalidates anything good that may be heard of it by tradition and report.[1]

The town's character for meanness is satirized by a younger contemporary of Ibn Jubayr, the poet Ibn al-Ta'áwídhí, who had long been domiciled in Baghdad and spoke with more extended experience behind him. In one of his satires he says:

> O thou whose goal is Baghdad, turn aside from a city in which wrong is at full tide and overflowing.
>
> If thou comest to satisfy a need, return; for its doors are closed against all that have hopes.

The days are no more—how far off that time!—when seekers (of knowledge) filled its dwellings, and the chiefs of its nobility dwelt in it.[1]

The traveller's contempt seems to have been reserved especially for the general mass of the citizens. As a man of learning, however, he was very appreciative of the scholarly qualities of the professors at the Niẓámiya *madrasa*, which, as we have seen, he visited on more than one occasion. He also attended other lectures and describes one of a series of sermons given every Thursday morning near the Badr Gate, which opened on to the great square in front of the royal palaces. From a raised belvedere that formed part of the women's quarters in one of the palaces, the Caliph with his mother and other women sat to listen to the lecture, which was open to all comers. When the gates were opened the great square rapidly filled with people who squatted waiting for the discourse to begin. The lecturer mounted the rostrum, and when he had removed his hooded gown from his head as a sign of respect for the place in which he stood, the Koran readers, seated on stools in rows in front of him, read a number of verses, after which he pronounced a eulogy on the Caliph and his mother, entitling her "The Most Noble Veil" and "The Most Compassionate Presence". The main part of the proceedings was a sermon, which drew tears from the audience and did not leave the preacher himself unaffected.[2]

In describing the city, Ibn Jubayr remarks on the ruin that had overtaken a great part of West Baghdad, which nevertheless still had seventeen populated quarters, each one a town in itself, possessing two or three public baths and as many as eight having Friday mosques. There were two bridges joining the two sides of the city, but the traffic between the two banks necessitated in addition the employment of innumerable boats that passed constantly back and forth, day and night. Pleasure boats added to the number, amongst them that of the Caliph, who was occasionally to be seen in a boat on the river.[1]

Most of the bazaars, crowded and busy, were on the east bank, where also lay three of the most important city mosques; the Caliph's adjacent to his palace, the Sultan's situated outside the walls and attached to the "Sultan's Palace", and the Ruṣáfa mosque, about a mile north of the Sultan's mosque. Numerous public baths were to be found in the city, most of them with walls covered with shining bitumen that looked to the beholder like black marble. Nearly thirty schools also graced the city, all of them, says Ibn Jubayr, on the east bank,[2] and all richly endowed with funds for payment of teachers' salaries and for maintenance grants for students. Amongst these institutions the Niẓámiya *madrasa* was supreme, being specially favoured by the Caliph Náṣir, who in A.H. 589 (A.D. 1193) built for it a library that he filled with thousands of valuable books.[3]

Such were some of the external indications of a renaissance at Baghdad. They were emphasized by a temporary increase in the regard shown to the Caliphate. In A.H. 567 (A.D. 1171) for example, the victorious Saladin, whilst in Cairo, deleted the name of the last

Fáṭimid Caliph, al-'Āḍid, from the *khuṭba* and substituted that of the Abbasid Caliph al-Mustaḍí. To celebrate this honour paid to their ruler, the inhabitants of Baghdad crowded into their decorated and illuminated streets and proclaimed their happiness with loud rejoicings.[1]

Eight years later, in the year of the accession of the Caliph Náṣir, the city was again decorated, and drums were beaten in joy at Saladin's overthrow and capture of the infidel lords of Ramleh and Tiberias.[2] In the same year also, an envoy from Saladin, accompanied by twelve Frankish prisoners in helmets and full armour and bearing lances and shields were seen in the city. Of these latter, one belonged to the king of the Franks and some of the lances had been captured from the Frankish "bishop". Amongst other gifts brought was "an image in stone, two cubits high and of exquisite workmanship, the sculptor having so contrived the lips that they smiled marvellously".[3]

Mustaḍí's son Náṣir, whose Shí'ite feelings[4] and jealousy for his own prestige would not let him be entirely friendly with the overthrower of the Fáṭimid Caliphate, almost forfeited the conqueror's loyalty when in A.H. 579 (A.D. 1183) he accused him of wrongly appropriating revenues that belonged to the Abbasid Caliphate, and of putting a slight on it in sending by the hand of a base-born Baghdadí the announcement of the fall of Edessa.[5] Somehow or other the danger of a break was averted, for four years later Saladin sent part of the booty of the battle of Ḥaṭṭín to Baghdad as tribute. It consisted of a great cross of bronze overlaid with gold and was said by tradition to have been the true cross.[1] This the Caliph Náṣir buried at the threshold of the *Báb al-Naubí*, "the Sentry's Gate", one of the gates of the Royal Precincts, leaving just enough exposed so that everyone that passed could trample and spit upon it.[2] It is very curious that only a few years later the practice arose of kissing this threshold which was now being defiled. When the Niẓám al-Dín ibn Sam'ání was sent by the Khwarizmsháh 'Alá al-Dín Muḥammad as an envoy to Baghdad he was made to alight at the Sentry's Gate and, in spite of his protests, was compelled to kiss the threshold. Similarly Abú 'l Hijá al-Samín and numbers of other men of all ranks of life were compelled to honour the threshold.[3]

The death of Saladin in A.H. 589 (A.D. 1193) was announced publicly in Baghdad[4] and the messenger who brought the news marched through the streets of the city with the coat of mail and the charger which, with a sum of money amounting in value to less than fifteen shillings, was all the property that the champion of Islam left for his heirs.[5]

In Persia as in the West, Náṣir's ambitions were flattered. In A.H. 590 (A.D. 1194) Tughril Sháh, the last of the Seljúqs, made a show of marching on Baghdad, and actually, to the consternation of the inhabitants, defeated an army sent out under the command of the vizier to meet him. However, the Khwarizmsháh 'Alá al-Dín Muḥammad, then in the full career of conquest, defeated the Seljúq in battle at Rayy, and having cut off his head, sent it stuck on a spear to

Baghdad, where it was exposed in front of the main gate of the royal palace.[1] At the same time the Khwarizm-sháh sent to Náṣir demanding recognition as Sultan and ordering the repair of the old Baghdad Palace of the Sultanate in which he proposed to live. In a fury at this piece of presumption and in spite of the Khwarizm-sháh's threat that he would march on Baghdad if his wishes were disregarded, Náṣir ordered the building to be demolished and every trace of it to be removed.[2] The Caliph's courage was justified, for the Mongols, the common destroyers both of Khwarizm and of Baghdad, descended on the Khwarizmian kings before ever they reached the city on the Tigris.

It was to be expected that the religious views of his subjects would not escape Náṣir's attentions. During his reign, probably in A.H. 588 (A.D. 1192),[3] the learned physician 'Abd al-Salám of Baghdad was accused by jealous rivals of being addicted to philosophy and of being so interested in the stars as to make it certain he was a star-worshipper and hence atheistical. Both he and his works were by Náṣir's orders examined, and being found unsatisfactory, the books were condemned to be burnt and carried out to one of the open spaces of the city. The sentence was carried out with great ceremony. A pulpit had been erected for the preacher, al-Máristání, who ascended it to deliver an oration, in the course of which he cursed all who had any dealings with philosophy, making particular reference to 'Abd al-Salám. He discoursed on each book separately, and, having denounced it, tore it across and threw it into the flames.[4] The Jewish *savant* and merchant Yúsuf al-Sabtí, who was a friend of the philosopher Maimonides, happened to be in Baghdad at the time on a business venture and afterwards told the biographer al-Qiftí what he had seen:

> "I went to the assembly", said he, "and heard the speech of Ibn al-Máristání. In his hand I saw Ibn al-Haitham's[1] book on astronomy in which he was pointing to a circle representing the heavens, and I heard him talk of it as a mighty calamity and an unspeakable disaster; a blank misfortune. He then tore it across and threw it into the fire. It was proof to me of his ignorance and fanaticism, for there is no irreligion in astronomy, on the contrary it is a pathway to faith and to knowledge of the omnipotence of God—in what he has ordained and established."

Al-Qiftí adds that 'Abd al-Salám was put into prison and remained there until A.H. 589 (A.D. 1193).[2]

During his reign of forty-five years (A.D. 1180–1225), a longer period of rule than that of any other Caliph, Náṣir had ample opportunity for imposing his will on the capital. Added to his Shí'ism as a potential danger to the peace of the community was his mania for spying, which made him, like another Hárún al-Rashíd, wander about the streets of the city at night and place his agents and informers in private houses and public meeting-places where they were least to be expected. Where his own pleasures were concerned he interfered without scruple in the affairs of his subjects, so that, for example, none but members of his own family were permitted to follow his special hobbies of pigeon-flying and shooting bullets with the crossbow. One independently-minded citizen, who refused to give up his shooting, was at last compelled to flee to Damascus to escape the sovereign's vengeance.

Consistently with this side of his character, Náṣir insisted that his sorrows must be shared by the citizens of his capital. When his mother, Zumurud Khátún, died in A.H. 599 (A.D. 1203), he ordered that the coffin—a very heavy one—should be carried all the way from the Qurayya quarter on the river bank to the burial ground at the tomb of Ma'rúf Karkhí, and that the mourners were to accompany it. The distance on foot was considerable and the day was hot, with the result that a number of the older persons in the procession collapsed on the roadside.[1] Again, fourteen years later, when his younger and favourite son died, the Caliph imposed his grief on the whole community. The bazaars were locked and trade was brought to a standstill, while the streets were covered with reed mats and ashes in token of mourning. In every quarter of the city the women were ordered to dress in the garments of sorrow and with loosened hair to appear in the streets beating their faces and breasts.[2]

Náṣir took particular interest in a certain society of notables of which there is mention in the annals of the day. It apparently had existed in Baghdad and the country generally for a considerable period, and seems to have been a sworn brotherhood of men of birth and distinction equivalent to an order of knighthood or perhaps a political association. Membership was coveted and was betokened by the wearing of special breeches and other garments of a distinctive pattern. Consequent on the indiscriminate awarding of such tokens of membership and the wholesale appointment of members, a jealous quarrel broke out at Baghdad. Swords were drawn and used, and the affair attracted the attention of Náṣir, who, in A.H. 604 (A.D. 1207–8), abolished the order as it stood and formulated an edict reconstructing it. Henceforward the Caliph was to be the source, origin and final arbiter of the order of *futuwwa* ("chivalry"), as it was called, of which every member had to obtain Náṣir's approval before being admitted. Amongst those excluded from membership were all criminals and in particular those who had committed murder or harboured a murderer. Those who were elected were enjoined to uphold the right and eschew the wrong. Finally the Caliph alone was to be empowered to present the garments of honour.[1] References to the order are scanty, but it may be presumed that it was destroyed with the Caliphate itself at the sack of Baghdad.

The Caliph resembled more than one of his ancestors in combining a grasping miserliness of character, which led him to fleece his subjects, with a mania for lavish building that displayed itself in bursts of constructive activity. In addition to the library of the Niẓámiya *madrasa*, in A.H. 589 (A.D. 1193) there was built the Ṭáhirid Palace of the Royal Precincts, and work was begun on a number of institutions in which the poor of each quarter might find food provided during the Fast of Ramaḍán, and in which pilgrims going to Mecca could be entertained. These institutions however were very short-lived and were pulled down or allowed to fall into ruin with the same absence of reason that led to their construction. Apart from such temporary structures, a number of city buildings suffered, not only from the perishable nature of the materials employed, but also from fire and flood. The library of the Niẓámiya *madrasa* was threatened more than once and its books only saved by the efforts of the students and staff. In A.H. 590 (A.D. 1194) a great flood washed away the walls of the old city of Manṣúr that were still standing, and in A.H. 601 (A.D. 1205) fire broke out in the Caliph's armoury, in which great numbers of weapons of war, as well as the bulk of his treasure, were stored. Every *saqqá* (water carrier), servant and workman in the neighbourhood was summoned to attack the flames, but even then enormous damage was done.[1] The city's recuperative powers were unable to keep pace with these destructive forces, and several more quarters relapsed into their original desert condition and became the haunts of wild animals. Both in A.H. 601 (A.D. 1205) and in A.H. 614 (A.D. 1217) there are reports that lions were killed in the Báb al-Azaj quarter and that fierce quarrels broke out when the inhabitants of the neighbouring Ma'múniya quarter refused to allow the subsequent triumphal processions to pass through their streets.[2]

CHAPTER XIV

City Ideals and Accomplishments

It may not be out of place here, before dealing with the catastrophe that removed Baghdad for centuries from amongst the cultural centres of Islam, to consider what view of life was held by those citizens who gave any thought to the matter at all, and to examine what ideal was set up by those interested in the less material requirements of existence. With regard to the outward conduct of life we have to some extent seen already what was regarded as normal and respectable, but this may be further illustrated by an examination of the lives of some citizens who were looked upon as queer and out of the ordinary. The descriptions of some Baghdad "characters" produced by Náṣir's long reign provide this further illustration. Even though the descriptions themselves may be apocryphal—but there is no real reason for doubting their authenticity—they may show by contrast what was regarded as everyday and usual, and incidentally prove that the Baghdadí leavened his normal seriousness with a considerable fund of humour.

An instance of the general run of humour is provided by the incident of a visit to Baghdad from an envoy from Persia. This ambassador, Abú 'l-Hijá al-Samín ("the Fat"), who has already been mentioned in another connection,[1] was met as he approached the city by a great crowd of notables and ordinary sightseers who surrounded his cavalcade and escorted it towards the city gates. In the mob was a potter, whose attention was caught by the visitor's comical figure. It was not merely that he was fat—obesity was common in a city where haste was regarded as of the devil[1]—but this visitor had a small head set on his broad shoulders and a huge paunch that covered the withers of the mule he was riding. The craftsman at once raced back to his alcove in the bazaar, and by the time the distinguished ambassador was passing, a large pot caricaturing him was hanging up full in his view. The joke pleased him and caught the fancy of the city, and for a time "Abú 'l-Hijá al-Samín" jars were to be found in every house.[2]

The fanaticism which characterized religion in the city in its less prosperous days led, as we have seen, to endless troubles. It made for hypocrisy and was not conducive to conversion, even though it might be only from one Sunní sect to another; and converts were inevitably regarded with suspicion. In A.H. 599 (A.D. 1203) there died al-Wajíh, who at the time of his death was a professor at the Niẓámiya *madrasa*. The fact indicates that he belonged to the Sháfi'í sect, but he had begun life as a Ḥanbalí and then, after an injury—real or imagined—from the members of his own sect, had joined the Ḥanafís. They too failed to please him, so that lastly he acquired membership of the community in which he died. An epigram written at his death throws very considerable suspicion on the honesty of al-Wajíh's motives for his various changes of belief, and implies—though without the delicate irony of the ode on the Vicar of Bray—that only death prevented his seeing what could be gained from all four Sunní sects.[1]

A far more interesting and important personage, who died in A.H. 602 (A.D. 1206), was Tashtigín ibn 'Abdulláh, a venerable traveller who had twenty-six times been the leader of the pilgrim train to Mecca and had been accustomed on these journeys to exercise the prerogatives of kings. On one occasion he suffered imprisonment, on a charge by the vizier Ibn Yúnus that he had been in friendly correspondence with Saladin, at a period when that warrior was out of favour with the Caliph. However, the charge was proved false and he was released. In the city he bore a character for great courage and haughtiness which was combined with a taciturnity that for a week together would prevent his uttering a word. It once drew the rebuke from a visitor that even Allah spoke to Moses. When he was past ninety years of age Tashtigín took a three hundred years' lease—the fact that this was possible may be noted in passing—of a piece of land on the Tigris bank for the purpose of building a house, and a professional storyteller went about the city carrying the good tidings that the Angel of Death was dead.[2]

So far as the religious beliefs of the city were concerned, the numerous occasions on which the annalists report fanatical outbreaks on the part of the citizens make the conclusion inevitable that the mass of the population was thoroughly unenlightened. That its bigotry was due to ignorance may be assumed for the plebs, but those higher in the social scale were often in no better case. Ibn al-Jawzí, during one Sunní-Shí'a riot, was asked to decide which of the two parties was in the right. The question was put to him in the common form of "Who is the best of men after Mohammed?" When he oracularly replied: "He whose daughter married the other", neither side was capable of probing the answer and discovering its ambiguity. Possibly neither side wished to inquire too closely into the meaning of the reply, in the desire that the great mufti's authority should be favourable to themselves. However that may be, the Sunnís interpreted his answer as meaning the Caliph Abú Bekr, their own hero, whose daughter 'Ā'isha married the Prophet Mohammed, while the Shí'a insisted he meant their own idol 'Alí, who married the Prophet's daughter Fáṭima.[1]

That there was, of course, a more enlightened condition amongst some of the citizens is clear from the literature of the period and from the existence of the numerous schools in the city. It may be assumed also that the higher standard of religious instruction was not entirely confined to the men whose profession was learning, and the fact that some citizens had ideals of their own concerning the things of the mind may perhaps be shown from the *Arabian Nights'* story of the debate between the slave girl Tawaddud and the *savants*. It would be difficult to date the story exactly, and though it is almost certainly later than the reign of Hárún al-Rashíd it may well be of Baghdad composition, from the stress laid in it upon the Sháfi'í doctrines.[2]

In an introductory part of the story the girl is asked in what branches of knowledge she excels; she replies: "I have knowledge of grammar, poetry, ecclesiastical law, interpretation of the Koran, and the meanings of words. Also I am acquainted with music, with the science of the laws of inheritance [a very complicated system of calculations] with reckoning and division and measuring, and with the legends of the ancients". Further she claims a very complete knowledge of the Koran with all its divisions and liturgical uses, and also knows which chapters were revealed at Medina and which at Mecca, and also which chapters abrogate others. Also she knows the *ḥadíth*, the vast body of traditions of the Prophet together with the indispensable chains of supporting authorities. The learned maiden then proceeds to number amongst her accomplishments an acquaintance with mathematics, geometry, philosophy, logic and the various branches of rhetoric. Moreover, not content with the theory of music, she asserts she is able to play the lute and to sing.

The Caliph is astounded that one so young should be so skilled in the arts and sciences, and demands she shall prove her claims before a committee of *savants*, consisting of readers of the Koran, men learned in the law, physicians, astronomers, philosophers and mathematicians. When all are assembled before the Caliph the girl is seated in a golden chair and the examination begins.

In reply to various questions concerning religious beliefs and duties she says that Allah is her lord and Mohammed her prophet; the Koran is her guide and the *ka'ba* at Mecca the object towards which she turns in prayer; all believers are her brethren; the good is her path; and the Prophet's practice her way of life. Her

[Photo: Hasso Bros. Baghdad

KAẒIMAIN MOSQUE

knowledge of Allah comes to her through the intellect, which is of two kinds: the one innate and the other acquired by training; its seat is in the first place the heart, where Allah deposits it; thence it ascends to the brain. The prime duties of her faith are to affirm that there is no god but Allah, to testify that Mohammed is his apostle, to pray, to give alms, to fast, to make the Mecca pilgrimage, to fight in the holy war and to avoid the unlawful. "Prayerful intent adds strength to Allah's worship"; so that preparation for worship demands the acts of purification, veiling the secret parts, rejection of defiled garments, standing in a pure place, facing the *qibla* (i.e. in the direction of Mecca), turning the heart to God, devotion, and glorification of the holy. Prayer itself is communion between the servant and his Master, and it has twelve (*sic*) qualities: it illumines the heart, gives light to the countenance, placates the Compassionate, enrages Satan, wards off calamity, prevents harm from foes, increases mercy, brings the servant nigh to his master and forbids what is wicked and unlawful.

The answers given to questions on general knowledge may also be regarded as representing the stage of science that had been reached in the centres of Arab learning in the twelfth century. Man is the microcosm, in whose various parts is to be found earth from the *ka'ba*, the east and the west, and who is compounded of the four elements of water, earth, fire and air. These elements correspond further to the four humours in him, phlegm, black bile, yellow bile and blood. Anatomically and physiologically man is made up of 360 veins,

240 bones and the three spirits, the vital, the animal and the natural, in addition to all the other organs, duly enumerated, in the right proportions. Also there are the five senses and the corresponding organs. The heart is in the left part of the chest, with the stomach in front of it, while the lungs are ventilators to the heart. In the head are five faculties called the "hidden sense-organs", which are the faculty of imagination, the fancy, the will, the faculty of conception and the faculty of retention.

With regard to disease, which is recognized by six rules derived from observation of various symptoms, the aphorism of the Prophet is held to be valid that "abstention from harmful food is the principle of all healing". Food is best prepared by women; if a tradition of the Prophet is followed, the food should consist of bread soaked in broth, though mutton is also regarded with favour. Salt meat should be avoided as having no virtue in it.

The best wine is that which has stood for eighty days or more and been pressed out of white grapes; "but", the girl adds as an afterthought, "it does not equal water, like which there is nothing on earth". The pomegranate and the citron are the best fruits, the endive the best vegetable, while the best scents are those of roses and violets.

In the realm of astronomy the girl shows acquaintance with twenty-eight stations of the moon, which are equivalent to the twelve divisions of the zodiac; she knows which the seven planets are:—namely Sun, Moon, Mercury, Venus, Mars, Jupiter and Saturn—and what their astrological qualities are, as well as the length of their occupation of each division of the zodiac.

For the rest, the knowledge shown on many points is bounded by the reported sayings of the prophet on them; but on the whole the standard is a high one. Even so it may fairly be applied to the attainments of a citizen of Baghdad in the twelfth century.

CHAPTER XV

The Downfall of the City

With the death of Náṣir the office of the Caliphate declined rapidly, till its end came at the fall of Baghdad to the Mongol hordes under Húlágú in A.D. 1258. Though the utter feebleness of Náṣir's successors was probably not worse than the condition of the Caliphs under the Buwayhids and the Seljúqs, yet the temporary access of strength under Náṣir made that weakness seem all the more pronounced. *Al-Fakhrí* emphasizes the point when speaking of a revolt against the Caliph Mustanṣir at Irbíl (the ancient Arbela), an unimportant town lying between the Greater and Lesser Zab rivers. An army was sent against the place and succeeded in reducing it, though only after a siege. News of this victory was sent by pigeon-post to Baghdad, where the information was received with great joy. "Now mark (the condition of) an empire", says the author, "in which such a trifle is posted on the emperor's gates as good news and the capital is decorated because of the fall of the citadel of Irbíl which is to-day one of the meanest and smallest of townships."[1]

Some faint flickers of the old life and spirit were visible on rare occasions, as when the Caliph Mustanṣir showed himself a true member of his line by building schools and hospitals for the citizens of Baghdad as well as places of shelter for travellers arriving in the city, who were there housed and fed at the public expense. He excelled himself in A.H. 631 (A.D. 1234) when he built a great new *madrasa* (the Mustanṣiriya) to eclipse the Niẓámiya which, after two centuries, was still in full activity. Special interest attaches to the new institution because its remains are still extant after a long and chequered career; in the sixteenth century as a retreat for brigands[1] and in more modern times partly as a busy café[2] and partly as a customs house. As for the position of the building in relationship to other well-known structures, it is probable that it stood just downstream of the Niẓámiya *madrasa*, and almost certainly it was included within the area of the palace enclosure, being "near the House of the Caliphate".[3]

Unlike the Niẓámiya, the Mustanṣiriya *madrasa* provided instruction in the doctrines and legal codes of all four Sunní sects. Two only of the chairs, those of the Sháfi'í and Ḥanafí codes are said to have been allotted to professors, while those of the Ḥanbalís and the Málikís were represented by assistant professors.[4] In addition it had a professor for the faculty of *ḥadíth* or traditions of the Prophet, and also a physician, whose duties were not only to attend to the health of the students, but to teach medicine; the porch in which the sick congregated also acting as a medical school. Generally, the number of students at the *madrasa* is reckoned as three hundred, divided equally amongst the four schools; but the figures are variously given.

A minaret in the modern *maḥalla* of Súq al-Ghazl, the old "Thread Bazaar", marks the remains of the mosque once known as the Jámi' al-Qaṣr, "The Palace

Mosque". This building, which was probably put up by the Caliph al-Muttaqí, was restored by Mustanṣir, who gave it an official connection with his *madrasa* by placing in it four benches, on which the students could sit and hold discussions after the prayers were over.[1]

The person who is said to have had charge of the building of the *madrasa*, Mu'ayyad al-Dín Ibn al-'Alqamí,[2] played a large part in the subsequent history of his city. Although he was a Shí'ite he became the vizier of the last Abbasid Caliph al-Musta'ṣim, a monarch whose taste for books and learning went with an utter incapacity for statesmanship. It so happened that at the end of the summer of the year A.H. 654 (A.D. 1256) a tremendous inundation swept over Baghdad and submerged even the upper stories of houses. During the confusion that was caused, gangs composed of the scum of the city went about plundering and robbing. At their head, rumour went, was the Dawátdár or Chancellor, Mujáhidu 'l-Dín Aybak, who saw in the sudden access of power which this brought him a chance of deposing the weakling Caliph and putting another Abbasid in his place. The rumour reached Ibn al-'Alqamí who warned al-Musta'ṣim. The Caliph summoned the Dawátdár, but that official, after denying the whole affair, in his turn accused Ibn al-'Alqamí of intriguing with the Mongols. In spite of the fact that, as subsequent disorders indicated, there was some foundation for Ibn al-'Alqamí's story, the Caliph decided to believe the Dawátdár.[3] Facts not in our possession may have led the sovereign to decide as he did, but more probably it was his dislike for his vizier's religious beliefs, for at that time the ancient antagonism between Sunní and Shí'a in the city was in a state of lively activity, and the Sunnites were accused by the vizier and others of having gone to the length of carrying off Shí'a women and children. The feud continued to rage even when Húlágú Khán, the Mongol conqueror, after putting an end to the power of the Isma'ílí Assassins in Persia marched down the great Khurásán highway towards Baghdad.

On the way, in September A.D. 1257, Húlágú sent an ultimatum to the Caliph bidding him surrender himself and demolish the outer wall of his capital. His evasive reply did not satisfy the conqueror, who ordered a Mongol army, then operating in Asia Minor under the general Bayjú, to march down on Baghdad. Bayjú advanced so as to attack the city on the west bank, while Húlágú himself was to come upon it from the east. The Caliph, as was intended, saw only the more immediate danger threatening from Húlágú, then on the Ḥulwán river. Against him, on his leisurely march down the Khurásán highway, was despatched a body of troops under the once suspect Dawátdár Aybak, but they had not advanced far beyond Bájisrá—scarcely a quarter of the way—when urgent messages came recalling them to oppose Bayjú's army, which had arrived unexpectedly at the 'Ísá canal, within striking distance of Baghdad. By a *détour* that involved a forced march, the Mongol army on the west bank had been able to cut off the royal force from its base, and by destroying dykes behind them, the invaders flooded the country and so hampered both pursuit and retreat.

Very great losses were inflicted on the army floundering helplessly in the mire and only the Dawátdár, with comparatively few men, was able to reach Baghdad in safety. On January 23rd, A.D. 1258, Bayjú occupied some of the quarters along the river on the west side of the city, including that in which the great 'Aḍudí hospital stood. It was not until some days afterwards that Húlágú arrived outside the walls on the east bank, where he built a fortified camp. Then the attack began, on all sides at once; the Mongol troops swarming like ants or locusts about the walls. In the sector commanded by Húlágú the mangonels made a break in the "Burji 'Ajamí" or Persian Tower, and the Caliph, in a futile effort to save further destruction, sent out his vizier Ibn al-'Alqamí in the company of the Nestorian Catholicos Makíkha to ask for terms. The Mongol commander however refused to receive them, and as they returned they were followed into the city by a flight of arrows bearing messages that cadis, merchants, 'Alids and others who might be disaffected towards the Caliph or who had not borne arms against the besiegers would be assured of their lives. The attack meanwhile continued without intermission for six days. Stones for the mangonels had to be brought from the Jebel Hamrín nearly eighty miles away, and, when they ran short, palm trees were cut down and the trunks hurled into the city.

On February 2nd the Burji 'Ajamí collapsed, but for three days the breach was defended so well that no entry was made. As soon as the defence weakened, however, the Mongols swarmed in, occupied the outlying quarters of the city and cleared the walls of the Caliph's troops. To make escape impossible by water, barriers were thrown across the river, and those who made efforts to flee by that way—amongst them the Dawátdár—were forced to return to the horrors of the siege. Some of the inner quarters still held out, and from them the Caliph again attempted to open negotiations, but both his gifts and his appeals for clemency were rejected with contempt. Such of the defending troops as deserted to obtain better terms for themselves were slaughtered without mercy; others who remained in the city hid themselves in holes in the ground and in the furnaces of the public baths, hoping to escape the inevitable massacre.

During a lull in the attack a number of the principal citizens came out to ask for an amnesty, telling the besieger that most of the inhabitants were eager to surrender, and asking for a truce while the Caliph and his son came out to the Mongol camp. The Mongol historian, Rashíd al-Dín, says that the conference might possibly have succeeded if, during its progress, an arrow from the city had not hit the Sultan's secretary in the eye. This incident seems merely to have been made an excuse for the savagery that followed, for it can scarcely be believed that Húlágú had not long before made up his mind to punish the city for its resistance.

When the fresh assault that followed on the west side reduced the Báb al-Baṣra quarter, where the Háshimites, the Caliph's kinsfolk, lived, the Caliph himself surrendered with three thousand cadis, shaikhs and principal officers of the city and State. Húlágú received them without any show of anger, and asked the Caliph to order his followers to lay down their arms. This they did and they were killed to a man, without mercy. Their slaying was followed in the city by a massacre of a most inhuman description. Even allowing for the exaggeration of annalists whose purpose was to create hatred of the infidel Mongols, it is clear that in the sheer lust of killing, the besiegers wiped out the majority of the inhabitants. The pestilential odours from the corpses lying unburied in the streets compelled Húlágú after a few days to leave a city that he would have been glad to ransack more thoroughly than he did.[1]

Though the Mongol conqueror professed no religious beliefs, his wife was a Christian.[2] It was probably for this reason that the Caliph had sent the Catholicos to be one of his emissaries to Húlágú, and that the Christians who had gathered in the Nestorian church—presumably the one in the Dár al-Rúm—at the invitation of the patriarch, found immunity from the general slaughter and plundering.[3] Húlágú further showed his favour to this patriarch (Makíkha II) by giving him the royal house known as the "Dawídár's (or Dawátdár's) Palace" to be turned into a church and a residence for himself, so that he was able later to live in great splendour.[4] According to the statement of one Christian authority, Mar Amr, the building lay on the Tigris bank, and this seems probable for the site of a royal palace. Another authority, Mar Jabalaha, says it was near the mosque built by the Caliph Muktafí "in his palace"[5]; which may or may not confirm the other statement. At any rate, all trace of a Christian church on the river bank has been lost.

In spite of his favourable treatment of the Christians and his unutterable cruelty towards the Moslems, Húlágú appears to have been not entirely indifferent to Moslem opinion. If *al-Fakhrí* is to be believed, he assembled in the Mustanṣiriya *madrasa* all the *'ulamá* who survived in the city after its fall and asked for their considered opinion on the question whether an unbelieving but just Sultan was inferior to a Moslem prince who was tyrannous and extortionate. The answer was given in favour of the former, though the doctors hesitated long about committing it to writing.[1]

Though he knew nothing about them, the conqueror had a great regard for the sciences[2] and for that reason spared the *madrasas* in the city. Even so their endowments were confiscated[3] and their libraries plundered.[4] Three-quarters of a century after the sack of the city the travellers Ḥamdulláh Mustawfí and Ibn Batúta found the two most important of such institutions in an excellent state of repair and apparently in normal working order. Yet it is significant that where the pages of the older biographers are filled with references to the men who had studied at Baghdad, those of the newer ones very seldom mention a man who visited its schools after the invasion. For those who grew up after the fall of Baghdad the centres of learning were Damascus, Aleppo or Cairo, and only very rarely are persons of any distinction mentioned as having been students in the old Abbasid capital.

On the whole, and apart from the dilapidations due to the siege engines, the damage deliberately wrought was not as great as is generally implied by the Moslem writers. The Caliph's own palace was not destroyed, and an inventory was made of all its contents which were carried off. Such buildings, however, as the Caliph's mosque and the shrine of Músá 'l-Jawád at Kaẓimain, which the Moslem population treated with especial reverence, were purposely dismantled out of revenge for the city's resistance. Yet this damage too was very shortly afterwards put right by a company of 3000 men under the command of two Mongol officers who were bidden to repair the main buildings and restore order in the city. Many of the city's artisans and tradesmen had escaped slaughter, and having nowhere else to go they had remained in their own houses or in such others as they could find habitable and unoccupied. Under the orders of Ibn al-'Alqamí, who had been sent to take over the administration of the city, as fast as they could they removed the corpses from the streets, rebuilt the bazaars and resumed normal life.[1]

Less than forty years after the catastrophe the author of the *Ta'ríkhi Waṣṣáf* visited the city, and though it had been reduced to a tenth of what it had once been, yet, in comparison with other well-known cities which had suffered in the same way under the Mongols, it was a paradise of ease and security, and its inhabitants were care-free and prosperous.[2] This condition of affairs lasted into the middle of the fourteenth century, when bitter struggles between rival Mongol chieftains—and afterwards between Persia and Turkey—for possession of the once-famous city extinguished almost all the life in it and left it moribund, until the events of recent years once again made it the capital of a kingdom.

NOTES

Page 6, note 1. *Kitáb al-Buldán*, ed. de Goeje, p. 235.
p. 6, n. 2. Yáqút, *Mu'jam al-Buldán*, ed. Wuestenfeld, I, 680.
p. 7, n. 1. D'Herbelot, *Bibliothèque orientale*, s.v. "Bagdad".
p. 8, n. 1. See al-Sharíshí's commentary on the thirteenth *maqáma* of Ḥaríri.
p. 12, n. 1. Ṭabarí, I, 2203 ff.
p. 16, n. 1. *Al-Fakhrí*, ed. Ahlwardt, pp. 190 f.
p. 16, n. 2. *Op. cit.* III, 274.
p. 18, n. 1. History of Baghdad, ed. G. Salmon, p. 1.
p. 18, n. 2. *Op. cit.* III, 276.
p. 19, n. 1. De Slane's translation of Ibn Khallikán († A.D. 1282), III, 555 ff.
p. 21, n. 1. Ṭabarí, III, 320.
p. 21, n. 2. *Op. cit.* III, 321.
p. 25, n. 1. Ed. G. Salmon, p. 11.
p. 25, n. 2. *Mu'jam al-Buldán*, ed. Wuestenfeld, I, 683.
p. 27, n. 1. See further von Kremer, *Culturgeschichte des Orients*, II, 172 ff.
p. 28, n. 1. Caussin de Perceval, "Notices anecdotiques sur les principaux musiciens arabes", *Journal Asiatique*, 1873, pp. 514 ff.
p. 29, n. 1. *Kitáb al-Aghání*, XVIII, 148.
p. 33, n. 1. A. Müller, *Der Islam*, I, 472 f.
p. 34, n. 1. Caussin de Perceval, *op. cit.* pp. 524 f.
p. 37, n. 1. *Al-Fakhrí*, ed. Ahlwardt, pp. 220 ff.
p. 38, n. 1. Ibn Khallikán, tr. de Slane, I, 202 f.
p. 39, n. 1. *Ibid.* I, 538, s.v. "Abu Dulláma".
p. 44, n. 1. Burton, Introduction to the *Arabian Nights*.
p. 44, n. 2. Von Kremer, *Culturgeschichte*, II, 59.
p. 50, n. 1. *Aghání*, VI, 77–81 [abridged], tr. by Caussin de Perceval, *op. cit.* pp. 529 ff.
p. 50, n. 2. C. de Perceval, *op. cit.* p. 543.
p. 58, n. 1. *Op. cit.* I, 310.
p. 59, n. 1. Ibn Khallikán, tr. de Slane, II, 107.
p. 60, n. 1. Von Kremer, *Streifzüge*, p. 43.
p. 60, n. 2. Abú 'l-'Atáhiya, *Díwán* (Beyrút, 1886), Introduction, p. 12.
p. 62, n. 1. Ibn Khallikán, tr. de Slane, I, 625.
p. 65, n. 1. Cf. von Kremer, *Culturgeschichte*, I, pp. 423 ff.
p. 67, n. 1. *Ibid.* II, 179 ff.
p. 68, n. 1. *Ibid.* II, 186 f.; Mas'údí, *Murúj al-Dhahab*, VIII, 152.
p. 68, n. 2. Von Kremer, *op. cit.* II, 188.
p. 70, n. 1. *Laṭa'if*, ed. de Jong, p. 71.

p. 71, n. 1. Ṭabarí, III, 971 f.
p. 78, n. 1. Ibn Khallikán, tr. de Slane, I, 649.
p. 79, n. 1. *Op. cit.* p. 4.
p. 82, n. 1. *Agháni*, XVIII, 43.
p. 83, n. 1. See Ṭabarí, III, 1008 ff.
p. 83, n. 2. Ṭabarí, III, 1009.
p. 83, n. 3. *Ibid.* III, 1010.
p. 85, n. 1. *Ibid.* III, 1023 ff.
p. 87, n. 1. Ibn al-Qiftí (ed. Lippert), s.v. "Banú Músá," p. 441. See *Fihrist*, II (notes) pp. 126 f.
p. 88, n. 1. *Fihrist*, p. 271; cf. Nicholson, *Lit. Hist. of the Arabs*, p. 359.
p. 88, n. 2. *Chahár Maqála* (Gibb Series), p. 55. The al-Kindí mentioned is not "the Arabian Philosopher" of that name, who was a Moslem.
p. 89, n. 1. *Agháni*, XVII, 15; quoted by von Kremer, *Streifzüge*, p. 42.
p. 89, n. 2. Ibn Khallikán, tr. de Slane, I, 478.
p. 89, n. 3. *Ibid.* I, 507.
p. 90, n. 1. *Mu'jam al-Udabá*, ed. Margoliouth (Gibb Series), VI, 5, 458.
p. 91, n. 1. See *Journal Asiatique*, 1873, pt. II, 583.
p. 94, n. 1. *'Iqd*, Cairo, 1316, III, 337 f.
p. 96, n. 1. See Ṭabarí, III, 1074 f.
p. 101, n. 1. Yáqút, *Mu'jam al-Buldán*, I, 684 ff.
p. 104, n. 1. Ṭabarí, III, 1343 ff.
p. 105, n. 1. See Deuteronomy vi, 4.
p. 105, n. 2. Ṭabarí, III, 1389 f.
p. 106, n. 1. *Ibid.* III, 1424.
p. 108, n. 1. *Ibid.* III, 1510 f.
p. 115, n. 1. Nöldeke, *Sketches from Eastern History*, tr. J. S. Black, p. 150.
p. 117, n. 1. Mas'údí, *Kitáb al-Tanbíh*, pp. 368 f.
p. 120, n. 1. D. S. Margoliouth, *The Table-Talk of a Mesopotamian Judge*, tr., p. 80.
p. 121, n. 1. See the edition by R. E. Brünnow (1886).
p. 126, n. 1. Yáqút, *Mu'jam al-Udabá*, ed. Margoliouth, VI, I, 37 ff.
p. 127, n. 1. Mas'údí, *Murúj al-Dhahab*, VIII, 125 f.
p. 130, n. 1. *Ibid.* VIII, 151 ff.
p. 130, n. 2. *Mirát al-Zamán*, B.M. MS. Or. 4619, anno 295.
p. 131, n. 1. Nöldeke, *Sketches from Eastern History*, tr. J. S. Black, p. 203.
p. 134, n. 1. Ṭabarí, III, 2226 ff.
p. 136, n. 1. From "A Greek Embassy to Baghdad", by G. Le Strange, *Journal of the Royal Asiatic Society*, 1897, pp. 37 f.

p. 137, n. 1. *Ibid.* p. 41.

p. 138, n. 1. Miskawaihi, *The Eclipse of the Abbasid Caliphate*, tr. D. S. Margoliouth, IV, 2.

p. 139, n. 1. D. S. Margoliouth, *Table-Talk*, tr., pp. 124 f.

p. 141, n. 1. Ibn al-Qiftí, p. 191.

p. 142, n. 1. *Ibid.* pp. 193 f.

p. 143, n. 1. *Abulḳâsim: ein bagdâder Sittenbild*, ed. A. Mez, 1902, p. 87.

p. 145, n. 1. Ibn al-Athír, anno 310, tr. E. G. Browne, *Literary History of Persia*, I, 360 f.

p. 146, n. 1. *The Eclipse of the Abbasid Caliphate*, tr. D. S. Margoliouth, IV, 44.

p. 146, n. 2. Ed. Ahlwardt, p. 306.

p. 146, n. 3. 'Aríb, ed. de Goeje, p. 96 n.

p. 147, n. 1. *The Eclipse of the Abbasid Caliphate*, tr. D. S. Margoliouth, IV, 135.

p. 149, n. 1. *Decline and Fall*, chap. LII.

p. 149, n. 2. A.H. 323, VIII, 229 f.

p. 150, n. 1. Ibn al-Athír, *l.c.*

p. 151, n. 1. Abú 'l-Maḥásin, ed. Juynboll, II, 305; Suyúṭí, tr. Jarrett, anno 333, p. 416.

p. 152, n. 1. Ḥamza of Isfahan, Berlin edn, A.H. 1340, p. 125.

p. 156, n. 1. Cf. Zaydán, *Islamic Civilization* (Arabic), I, 187.

p. 157, n. 1. F. Krenkow, "Al-Khatíbu 'l-Baghdádí", *J.R.A.S.* Jan. 1912, p. 71.

p. 157, n. 2. Yáqút, *Mu'jam al-Udabá*, ed. Margoliouth (Gibb Series), VI, I, 73.

p. 159, n. 1. *Masálik al-Mamálik*, ed. de Goeje, Leyden, 1870, pp. 83 ff.

p. 160, n. 1. Ibn al-Athír, VIII, 407; *Mir'át al-Zamán*, fol. 155 *a*.

p. 160, n. 2. Mirkhwánd, Buyids, ed. and tr. F. Wilken, 1835, pp. 73 f.

p. 161, n. 1. A.H. 361.

p. 162, n. 1. *Mir'át al-Zamán*, A.H. 350.

p. 163, n. 1. *Rawḍat al-Ṣafá*, pt. IV [vol. I of Ṭihrán edn of A.H. 1270, no pagination].

p. 164, n. 1. D. S. Margoliouth, *Table-Talk*, tr., p. 228.

p. 164, n. 2. Al-Bírúní, *Chronology of Ancient Nations*, tr. Sachau, p. 258.

p. 164, n. 3. The location of the exact site has not been settled. Ibn Baṭúṭa, who visited Baghdad about the middle of the fourteenth century, in his *Book of Travels* (pt. II, p. 108 of Defrémery and Sanguinetti's edn) talks of the ruins of the hospital and the mosque of the Khuld Palace as being in the quarter of Báb al-Baṣra, where also stood and stands the tomb of the saint Ma'rúf Karkhí. This tomb is now in the neighbourhood of the quarter known as Báb al-Síf—between the two bridges on the west bank. On the other hand, the old wall of Babylonian bricks, above the upper bridge and known as al-Sinn, has been identified as part of the ruins of the Máristán.

p. 165, n. 1. The *Travels* of Ibn Jubayr (Gibb Series, vol. v), pp. 225 ff.

p. 165, n. 2. Or. 8293.

p. 165, n. 3. Ed. Margoliouth (Gibb Series, vol. VI, 7), 243.

p. 166, n. 1. Khanikof, *Mémoire sur Khacani*, p. 95.

p. 166, n. 2. Al-Qiftí, ed. Lippert, p. 283.

p. 167, n. 1. *Mir'át al-Zamán*, A.H. 378.

p. 168, n. 1. The MS. of Mir'át al-Zamán has Fakhr al-D. (by error). Possibly Fakhr al-Mulk, the Buwayhid viceroy, is intended. See Ibn al-Athír, IX, 157 f.

p. 168, n. 2. *'Íd al-Qurbán* (10th of the month of Dhú 'l-Ḥijja).

p. 168, n. 3. *Mir'át al-Zamán*, anno 402.

p. 169, n. 1. *Ibid.* anno 403 (fol. 199 *b*).

p. 170, n. 1. X, 5.

p. 170, n. 2. Nicholson, *Literary History of the Arabs*, p. 267.

p. 170, n. 3. *Letters*, ed. Margoliouth, p. 66.

p. 171, n. 1. Ibn al-Athír, A.H. 409, IX, 216.

p. 171, n. 2. *Ibid.* IX, 216 f.

p. 172, n. 1. *Ibid.* IX, 246.

p. 172, n. 2. *Ibid.* IX, 254 f.; *Mir'át al-Zamán*, anno 418 (fol. 214 *a*).

p. 174, n. 1. *Mir'át al-Zamán*, anno 424 (fol. 224 *a*).

p. 175, n. 1. *Ibid.* anno 426.

p. 176, n. 1. *Ibid.* anno 426.

p. 176, n. 2. *Ibid.* anno 431.

p. 176, n. 3. "of the companions (of the Prophet)—ask therefore for God's compassion upon them."

p. 177, n. 1. This account is given by Ibn al-Jawzí, anno 442. It is omitted from the editions of Ibn al-Athír, though it must have been included in his original text, for in his summary of the events of the year 443 he speaks of the break-up of the strange "alliance of which we gave an account during the record of the past year".

p. 178, n. 1. Ed. A. Mez.

p. 179, n. 1. *Ibid.* pp. 13 f.

p. 180, n. 1. *Ibid.* p. 24.

p. 180, n. 2. *Ibid.* p. 35.

p. 180, n. 3. *Ibid. loc. cit.*

p. 181, n. 1. *Ibid.* p. 36.

p. 181, n. 2. *Ibid.* p. 38.

p. 182, n. 1. *Ibid.* pp. 38 ff.

p. 182, n. 2. *Ibid.* p. 41.

p. 182, n. 3. *Ibid.* p. 46.
p. 182, n. 4. *Ibid.* p. 49.
p. 182, n. 5. *Ibid. loc. cit.*
p. 182, n. 6. *Ibid.* p. 50.
p. 183, n. 1. *Ibid.* p. 51.
p. 183, n. 2. *Ibid.* p. 81.
p. 184, n. 1. *Mir'át al-Zamán*, anno 444 (fol. 273 *b*).
p. 186, n. 1. Ibn al-Athír, IX, 420 f.
p. 187, n. 1. *Ibid. loc. cit.*
p. 187, n. 2. Al-Bundárí (ed. Houtsma), p. 13.
p. 188, n. 1. Ibn al-Athír, IX, 436.
p. 188, n. 2. Al-Bundárí, pp. 13 f.
p. 189, n. 1. *Zubdat al-Tawáríkh*, B.M. MS. Stowe Or. 7, fol. 12 *b*.
p. 190, n. 1. Koran, III, 25.
p. 190, n. 2. Ibn al-Athír, A.H. 450, IX, 443.
p. 191, n. 1. *Ibid.* IX, 445.
p. 193, n. 1. Ed. F. Wuestenfeld, Göttingen, 1848, vol. II, p. 276, s.v. "Ṭús".
p. 193, n. 2. Ibn Khallikán, tr. de Slane, I, pp. xxviii f.
p. 194, n. 1. Cf. L. Massignon, "Les medresehs de Bagdad", *Bull. de l'Institut français d'Arch. orient.* VII, 77 ff.
p. 194, n. 2. Ibn al-Athír, XI, 100.
p. 194, n. 3. *Mir'át al-Zamán*, anno 457.
p. 194, n. 4. Ibn al-Athír, X, 38; Ibn Khallikán, ed. Wuestenfeld, IV, No. 410, p. 113.
p. 194, n. 5. The *Mir'át al-Zamán*, anno 457, says the school was intended from the beginning for the Sháfi'í sect.
p. 195, n. 1. Ibn al-Athír, X, 141.
p. 195, n. 2. '*Uyún al-Ta'ríkh*, Cambridge MS. Add 2922, fol. 36 *a*.
p. 196, n. 1. Ibn al-Athír, X. 123.
p. 196, n. 2. For the meaning cf. Ibn Jubayr (Gibb Series), pp. 219, 229.
p. 196, n. 3. Ibn Khallikán, tr. de Slane, IV, 434, note (6).
p. 196, n. 4. *Bústán*, VII, l. 147 (ed. Graf, p. 341).
p. 196, n. 5. Ibn Khallikán, tr. de Slane, IV, 417 f.
p. 196, n. 6. *Ibid.* IV, 432.
p. 196, n. 7. Here called *faqíhs*.
p. 196, n. 8. ? *Semecarpus anacardium*.
p. 196, n. 9. Ibn Khallikán, tr. de Slane, IV, 427.
p. 197, n. 1. Ibn al-Athír, XI, 115.
p. 198, n. 1. Al-Bundárí, p. 33.
p. 198, n. 2. *Ibid.* p. 32.
p. 198, n. 3. Yáqút, *Mu'jam al-Buldán*, I, 826.

p. 199, n. 1. Al-Bundárí, p. 80; Ibn al-Athír, x, 103 f.

p. 199, n. 2. For details see Le Strange, *Baghdad*, pp. 283 f. and Ibn al-Athír, x, 156.

p. 199, n. 3. Ibn al-Athír, x, 172.

p. 200, n. 1. *Ibid.* x, 435.

p. 201, n. 1. *Ibid.* x, 329.

p. 201, n. 2. *Ibid.* x, 63, 71–74; al-Bundárí, p. 52.

p. 202, n. 1. *Al-Fakhrí*, pp. 344 f.

p. 202, n. 2. Ibn al-Athír, x, 123.

p. 203, n. 1. *Ibid.* x, 317 f.

p. 203, n. 2. *Ibid.* x, 63.

p. 203, n. 3. Cf. the *Mejelle*—the codification of Ḥanafi law, Eng. trans. by C. R. Tyser and D. G. Demetriades, Nicosia, 1901.

p. 203, n. 4. Ibn al-Athír, x, 173.

p. 204, n. 1. *Ibid.* x, 156.

p. 204, n. 2. *Ibid.* x, 134 f.; cf. Le Strange, *Baghdad*, pp. 240, 339, etc.

p. 204, n. 3. *Op. cit.* x, 135.

p. 205, n. 1. Cf. Abú 'l-Fidá, *Annales*, ed. Reiske, III, 284 ff.

p. 205, n. 2. Ibn al-Athír, x, 157.

p. 205, n. 3. *Ibid.* x, 245.

p. 206, n. 1. Michaud, *Hist. des Croisades*, I, 261.

p. 206, n. 2. Ibn al-Athír, x, 192.

p. 208, n. 1. Al-Bundárí, p. 91.

p. 208, n. 2. *Ibid.* p. 95.

p. 209, n. 1. *Ibid.* p. 99

p. 209, n. 2. *Ibid.* p. 103.

p. 209, n. 3. *Ibid.* p. 101.

p. 209, n. 4. *Ibid.* p. 103.

p. 210, n. 1. *Ibid. loc. cit.*

p. 211, n. 1. Ibn al-Athír, x, 338 f.

p. 211, n. 2. *Ibid. loc. cit.*

p. 211, n. 3. *'Uyún al-Ta'ríkh*, Cambridge MS. Add. 2922, fol. 1 *b*.

p. 212, n. 1. Al-Bundárí, p. 137.

p. 212, n. 2. *Ibid. loc. cit.*

p. 213, n. 1. Ibn al-Athír, x, 428.

p. 213, n. 2. *Ibid.* x, 429.

p. 214, n. 1. *Ibid.* x, 435.

p. 214, n. 2. *Ibid.* x, 430.

p. 215, n. 1. *Ibid.* x, 441 f.

p. 216, n. 1. Called the "Nubian Gate" in G. Le Strange's *Baghdad during the Abbasid Caliphate*. The name occurs in the Arabic texts either as *Báb al-Nauba* or as *Báb al-Naubí*, which Mr Le Strange reads as *Báb' al-Núbí*.

p. 217, n. 1. Ibn al-Athír, x, 447 ff. Bundárí, p. 152.

p. 217, n. 2. Ibn al-Athír, x, 476 f. Bundárí, pp. 158 f.

p. 218, n. 1. Ibn al-Athír, xi, 16 f.

p. 218, n. 2. Bundárí, p. 178, and for other views on the murder, *J.R.A.S.* 1902, pp. 788 ff.

p. 220, n. 1. Ibn al-Athír, xi, 26.

p. 220, n. 2. *Ibid.* p. 28.

p. 221, n. 1. *Ibid.* p. 40.

p. 221, n. 2. *Ibid.* p. 59; cf. *ibid.* p. 63.

p. 222, n. 1. Bundárí, p. 216; Ibn al-Athír, xi, 78.

p. 222, n. 2 Ibn al-Athír, xi, 106; *Zubdat al-Tawáríkh*, B.M. MS. Stowe Or. 7, fol. 71 *b*.

p. 222, n. 3. *Zubdat al-Tawáríkh*, fol. 72 *a*; Bundárí, pp. 234 ff.

p. 223, n. 1. Chau Ju-Kua, translated by F. Hirth and W. W. Rockhill, St Petersburg, 1911.

p. 227, n. 1. *Ráḥat al-Ṣudúr* (Gibb Series), p. 268.

p. 227, n. 2. Ibn al-Athír, xi, 140 ff.; Bundárí, pp. 246 ff. *Ráḥat al-Ṣudúr*, pp. 267 f.; *Zubdat al-Tawáríkh*, fols. 74 *a*–78 *a*.

p. 227, n. 3. *Zubdat al-Tawáríkh*, fol. 74 *b*.

p. 228, n. 1. Ibn al-Athír, xi, 164.

p. 228, n. 2. Cf. *The Itinerary of Benjamin of Tudela*, ed. M. N. Adler (1907), p. 36.

p. 229, n. 1. *Ibid.* p. 42.

p. 229, n. 2. Their number is put in different MSS. either as 1000 or 40,000; the former too low, the latter probably too high. Cf. Mez, *Die Renaissance des Islams*, 1922, p. 33, note 9.

p. 230, n. 1. Mez, *op. cit.* pp. 54 ff.

p. 230, n. 2. Cf. Lane-Poole, *Mohammedan Dynasties*, p. 165.

p. 230, n. 3. Cf. Steinschneider, *Arabische Lit. der Juden*, § 149.

p. 230, n. 4. *Emeḳ habacha*, tr. M. Wiener, who gives the original Judaeo-Arabic, pp. xxv–xxvii; De Sacy, *Chrestomathie arabe*, i, 363.

p. 231, n. 1. Ibn al-Qiftí, ed. Lippert, pp. 343 f.; Bar-Hebraeus, ed. Ṣalḥání, pp. 364 f.

p. 233, n. 1. Cf. Chau Ju-Kua, his work on the Chinese and Arab Trade in the twelfth and thirteenth centuries; translated by F. Hirth and W. W. Rockhill, St Petersburg, 1911, pp. 102–104 and notes, pp. 104–110, with literature there cited.

p. 233, n. 2. (Gibb Series, vol. v), p. 216.

p. 234, n. 1. *Ibid.* p. 218.

p. 235, n. 1. *Díwán*, ed. D. S. Margoliouth, No. 24, p. 47.

p. 235, n. 2. Ibn Jubayr, pp. 222 f.

p. 236, n. 1. *Ibid.* p. 227.

p. 236, n. 2. Ibn al-Athír (xi, 211) mentions a Ḥanabalite *madrasa* in the Bāb al-Baṣra quarter, on the west bank, built by the vizier Yaḥyá b. Mohammed, who died in A.H. 560 (A.D. 1165).

p. 236, n. 3. Ibn al-Athír, XII, 67.

p. 237, n. 1. *Ibid.* XI, 241 ff.

p. 237, n. 2. Al-Subkí, *Ṭabaqát al-Sháfi'iya*, B.M. MS. 6523, fol. 193 *a*.

p. 237, n. 3. *Ibid.* fol. 193 *b*.

p. 237, n. 4. Abú 'l-Fidá, *Annales*, ed. Reiske, IV, 328; Suyúṭí, tr. Jarrett, p. 475.

p. 237, n. 5. Bar-Hebraeus, *Chron. Syr.* tr. Bruns and Kirsch, pp. 414 f.; *Mir'át al-Zamán*, ed. Jewett, p. 241.

p. 238, n. 1. Ibn al-Athír, XI, 353.

p. 238, n. 2. Abú Sháma (Shiháb al-Dín al-Muqaddasí), *Kitáb al-Rawḍatayn*, II, 139; cf. Le Strange, *Baghdad*, pp. 274 f.

p. 238, n. 3. Cf. (i) the article in al-Muqtabas, vol. III (Cairo, 1326), p. 96, on a fragment of Ibn al-Sá'í's history *Al-Jámi' al-Mukhtaṣar*, containing the years 595–606; and (ii) *Mukhtaṣar Mir'át al-Zamán*, B.M. MS. Add. 23,279, fol. 84 *b*, anno 593.

p. 238, n. 4. Abú Sháma, II, 214 *ad fin.*

p. 238, n. 5. Suyúṭí, tr. Jarrett, p. 479.

p. 239, n. 1. Al-Dhahabí, B.M. MS. Or. 52, fol. 65 *a*.; Ibn al-Athír, XII, 70.

p. 239, n. 2. Ibn Khaldún, *History*, III, 529; Suyúṭí, *op. cit.* pp. 479 f.

p. 239, n. 3. Cf. *Journal Asiatique*, 1842, XIV, 20.

p. 239, n. 4. Bar-Hebraeus, ed. Ṣalḥání, pp. 414 f.

p. 240, n. 1. A famous mathematician of Basra, d. A.H. 430 (A.D. 1038).

p. 240, n. 2. Ed. Lippert, pp. 228 f.

p. 241, n. 1. *Mukhtaṣar Mir'át al-Zamán*, fol. 113 *a*.

p. 241, n. 2. Ibn al-Athír, XII, 210; *Mir'át al-Zamán*, ed. Jewett, p. 375.

p. 242, n. 1. Ibn al-Athír, XII, 286; Al-Muqtabas, III, 96; cf. Dozy, *Supplément*, II, 211.

p. 243, n. 1. *Mukhtaṣar Mir'át al-Zamán*, fol. 119 *a b*.

p. 243, n. 2. Ibn al-Athír, XII, 133, 216.

p. 244, n. 1. P. 238.

p. 245, n. 1. Ḥamdulláh Mustawfí (in *Nuzhat al-Qulúb*, tr. Le Strange, p. 42) says that obesity was characteristic of the Baghdadí.

p. 245, n. 2. *Mukhtaṣar Mir'át al-Zamán*, fol. 84 *b*.

p. 246, n. 1. *Ibid.* fol. 115 *a*.

p. 246, n. 2. *Ibid.* fols. 120 f.

p. 247, n. 1. Ibn Khallikán, ed. Cairo, 1310, I, 279, tr. de Slane, II, 97 f.; Suyúṭí, tr. Jarrett, p. 475.

p. 247, n. 2. The story covers Nights 438–460; *Alif Layla*, ed. Macnaghten, II, 493 ff. I am indebted for the reference to Mr J. Leveen of the British Museum.

p. 252, n. 1. *Op. cit.* ed. Ahlwardt, p. 37.
p. 253, n. 1. Cf. C. Huart, *Hist. de Bagdad*, p. 37.
p. 253, n. 2. *Qahwat Rás al-Jisr.*
p. 253, n. 3. Abú 'l-Fidá, *Ta'ríkh*, Stambúl edn, 1286, III, 179.
p. 253, n. 4. Al-Machriq, vol. V, 1902, p. 164.
p. 254, n. 1. *Ibid.* X, 80 ff., 391 ff.
p. 254, n. 2. *Ibid.* V, 164.
p. 254, n. 3. Quatremère, *Histoire des Mongols*, pp. 224 f.
p. 258, n. 1. *Ibid.* pp. 278 ff.
p. 258, n. 2. Al-Ṣafadí, B.M. MS. Add. 23,359, fol. 235 *b*.
p. 258, n. 3. Cf. D'Ohsson, *Hist. des Mongols*, III, 241.
p. 258, n. 4. *Maris Amri et Slibae de Patriarchis Nestorianorum Commentaria*, ed. H. Gismondi, 1897, II, 120 f.
p. 258, n. 5. J. B. Chabot, *Histoire du Patriarche Mar Jabalaha III*, 116 f.
p. 259, n. 1. *Op. cit.* ed. Ahlwardt, pp. 19 f.
p. 259, n. 2. Al-Ṣafadí, *loc. cit.*
p. 259, n. 3. Cf. L. Massignon, "Les medresehs de Bagdad."
p. 259, n. 4. Cf. E. G. Browne, *Lit. Hist. of Persia*, II, 484.
p. 260, n. 1. Quatremère, *loc. cit.*
p. 260, n. 2. *Op. cit.* ed. von Hammer, pp. 52, 117.

BIBLIOGRAPHICAL LIST OF AUTHORITIES

Abú 'l-'Atáhiya. *Díwán* Beyrút, 1886.

Abú 'l-Faraj (Bar-Hebraeus). *Ta'ríkh al-Duwal.* Beyrút, 1890.

—— *Chronicon Syriacum.* Ed. and tr. Bruns and Kirsch. 2 vols. Leipzig, 1789.

—— *Chronicon Ecclesiasticum.* Ed. and tr. Abbeloos and Lamy. 3 vols. Louvain, 1872–7.

Abú 'l-Fidá. *Annales.* Ed. J. Reiske. 5 vols. Copenhagen, 1786.

—— *Ta'ríkh al-Bashar*, 4 vols. Stambúl A.H. 1286.

—— *Geography.* Ed. Reinaud and de Slane. Paris, 1840.

Abú 'l-Maḥásin ibn Taghribardí. *Al-Nujúm al-Ẓáhira.* Ed. T. G. Juynboll. 2 vols. Leyden, 1852–61.

Abú Sháma. *Kitáb al-Rawḍatayn.* Cairo, A.H. 1287.

Abú 'l-Ṭayyib Muḥammad ibn Isḥáq. *Kitáb al-Muwashshá.* Ed. R. E. Brünnow. Leipzig, 1886.

Al-Bírúní. *Chronology of Ancient Nations.* Tr. E. Sachau. London, 1879.

Alif Layla wa-Layla. Ed. W. H. Macnaghten. 4 vols. Calcutta, 1831–42.

H. F. Amedroz and D. S. Margoliouth. *The Eclipse of the Abbasid Caliphate.* Oxford, 1920–1.

'Aríb. *Tabari Continuatus.* Ed. M. J. de Goeje. Leyden, 1897.

Benjamin of Tudela. *Itinerary.* Ed. and tr. A. Asher. London, 1840.

—— *Ibid.* Ed. and tr. M. N. Adler. London, 1907.

—— *Die Reisebeschreibungen....* Ed. and tr. L. Grünhut and M. N. Adler. Frankfurt, 1903–4.

C. Brockelmann. *Geschichte der Arabischen Literatur.* 2 vols. Weimar, 1898–1902.

E. G. Browne. *A Literary History of the Arabs.* 2 vols. London, 1909.

R. F. Burton. *The Thousand and One Nights.* 6 vols. London, 1887.

J. B. Chabot. *Histoire de Mar Jabalaha III.* Paris, 1895.

Chau Ju-Kua. Tr. F. Hirth and W. W. Rockhill. St Petersburg, 1911.

Al-Dhahabí. *Ta'ríkh al-Islám.* British Museum MS. Or. 52.

R. Dozy. *Essai sur l'histoire de l'Islamisme.* Paris, 1879.

—— *Supplément aux Dictionnaires arabes.* 2 vols. Leyden, 1881.

I. Goldziher. *Muhammedanische Studien.* 2 vols. Halle, 1889–90.

I. Guidi. *Tables alphabétiques du Kitáb al-Aghání.* Leyden, 1895–1900.

Ḥamdulláh Mustawfí. *Nuzhat al-Qulúb*. Ed. and tr. G. Le Strange. Gibb Memorial Series, 1915, 1918.
Ḥamza of Isfahan. *Ta'ríkh Siní Mulúk al-Arḍ*. Berlin, A.H. 1340.
D'Herbelot. *Bibliothèque orientale*. 2 vols. Paris, 1776–80.
Ibn 'Abdi Rabbihi. *Al-'Iqd al-Faríd*. Cairo, A.H. 1316.
Ibn Abí Uṣaybi'a. *'Uyun al-Anbá*. Ed. A. Müller. Königsberg, 1884.
Ibn al-Athír. *Kitáb al-Kámil*. Ed. C. J. Tornberg. 14 vols. Leyden, 1851–76.
Ibn Baṭúṭa. *Travels*. Ed. and tr. Defrémery and Sanguinetti. 6 vols. Paris, 1877.
Ibn Jubayr. *Travels*. Ed. M. J. de Goeje. Gibb Memorial Series, 1907.
Ibn Khaldún. *Kitáb al-'Ibar*. 7 vols. Bulaq, A.H. 1284.
Ibn Khallikán. *Wafayát al-A'yán* (Biographical Dictionary). Tr. M. de Slane. 4 vols. Paris and London, 1842–71.
Ibn al-Qiftí. *Ta'ríkh al-Ḥukamá*. Ed. J. Lippert. Leipzig, 1903.
Ibn al-Tiqtaqí. *Al-Fakhrí*. Ed. Ahlwardt. Gotha, 1860.
Imád al-Dín. In *Recueil des Textes relatifs à l'Histoire des Seldjoucides*. Vol. II. Ed. M. T. Houtsma. Leyden, 1889.
Iṣṭakhrí. *Masálik al-Mamálik*. Ed. M. J. de Goeje. Leyden, 1870.
Joseph ben Joshua Hakkohen. *Emek Habacha*. Tr. M. Wiener. Leipzig, 1858.
Journal of the American Oriental Society. Vol. 44.
Journal Asiatique. 1873.
Journal of the Royal Asiatic Society.
Khanikof. *Mémoire sur Khacani*. Paris, 1865.
Kháqání. *Tuḥfat al-'Iráqayn*. Lucknow, A.H. 1294.
Al-Khaṭíb al-Baghdádí. *L'introduction topographique à l'histoire de Baghdadh* par G. Salmon (Bibliothèque de l'École des Hautes Études, vol. CXLVIII. Paris, 1904).
Kitáb al-Aghání. Bulaq ed. 20 vols. A.H. 1284–5.
A. von Kremer. *Culturgeschichtliche Streifzüge auf dem Gebiete des Islams*. Leipzig, 1873.
—— *Culturgeschichte des Orients unter den Chalifen*. 2 vols. Vienna, 1875–7.
Al-Kutubí. *'Uyún al-Tawáríkh*. Cambridge MS. Add. 2922.
—— *Fawát al-Wafayát*. Bulaq, A.H. 1283.
S. Lane-Poole. *The Mohammadan Dynasties*. London, 1894.
G. Le Strange. *Baghdad during the Abbasid Caliphate*. Oxford, 1900.
—— *The Lands of the Abbasid Caliphate*. Cambridge, 1905.
Al Machriq. Vols. V and X. Baghdad, 1902 and 1907.
D. S. Margoliouth. *Letters of Abú 'l-'Alá al-Ma'arrí*. Oxford, 1898.
—— *The Table-Talk of a Mesopotamian Judge*. London, 1921.

Maris Amri et Slibae Commentaria. Ed. H. Gismondi. 2 vols. Rome, 1897–9.

L. Massignon. "Les medresehs de Bagdad." *Bulletin de l'Institut français d'Archéologie orientale*. Vol. VII.

Mas'údí. *Murúj al-Dhahab*. (Maçoudi. *Les Prairies d'Or*.) Arabic text and French translation by B. de Meynard and P. de Courteille. 9 vols. Paris, 1861–77.

—— *Kitáb al-Tanbíh*. Ed. M. J. de Goeje. Leyden, 1893.

Máwardí. *Kitáb al-Aḥkám al-Sulṭániya*. Ed. R. Enger. Bonn, 1853.

The Mejelle. The codification of Hanafi law. English translation by C. R. Tyser and others. Nicosia, 1901.

A. Mez. *Abulḳâsim, ein bagdâder Sittenbild*. Heidelberg, 1902.

—— *Die Renaissance des Islams*. 1922.

Michaud. *Bibliothèque des Croisades*. Vol. I. Paris, 1829.

Mirkhwánd. *Mirchond's Geschichte der Sultane aus dem Geschlechte Bujeh*. Ed. F. Wilken. Berlin, 1835.

Mukhtaṣar Mir'át al-Zamán. British Museum MS. Add 23,279

A. Müller. *Der Islam im Morgen- und Abendland*. 2 vols. Berlin, 1885–7.

Al-Muqtabas. Vol. III. Cairo, A.H. 1326.

Al-Nadím al-Baghdádí. *Al-Fihrist*. Ed. G. Fluegel. Leipzig, 1871.

R. A. Nicholson. *A Literary History of the Arabs*. London, 1907.

Niẓámí 'Arúḍí. *Chahar Maqala*. Ed. Mirza Muhammad Qazvini. Gibb Memorial Series, 1910.

T. Nöldeke. *Sketches from Eastern History*. Tr. J. S. Black. London, 1894.

M. d'Ohsson. *Histoire des Mongols*. 3 vols. Amsterdam, 1834–5.

Qazwíní. *Áthár al-Bilád*. Ed. F. Wuestenfeld. Göttingen, 1848.

E. Quatremère. *Histoire des Mongols*. Paris, 1836.

Al-Rawandí. *Ráḥat al-Ṣudúr*. Ed. Md. Iqbal. Gibb Memorial Series, 1921.

S. de Sacy. *Chrestomathie arabe*. 2nd ed. 2 vols. Paris, 1826–7.

Sa'dí. *Bústán*. Ed. Graf. Vienna, 1857.

Al-Ṣafadí. *Al-Wáfi bi'l-Wafayát*. British Museum MS. Add. 23,259.

Sibṭ ibn al-Jauzí. *Mir'át al-Zamán*. British Museum MS. Or. 4619. (Published in facsimile by J. Jewett. Chicago, 1907.)

M. Steinschneider. *Die Arabische Literatur der Juden*. Frankfurt, 1902.

Al-Subkí. *Ṭabaqát al-Sháfi'iya*. British Museum MS. Add. 6523.

Suyúṭí. *History of the Caliphs*. Tr. from the Arabic by H. S. Jarrett. Calcutta, 1881.

Al-Ta'áwídhí. *Díwán*. Ed. D. S. Margoliouth. Cairo, 1903.

Ṭabarí. Ed. M. J. de Goeje and others. Leyden, 1879–1901.
Ta'ríkh-i Waṣṣáf. Ed. and tr. Hammer Purgstall. Vienna, 1856.
Tha'álibí. *Laṭá'if al-Ma'árif.* Ed. P. de Jong. Leyden, 1867.
G. Weil. *Geschichte der Chalifen.* 3 vols. Mannheim, 1846–51.
F. Wuestenfeld. *Die Geschichtschreiber der Araber und ihre Werke.* Göttingen, 1882.
—— *Die Academien der Araber.* Göttingen, 1837.
Ya'qúbí. *Kitáb al-Buldán.* Ed. M. J. de Goeje. Leyden, 1892.
Yáqút. *Mu'jam al-Buldán.* Ed. F. Wuestenfeld. 5 vols. Leipzig, 1866.
—— *Dictionary of Learned Men.* Ed. D. S. Margoliouth. Gibb Memorial Series, 1908–26.
G. Zaydán. *History of Islamic Civilization* (Arabic text). 5 vols. Cairo, 1902–6.
Zubdat al-Tawárikh. British Museum MS. Stowe Or. 7.

INDEX

[A hyphen before a word denotes the omission of *al.*]

The references are to pages.

-'Abádí, 221 f.
Abbasids, 13 f. and *passim*
'Abd al-Salám, 239 f.
Abú 'l-'Alá al-Ma'arrí, 170
Abú 'l-'Atáhiya, 37 f., 60
Abú Duláma, 39
Abú 'l-Faraj, 156 f.
Abú Ḥanífa, 19
Abú 'l-Hijá al-Samín, 238, 244 f.
Abú Manṣúr al-Maybudí, 209
Abú Muslim, 13
Abú 'l-Muṭahhar, 143 f., 178 ff.
Abú Nuwás, 60
Abú 'l-Qásim of Baghdad, *see* Abú 'l Muṭahhar
Abú Riyásh, 157
Abú Shujá', 201
Abú 'l-Taiyyih, 121 f.
'Aḍud al-Dawla, 163, 164, 166
Aḥmad ibn Ḥanbal, 144, 149, 177
Aḥmad ibn Naṣr, 102 f.
'Alí, the Caliph, 12, 13, 114
'Alí ibn 'Ísá, 141, 144
Alp Arslán, 192, 193
Amín, 70–9
Amír al-Umará, 153, 154
Anbár, 14, 57, 221
Anúshírwán, 209
Architecture, 180
'Aríb, 145
-Ash'arí, 294 f.
Assassins (Isma'ílí), 133, 192, 204, 207, 209, 210, 218
Atábegs, 219
'Attábiyín quarter, 211
Báb al-Azaj quarter, 185, 243
Báb al-Baṣra quarter, 171, 176, 191, 202, 224, 257
Báb al-Nawbí, *see* Sentry Gate
Baghdad, building of, 19 f.
  gates, 21 f.
  the name, 7–9
  planning of city, 18
  quarters, 23
  site, 6, 7, 15, 16, 17
  streets, 23
  walls, 21 f., 222, 224
Baghdadís, character of, 234
Bahá 'l-Dín (Bohaddin), 196
Baládur, 196
Banú Músá, 87
Baríd ("post" system), 106, 208
Barkyáruq, 205, 207
Barmecides, 20, 40, 43, 51–8
Basásírí, 188–92
Baths, public, 125, 203, 204, 236, 257
Bazaars, 22, 29, 32 f., 44 f., 67 f., 157, 168, 180, 236, 260
Benjamin, Rabbi, of Tudela, 9, 228–31
Bímáristán-i 'Aḍudí, 164 f., 198, 199
Blaeu, Jean, 9
Booksellers, 157
Bottle factory, 166, 223
Bridges, 40 f., 69, 226 f., 236
Brigands, 82 f., 151, 167, 173–5, 176, 221, 253
Bukht Yishú', 55, 66 f., 106

-Burjumí, 173 f.
Bursuqí, 212 f., 214
Buwayhids, 152 f., 159, 178, 184 f., 186, 200, 215

Canals, in and near Baghdad, 16, 17, 23 f., 224
Carmathians, 133–5, 147
Charlemagne, 50
"Chief of the Captivity", 229, 230 f.
Chóu K'ü-feï, 223, 231 f.
Christians, 6, 7, 15, 16, 26, 65–7, 104 f., 108, 162, 163, 165, 168 f., 258, 259
Church (Latin), 132
(Nestorian), 258
of St Mary, 26
Crossbow, 240
Crucifixion, 190
Crusaders, 206, 207, 210, 211
Ctesiphon, 2, 5, 11, 12, 20, 26, 131

Damascus, 13, 14
Dár al-Rúm, 67, 162, 233, 258
David Alroy, 229 f.
Dawatdár Aybak, 254, 258
Di'bil ibn 'Alí, 89
Dress, 2, 3, 4, 53, 80, 90, 104 f., 122 f., 189, 195, 203, 232, 235, 241
Dubays, 212–14, 215, 217

Education, 62, 122, 165, 169 f., 192–7, 211 f., 229, 236, 247 f., 252
Etiquette, 122 f.

Fadhl ibn Yahyá, 52
Fakhrí, 35, 53, 138, 146, 252, 259
Famine, 151 f.
Fanaticism, 245
Fáṭimids, 189, 206, 237
Ferrymen, 199, 203
Festivities, 68 f., 70 f., 174, 176, 237
Floods, 198 f., 228, 243, 254
Food, 123 f., 181 f., 232, 250
Furniture, 180 f.
Futuwwa, 241 f.

Galland, Antoine, 10
-Ghazálí, 195
Ghuzz, 184
Guilds, 67 f.

Ḥákim al-Wádí, 27 f.
-Ḥalláj, 145, 146
Ḥamdulláh Mustawfí, 259
Ḥanafites, 209, 245
Ḥanbalites, 144 f., 148 f., 201
Ḥarím (Royal Precincts), 158, 199, 206, 228
Hárún al-Rashíd, Caliph, 34, 42–58
Ḥasan al-Sabbáḥ, 207
Hashimites, 88, 111, 168, 171, 177, 189, 257
Hibatulláh Abú 'l Barakát, 231
Hibatulláh ibn Sá'id, 165 f.
Hospitals, 140, 141, 164 f., 198, 211, 212, 229, 252, 253
Húlágú, 133, 255–9
Humour, 244–6
Humours (the four), 249
Ḥunayn ibn Isḥaq, 89

Ibn al-Alqamí, 254, 260
Ibn al-Athír, 144, 149, 188, 191, 204, 214
Ibn Baṭúṭa, 259
Ibn al-Furát, 138 f., 146, 147

Ibn Jámi', 35, 45–50
Ibn al-Jawzí, 162, 175, 246 f.
Ibn Jubayr, 165, 197, 233–6
Ibn Khallikán, 196
Ibn al-Máristání, 239 f.
Ibn Miskawayhi, 144, 145
Ibn Sahlán, 171
Ibrahím al-Ḥarbí, 125 f.
Ibrahím ibn al-Mahdí, 70, 81–5
Ibrahím al-Mauṣilí, 35, 45, 50
Insignia, of the Caliph, 187, 212
of the Seljúq Sultan, 188
'Ísá canal, 117
Isḥaq ibn Ibrahím, 90–4
Iṣṭakhrí, 157 f.

Ja'far ibn Yaḥyá, Barmecide, 52–5
Jámi' al-Qaṣr, 253 f.
Jews, 6, 27, 65 f., 104 f., 142, 169, 173, 202 f., 229 f., 231, 239, 240

Karbúqá, 205, 206
Karkh, 6, 29, 158, 161, 167, 168, 170, 171, 178, 186, 187, 190 f., 202, 224, 229
Kaẓimain, 2, 41, 177, 260
Kelleks (skin rafts), 44
Kerbelá, 105 f., 159
Khálid ibn Barmak, 20, 28, 42, 51
Kháqání, 166, 223
-Khaṭíb, al-Baghdádí, 18, 135
-Khaṭíbí, 208 f.
Khuld Palace, *see* Qaṣr al-Khuld
Khurásán gate, 21, 31
highway, 40
Khuṭba, 81, 170, 172, 174, 185, 189, 191, 205
Khwárizmsháhs, 238 f.
-Kindí, 88
Kitáb al-Aghání, 156
Kitáb al-Muwashshá, 121
Knighthood, *see Futuwwa*
Koran, 102 f., 103, 169, 197, 213, 235, 248

Law and order (*see also Muḥtasib*), 127–30, 175
Learning, 87 f., 162, 235
Libraries, 170, 236, 259
Lions (and other wild animals), 71, 234

Madínat al-Salám, 8
Mahdí, Caliph, 19, 30, 31–40, 42
Maḥmúd (Seljúq Sultan), 212, 215–17
Maimonides, 240
Makíkha II (patriarch), 258
-Malik al-Raḥím, 185 f.
Maliksháh, 199, 204, 205
Ma'mún, Caliph, 69, 72 f., 74, 79 f., 81, 85, 86–97, 167, 219
Ma'múní palace, 118, 119, 120, 131 f.
Ma'múniya quarter, 243
Manṣúr (Abú Ja'far), Caliph, 5, 8, 14–17, 18, 19, 21, 27 f., 29, 30, 31, 51
Mar-Abá Elias III, 232
Mar Amr, 258
Mar Jabalaha, 258
Marco Polo, 91
Ma'rúf Karkhí, 241
Mas'úd (Seljúq Sultan), 217 f., 218, 219 f., 222
Mas'údí, 76, 126
Medina, 11, 12, 13, 27
Mercenaries, Turk, Berber, etc., 99 f., 106, 107, 109, 110, 111–13, 117, 118, 148, 150, 151, 152, 154, 167, 171, 173, 185, 186

Mint, the, 25
Mohammed al-Júzaqání, 209
Mongols, 239, 252 ff.
Mosques, 19, 132, 161, 189, 200, 210, 222, 236, 260
Mu'áwiya, 12, 13
Mu'aẓẓam, 19, 41
Mu'aẓẓam Gate, 200
-Muhallabí, 156, 157, 159
Muḥarram ceremonies, 159 f., 168
Muḥtasib, 63–5, 140
Mu'izz al-Dawla, 153, 155 f., 159, 162
Mukharrim quarter, 40, 114
Muntafiq, 214
Muqtadí, 203
Muqtadir, 135, 138–40, 147
-Muqtafí, 220
Muruwwa (honourable conduct), 122
Músá (al-Hádí), Caliph, 34, 42
Music, 33, 34, 143, 182
Musta'ín, 107–14
-Mustanṣir, Abbasid Caliph, 252 f.
  Fáṭimid, 170
Mustanṣiriya *madrasa*, 253 f., 259
Mustarshid, 215, 216, 217
Musta'ṣim, 254
Mustawfí Aziz al-Dín, 211, 212
Mustaẓhir, 199
-Mu'taṣim, 98–100, 118
Mutawakkil, 104, 105
Mu'tazz, 107, 108
-Mutí', 161, 162
-Muttaqí, 154

Nahrawán canal, 32
Naqíb, 161 f., 214
Náṣir (Caliph), 237 f., 239, 240, 241, 252
Náṣir al-Dawla, 154, 155
Nestorians, 26, 232, 256
Niẓamiya *madrasa*, 192–7, 199, 201, 235 f., 242, 245, 253
Niẓám al-Mulk, 192–5, 199, 201, 203 f., 207, 208

Observatory, 88, 167
Omar Khayyam, 192

Palace of the Golden Gate, 24 f., 30
Palace of the Sixty, 164
"Paradise", Castle or Palace, *see Qaṣr al-Khuld*
Persians, 13, 14, 26, 28, 152, 155, 209, 222
Pietro Della Valle, 9
Pigeon-flying, 240
Pigeon-post, 252
Planets, the seven, 250
Plague, 228
Police, *see Muḥtasib*
Poverty and poor, 45, 59, 62
Processions, 68 f., 127, 130 f., 143, 136 f., 187, 190, 239, 244
Professions, 38, 62 f., 66
Prostitutes, 203

-Qá'im, 203
Qaṣr al-Khuld, 31, 40, 52, 53–5, 120, 164
Qazwíní, 193
-Qiftí, 240
Quffas, coracles, 2, 44
Qurayya quarter, 241
-Qushayrí, 201

-Ráḍí, 149, 150
Raḍíy al-Dín, 197
Ramaḍán, 171, 176, 242
Raqqa Gate, 186, 187
Rashíd al-Dín, 257
Raymund of Toulouse, 207

Religious ideas, 247–9
Roe, Sir Thomas, 9
Round City, the, 31, 45, 120, 162
Ruṣáfa, 30, 32, 39, 114, 158, 162, 189

Ṣadaqa, 212, 217
Sa'dí, 196
Saffron Street, 191
Saladin, 196, 221, 236 f., 238, 246
Samarra, 100 f., 102, 107, 108, 109, 117
Samuel ibn 'Abbás, 230
Sanjar, 212, 221
Schools, *see* Education
Science, 249–50
Seljúqs, 184–227, 238
Sentry Gate (Bab al-Nawbí), 216, 238, 266
Sháfi'ites, 149, 247
Shammásiya gateway, 108, 110, 111, 112, 136, 224
  quarter, 40, 52, 114
Sharaf al-Mulk, 198
Shi'ism and Shi'ites (*see also* Sunnites), 152, 159 f., 161, 167, 171, 173, 176 f., 185, 186, 189, 191, 202, 237, 240, 246 f.
Shipping, 44
Sieges of Baghdad, 74–7, 108–14, 150, 219 f., 223–7, 255–60
Sinán ibn Thábit, 140–42
Singers, 27, 34, 45, 59, 143 f., 182 f., 203
Siyáṭ, 34 f., 45
Storytellers (*ráwís*), 176
Sunnites, 152, 167, 176–8, 189, 201, 202, 246 f., 253, 255
Súq al-Ghazl, 132, 253
Súq Baghdad, 11
Súq al-Madrasa, 201
Súq al-Thaláthá, 7, 155, 201
Súrá, 142
Synagogues, 228 f.

Ṭabarí, 7, 12, 14, 16, 18, 21, 70, 135, 144 f., 149
Table-manners, 123
Táj Palace, 131 f., 163, 197
Tavernier, 9
Taverns, 34
Tawaddud, 247 ff.
Taxation, 33, 34, 176, 200
Thábit ibn Sinán, 165
Trade and traders, *see* Baghdad bazaars
Tughril Beg, 184–92
Turks, *see* Mercenaries
Tushtigín ibn 'Abdulláh, 246
Tutush, Táj al-Dawla, 198

-Wajíh, 245
Waṣṣáf, 260
Wáthiq, 102, 103, 104
Wine, 176, 182, 203, 250
Women, position of, etc., 61 f., 123, 125, 140, 235

Yahyá ibn Khálid, the Barmecide, 43, 51
Ya'qúb ibn Dá'úd, 35–7
Ya'qúb ibn Layth (Coppersmith), 115 f.
Ya'qúbí, 6
Yáqút, 25, 157, 165
Yúsuf al-Dimishqí, 194
Yúsuf al-Sabtí, 240

Zangí (Atabeg), 217, 220
Zanj (negro slaves), 115, 116, 117, 133
Zubaida, wife of Hárún, 51, 69
Zuṭṭ (? gypsies), 98